To
Dad
Happy Birthday 1926-198?
Best Wishes
Peter Paul
Jacqui e Jenni
x xxx

A Clown Too Many

A Clown Too Many

LES DAWSON

ELM TREE BOOKS · LONDON

First published in Great Britain 1985
by Elm Tree Books/Hamish Hamilton Ltd
Garden House, 57–59 Long Acre, London WC2E 9JZ

British Library Cataloguing in Publication Data

Dawson, Les
  A clown too many.
   1. Dawson, Les   2. Comedians – Great Britain –
  Biography
  I. Title
  791'.092'4   PN2598.D3
   ISBN 0-241-11577-9

Photoset by Rowland Phototypesetting Ltd
Bury St Edmunds, Suffolk
Printed in Great Britain by
St Edmundsbury Press, Bury St Edmunds, Suffolk

This book is dedicated to my wife Meg, and my three children, Julie, Stuart and Pamela: without them, I would have achieved nothing.

Shakespeare wrote, 'When you find a friend, bind him to your soul with hoops of steel.' I dedicate this book also to my friends, because when a man has love and friends, he has the greatest gifts of all.

To my enemies, hopefully small in number, I also dedicate this book, because your dislike tempered the sword of my determination to find satisfaction.

The final dedication is to all comedians, who have the loneliest job in show business.

Acknowledgements

The author and publishers would like to thank the following for permission to reproduce photographs in this book:

H. Goodwin (p.4, with Syd Lawrence)
Doug McKenzie/Professional Photographic Services (p.4, with HM The Queen; p.14; p.15, with the Duke of Edinburgh; p.16, as King Rat)
Yorkshire Television (p.5, both pictures; p.9, with Ray Galton and Alan Simpson; p.10, Dawson's Electric Cinema)
South West Picture Agency Ltd (p.6, signing session)
Brian Moody/Scope Features Ltd (p.7)
Syndication International (p.9, with Eric Sykes and Hattie Jacques)
Don Smith/Radio Times (p.11, Ada Sidebottom)
Christopher Ridley (p.12, The Dawson Watch)
BBC (p.12, with Shirley Bassey, a BBC Copyright Photograph)
Blackpool Gazette and Herald Ltd (p.13, Garth House)
Norman Butler, FRPS (p.13, the family; p.16, the famous face)

Every effort has been made to trace the owners of copyright for photographs used in this book. Should any omission have been made, we apologise and will be pleased to make proper acknowledgement in any future editions.

Contents

Prologue

I would like to think that this book is not merely the story of one man's journey through the wayward and vicissitudinous corridor of Life, but that it is also the history of an epoch in which turbulent change was the most dominant and challenging factor. Within the short period that is the backcloth to my existence, I have known gaslit hovels, dirt and poverty. . . . Cobbled streets and lumbering trams; bleak women in clogs and shawls, filing in silence towards the brooding mills. I witnessed the emerging vista of urban materialism, science, supersonic travel, the dawn of the Atom; all goaded into maturity by a major war and lesser strifes that would one day balk the spiritual progress of Mankind.

From the beginning of the 1930s, until the present day, the pace of change was bewildering; too sudden a metamorphosis for humanity to assimilate it properly. The society of the early Thirties was akin to a theatre: one bought a ticket according to one's station in life. The well-to-do purchased a box or a fauteuil, the middle class sat in the front stalls or upper circle, and the deprived and poor were squeezed in the gallery together. But despite the system, all were a part of the show. Today, we seem to be prisoners of our possessions, as Oscar Wilde tartly put it, 'living up to one's blue china.'

Today we tend to close our doors on the show we call life, and we are the lonely rooms in cities that are dying for the want of a community more interested in people than possession. Grey suburbia is an enticing cancer of a habitat, and so decays the metropolis as the breath of understanding is stilled.

Granite towers house people who now have no contact with their neighbours; children cannot mix, and therefore lose the sense of companionship and tolerance. There was a time when one could tell the seasons by a child at play: hopscotch, whip and top, kick-can, Molly dancers, May day . . . whatever happened to it all? Present day observers might have been appalled at the sight of me as a small boy, poking at grids in the mean streets, and yet in those days, nobody locked their doors, old citizens never died for want of caring, no child ever lacked supervision. Every street was a commune. Each one had its amateur midwife, undertaker, judge and medical advisor. There was a 'knocker up' to get you to work if you had any; and there was always a pawnbroker's menage, where a well worn coat could always glean a copper for bread. If two men fought, it was with fists and fair play, and all the policemen were beefy Sons of Erin, who corrected an offender with a judicial clout, not a charge sheet.

In those times, people did not rely on the promises of a government to mould their lives – they did it for themselves, despite the hardships endured, and that in turn bred respect and comradeship. Today, of course, we look back on that era and scorn it, as we pat our shimmering limousines and colour television sets that have helped to increase the envy of diverse economic strata, and construct new class distinctions within one class of society.

So here I stand, a man of my time and of that time, and with all the errors that go with them.

Les Dawson

BOOK ONE

1931–1964

RETROSPECT

The Royal Command Performance of 1973 was finally over, and I had played my part in it. I had received a most sincere approbation from the glittering audience, and now I awaited the arrival of Her Majesty the Queen. As I stood ranged alongside the famous luminaries of the entertainment world, I could not avoid pondering on the whim of capricious fate that had snatched a working class lad from the Manchester slums, and thrust him into the sparkle of high echelon show business.

Whilst on the stage of the London Palladium, I had glanced at the Royal Box, and had been rewarded by the sight of the sovereign and her entourage laughing at my patter. But even that spectacle was outshone by the look of happiness on my wife's face, as she sat in the front row of the stalls. We had been through so much together, and now she was a partner in the success that I had attained in my first Royal Command Show.

As I shook the hand of the monarch, varied scenes scampered through my mind. . . . The heartaches, once so poignant, now made impotent on this great occasion. With wry amusement, I wondered how had I got here? Me, Les Dawson, slum kid, warehouse worker, apprentice electrician, soldier, boxer, insurance agent, pub pianist, singer; oft times failed writer and poet, vagrant, vacuum cleaner salesman, washer-up in London cafés, coward, drinker. . . A narrative of dead end jobs, as I went on, always dreaming. . . . Door to door refrigerator rep, seller of plastic bottles, strip club compère, labourer, failure, but always the dreamer. Perhaps that was the reason for my whole existence. There and then I decided that I would write it all down one day, the story of a comedian . . . and why not? For is life anything more than a comedy of errors?

AUDITION

Grimy hunched warehouses severing the skyline with dissipated profiles that lurch above narrow tenements gazing eyeless on to litter-pitted streets. Garish pools of pallid illumination retching from the open maws of public houses and twisting to freedom with wreaths of tobacco smoke. Under the splash of light from rusty lamp standards, small knots of unemployed men standing in desperate, defiant stances, as their pride ebbs away. Stout women gossiping on door stoops with their arms folded across soiled pinafores, darting glances of laser intensity at passers-by. Old men sitting in chairs, waiting for death as they dream of what might have been. Carts trundling by with waving oil lamps casting grotesque shadows on soot-grimed walls; black-clad nuns scurrying on errands of mercy, jostling in convoy with crippled buskers and Somme survivors. Shrieking children and lovers, oblivious of their surroundings, edging through the winding cobbled streets, past solemn people with empty bellies who press their noses against the shop windows in silent yearning . . . and always the children: teeming running fighting children, never pausing for breath as they dart down drain-blocked alleyways . . . Collyhurst, Manchester in 1931.

In a two-up and two-down house in Thornton Street, which lay just off Queen's Road, Julia Dawson arched her back in agony and on February 2nd, in the early hours of the morning, gave birth to a son. She named him after her husband, Les Dawson, and thus, in a cramped room lit by sickly gas, I took my place in society.

In that humble dwelling lived my mother and father, my grandparents David and Ellen Nolan and my mother's brother, Tom. How they all managed to co-exist in such tiny quarters remains an enigma. The kitchen had a stone-flagged floor and bare walls, and on the battered stove would be found the eternal stock pot: everything went in it, scraps from previous meals, potato peelings, and, for sure, many a cockroach too.

It was a constant fight for cleanliness: the property should have been condemned by Cromwell, and laid to waste. Dampness glistened on the walls and weakened the lungs; furtive mice on hopeless quests for food became ever bolder.

My grandfather was a heavy drinker and public house wit. His nose was a sonnet to booze, the veins distended and purpling; his eyes were watery and faded. What money he earned went into the hands of the innkeeper, and yet in his fashion, he was a good man. During the First World War, he had deserted from the front, and made his way back home. When the army reclaimed him, he was punished by being tied to the wheel of a gun carriage.

Grandmother was a tiny round lady of Irish descent and she had a temper that was both volatile and volcanic. When she took a drink, "me tipple" as she was prone to call it, her stories about the troubles in Ireland would lead her to tears and eventually to singing "They're hangin' men and women for the wearing o' the green". At the age of seventy-two, upon hearing that her brother had slighted her in a pub, she loaded her handbag with a flat iron, confronted her brother and felled him with a fearful blow to his cropped head.

My mother had the dark beauty found only in a slum child. It is a beauty that haunts the beholder; the eyes speak volumes of experience beyond years, the pale face is a tone poem of wonder and tragedy. She cried and laughed a lot, did Julia, and she cushioned me with love. My father was an orphan from a district called Blackley: his relatives had shunned him and his brother Arthur on the death of their parents, and yet one was conscious that he came from a fairly middle class background. How they met, I know not, but they shared a close relationship that thwarted the economic hardships of the times.

My uncle Tommy was a street fighter, who cared for no man. His brawls became a legend in an area renowned for hard men. Collyhurst possessed a gymnasium called Fleming's which is part of Manchester folklore: it was there that great boxers were culled from the streets, names like Johnny King, Jock McAvoy, Jackie Brown . . . my uncle, Paddy Ryan . . . Len Johnson and the Cusacks: they fought for pennies in arenas like the "Blood Tub" in Ardwick Green, where the sight of blood was a stimulus for the crowds. Fighting was more than a temporary escape from the ghetto of despair, it was a way of life.

In every street from Red Bank tenements to the hovels of Miles Platting and Ancoats, at the drop of a hat, young bulls would flail into one another to prove manhood and to establish a shred of community standing. My first memories as a toddler are of Uncle Tommy sparring with me, teasing me to lash out with chubby fists at his dancing figure.

I remember red trundling trams grating up Oldham Road in a sea of sparks; women breast-feeding their young in public places; treacle toffee and sticky buns on groaning wooden tables in the middle of the streets on Bonfire Night. . . . Flames everywhere licking the sooty sky with crimson fingers; wide-eyed kids lost in awe at the spiralling rockets, and the jangling music from creaking pianos in the pubs.

On Saturday nights they all would congregate in our house and drink and eat the poor fare of cheese and pickles. They would shout and laugh and argue and the stories would get more and more risqué. I recall hiding under the table with other toddlers, listening to them and wanting to grow up and join them, not to have to lie in a trundle bed, narrow and cold.

At quite an early age I was aware of my parents' despair. My dad was a labourer in the building trade, and when he was in work, I would see my mother rubbing his torn shoulder where the hod had lain. His hands were calloused and angry red, but work gave him not only money, but pride. Christmas presents for me consisted of an apple or an orange, and a second hand toy. . . . But always there was love. My father did many things to keep his little family clothed: he was a card sharp and a rogue, a back-street gambler, a billiard-hall marker, anything that would ensure his family's survival. He was arrested occasionally, but the police had a great deal of sympathy for those hardy Manchester folk, and invariably, they'd let him and his friends go free or turn a blind eye. Uncle Tom got married and he and his wife were living with us all. Dad decided we would have to leave, and so one foggy night in October, escorted by the wan streetlamp pools of brightness, we pushed our furniture on a cart all the way to Moston Lane, and the new home: well, not new in the proper sense of the term, it was just another slum really, but by leaving Collyhurst, we had a feeling of making a fresh start.

Mother cried as my father and Tommy brought the cart to a halt at the house. I remember being perched on top of our burst sofa listening to my grandmother whisper, "God bless all who will live in this house." With that, she gave mother some salt and a piece of coal in the time-honoured tradition.

I commenced school, Moston Lane Infants' Elementary, which lay adjacent to our house, and settled in quite easily. It was a period of upheaval: in Spain, the Civil War was decimating idealism; Europe had spewed forth Hitler and his Satanic desires; the depression made a cult out of Oswald Mosley and his Blackshirts. . . . My father joined the Fascists, for one reason only: he needed a shirt no matter what colour. Manchester in the Thirties.

My education was a very basic one; as the name implies, elementary, but even that limited scope was interrupted by the drums of war. I remember excitedly trying on gas masks in the school yard; watching young territorial soldiers marching into regular service, and seeing a dignified lady in a black dress being dragged into a police van accused of being a German spy. . . . The scum rose at this time and started throwing bricks at Italian ice cream shops. . . . Hate was in the air.

Those same Italians we now abused were the very ones we saluted on Whit Week walks through the heart of Manchester: adults and children walking in a show of faith to God; banners held aloft and tinny bands leading all the churches of various denominations on one day of unification. Whit Week meant that kids would be sure of a pair of shoes, some new, most second hand, but the first pair of the year and the last. Out of the blue, my family moved to a rented flat in New Moston, on Lightbowne Road; it was small but clean, and it had a garden, which was something I had never seen before: the green of the grass fascinated me for ages. War broke out as I started at a new school, a school I would stay at until I reached eleven years of age.

About this time, my mother gave birth to a stillborn baby

and I was thus to remain an only child. The war claimed my father: he was drafted into the Royal Engineers and almost immediately sent overseas. The air raids began in earnest now: I recall the enemy planes tracering the skies, and the puff of smoke skirting them, as the artillery on Broadhurst Fields hammered at the attacks. Mother got a job cleaning and it helped to maintain us, there was rationing and the Black Market, fiddles, under the counter deals, and every Saturday, I'd go with mother to a pit-head slag heap and spend hours picking coal to keep us warm.

Like all the other kids, I longed to be a soldier; we played interminably on the streets, Germans and English, all dying the most spectacular of deaths.

One day while I was on the way to school – we had to walk of course in those days – a German plane screamed down and machine gunned us, and we kids threw ourselves into heaps on the ground. . . . The adult war was now our war.

Mother and I had to leave our home and go into a rest centre, because a large unexploded bomb, fin visible, was stuck in the back garden. In the rest centre I found something out about myself . . . a flaw in my make-up that would haunt me for all time. A boy half my size across the shoulders hit me in the face during a childish fracas, and I yelled for mercy and ran away. . . . I was a coward then, and I still am.

At the age of eleven, I left the primary school and returned to Moston Lane Elementary. I had sat for an admittance examination to North Manchester High School, and had failed to secure a place. The war was slowly turning in favour of the allies, and there was an air of optimism in people's attitudes. My father was serving in the Eighth Army, and his letters were the only thing that stopped Mother from sinking into a pit of loneliness. About this time, Mother and I were rehoused, and we moved our scant belongings to No. 21 Keston Avenue, Higher Blackley. It was a small corporation house with a cramped lawn, but it was like living in the Albert Hall after the flat we'd had.

My life then was like the lives of all the other boys my age: hanging around street corners, brawling, looking at girls as the sex drive meshed into gear; delivering newspapers in order to supplement the family income, and playing truant from school, with petty pilfering on the side.

Again, the cowardice that lurked in my make-up reared its unsavoury head, when a pugilistic-looking lad called Dunn picked a fight with me. . . . As I would in years to come, I went to jelly, and damn near fell to my knees in front of the whole class.

We fought surrounded by a tight knot of silent schoolboys. Again and again the fists rained upon my face and chest, and I did not retaliate. Dunn was quite contemptuous of me, and understandably so, as I tried to back away, only to be pushed by the crowd into the path of my adversary. Then I hit Dunn with one punch and it was over. One punch and he went down as if pole-axed. Nobody said a word to me, the crowd about-turned and left the scene. Dunn staggered to his feet and shook my hand; he, too, remained silent, and at last alone, I sat and cried. In those formative years, I strived to find something that would give me access to juvenile society, a key to friendship. Even then, I knew that without affection, my character would flounder.

At school I did not excel at sport. When I played football, I was known as the "Grey Ghost", not because of my speed and dexterity with the leather sphere, but on account of the uncanny pallor of my knees. Because I suffered from hay fever, I couldn't swim for any length of time before puffing like a second hand grampus. Academically, I was much below par; the one thing I did possess, and it was nurtured in my lonely state, was a vivid imagination, and I began to set down in words the meanderings of my thoughts.

These days, a lot of hot air is talked about educational facilities. As far as I am concerned, a child can be developed in a tin hut; it's the quality of the teacher that matters, not the housing. At Moston Lane School, there was one teacher who breathed life into the lessons. I shall never forget Bill Hetherington. A tall, grey, spare man with a heavily creased, yellow-tinged face, he inspired and gave confidence, and his use of the cane was a positive legend. Bill Hetherington was at heart an actor, and I firmly vouchsafe that every teacher should be one. When he took a lesson in history, by his very mannerisms and speech, he transported all the boys in that class to Mary Queen of Scots' execution. . . . When he described the Battle of Agincourt, I was a spectator, and with his description of Waterloo, I endured the agony of old Bonaparte's defeat.

One day, Bill had me in front of the whole form and he took me to task about my maths and geography, two subjects about which even he could not enthuse me. I had been bent over and given six of the best, and it was hard for me not to sob openly with pain and humiliation. "Before Dawson goes back to his seat, I'd like to say a word about his essay from yesterday," Bill said quietly. The class hooted: more fun from Dawson was in the offing. I stood there in my ill-fitting shorts and the ripped cardigan that had a safety pin to secure it, and I crimsoned with chagrin. Bill began to read my essay, and I still recall that written exercise – it was called "A Winter's Day". "Mantles of white gentleness caress a sullen earth, and the stark trees bow their powdered heads like stately escorts."

When Bill had finished reading it, the sniggers from my classmates grew into an explosion of laughter. Bill waited until the wave of mirth had died down, cocked his head in a puzzled fashion, and he said, "His maths are appalling, indeed, poor Dawson seems not to grasp most subjects, but this essay, young man. . . ." I waited for it. An eleven-year-old boy in the almost traditional garb of poverty. An eleven-year-old boy with badly cut hair and a begrimed face. An eleven-year-old solitary lad who had a great depth of inferiority within his soul, waited for yet another crippling indictment. "This essay, Dawson," said Bill looking at me with something akin to compassion, "is superb. . . . Your words have created a picture in my mind, and you have the talent to be a fine writer. Splendid, my boy."

I could not believe my ears. When Bill patted me on the shoulder, I forgot the burning sensation in my buttocks, and I stood ten foot tall.

It was about this time that I found the key that would admit me into the schoolyard society. . . . It was simple: I became the daft one, the idiot, the one who made all the others laugh. It wasn't really all that hard to do. I was small and chubby, I could pull sidesplitting faces, and I had a gift for mimicry. I made my entrance on the stage of existence.

FIRST READ THROUGH

The war ended and all the land was bright with the fires of victory. . . . VE Night: Germany defeated and laid to waste. In every town, city, hamlet, from the storm-tossed Hebrides to the pastoral tranquillity of the Cotswolds, Britons started to live again, and the feverish celebrations took on the appearance of wholesale Roman orgies. There was dancing in the streets, feckless drunkenness, and open fornication in the shadows. Forgotten now, the bombing and the slaughter. . . . Forgotten now, the dreaded drone of the enemy rockets and flying missiles. . . . Gone forever the memory of death and the scream of mutilation. Peace once more.

The girls wore the nylon stockings given to them by American soldiers in return for their virginity, and the legend of England's "cheap" womanhood became a fact. As many a returning British serviceman found to his bitter cost, the Poles, the Dutch, the Americans and the Free French had denuded Britain's females of all modesty and dignity. . . . Our men weren't wanted, and terrible deeds were perpetuated through hostile frustration. Peace once more.

To me, the war held few memories. Oh in later times I would tell my children about seeing corpses lying twisted in burning debris: of the deafening boom of bombs exploding; of the night I was camping out with my friend Ken Cowx in Ashworth Valley and we narrowly escaped being held hostage by two escaped German prisoners-of-war. . . . But my memories of wartime are really of the emerging spots of adolescence; furtive shaming masturbation or fumbling embraces with girls; trying to sprout a moustache to look older in order to gain admittance to public houses; throwing up in alley ways. . . . Growing up.

This was an era of abandonment, of the jitterbug in sweating halls, of young men yearning for seduction: and shortly it was the era of the Atomic Bomb. Nuclear fission brought Japan to her knees and altered the future of Mankind . . . and on we youngsters jitterbugged. My father returned home from the conflict, and he was a stranger to me. Those vital years of my life, he had missed and it was to be a long time before our relationship softened.

In an effort to fight my innate cowardice, I joined a youth club and started to box as an amateur; in an attempt to discourage my opponents, I let the stubble grow on my chin. I must say that I looked the part of a pugilist – heavy in the shoulders and big in the arms, and I could punch. . . . The trouble was, of course, my heart wasn't in it.

There was a lad who terrified me. Physically strong, he was a street fighter and always in trouble with authority. He finished up doing many years in prison, as many of my contemporaries did: we were a lost generation, the discipline wasn't there, either at home or at school. The street fighter joined the boxing club and took a dislike to me straight away. I stayed away from the club in order to avoid a confrontation, but one night in a public house, he and some of his cohorts dragged me outside, and he warned me that if I didn't box him, he'd beat me up in the street – and that meant boots and a razor slash.

The club that night was full of warring gangs, some for me, but most for him. The girls had egged the boys on, and there was a smell of violence in the air. The smoke hung in shreds around the ring, as the crowd punished their lungs with cigarettes. The lights dashed a lagoon of brightness over our heads as we prepared for the fight. My stomach was tied up in knots and I felt sick. My antagonist looked positively awesome and much older than his fifteen years, and I hoped that I wouldn't evacuate my bowels. . . .

The bell went and we circled each other like predators; he flicked a left hand at me and caught my cheekbone, God that hurt. . . . Another flurry of left hands, a right cross . . . I taste blood, my nose is running with the claret. . . . Again he hurts me; please stop this, please. He can smell my fear

and he hits me at will: I back away, my hands at my side . . .
I have no defence against the crippling punches on face and
torso. One round over. An anxious official, peering at my
injuries, ponders whether or not the contest should be
stopped.

Suddenly, as I sat there on the stool waiting for the fight
to resume, a calmness came over me, a calmness that was to
be a weapon for me in later life. The calmness of fatalism –
what will be will be. It is an axiom that I have often followed,
an acceptance of things as they are; a character weakness
maybe, but one that I have found is a saviour for my nerves.

He hits me again, and this time I hit him back with a right
hook. . . . His lip bursts open and a frightened look replaces
his angry expression. Again I punch him, I don't care if I lose
as long as I hurt him . . . and I do hurt him. . . . We close
and we flail at each other's bodies; the crowd cry for more
blood and we oblige them. The bell signals the end of the
second round but I must not have heard it, for I go on
punching my enemy. My trainer drags me back to my corner
and he seems delighted. Why? He says loudly, "You win,
son, he's not coming out for the third round." I can smell
my sweat and my animal odour and the roars from the crowd
make my senses reel; he comes across, the boy I once feared
and he puts my arm in the air, and he says in my ear, "You
can't half bleedin' fight, Dossy."

He used my nickname and that meant acceptance. Indeed
it was, and that was a lesson learned.

I started work at the tender age of fourteen summers in the
drapery department of the Co-operative Wholesale Society,
Balloon Street, Manchester. My weekly wage, for dragging
basketwork skips through winding labyrinths from one
underground vault to another, was twenty-one shillings. It
was hard toil and our hands became calloused and torn off
the ropes by which we pulled the skips. However, we lads
still contrived to turn the daily drudge into something akin
to Le Mans.

Frankly, it was a soul-destroying job, and I began to hate
the mound of parcels that resembled a sort of Alpine range
when we wandered into the catacombs first thing in a morning. It was there, in that cavern of commerce, that a new side

of life made its presence known: a man tried to rape me. He was a fat, balding, perspiring type who ran the goods hoist. I must confess that I had noticed him staring at me on quite a few occasions as I went about my humdrum tasks, but never for a moment did I imagine that he had me down as a homosexual partner. He grabbed me one lunchtime and virtually dragged me behind a sort of partition, where the workers sat to have their morning break. While he fumbled eagerly to remove my trousers, I hit him with a crowbar and as he staggered back, I ran off like a startled gazelle. . . undamaged but scared to hell.

That incident was a whole new insight into the human condition, and it left a mental scar for a considerable period.

That same evening when I arrived home, I scanned my image in the mirror. . . . Doubts scampered through my mind: did I look as if I would welcome another man's attentions? Then, of course, homosexuality was a subject of grave taboo, and it was unthinkable even to consider such things. . . .

I reached the stage where I couldn't take any more of the dead-end drapery boredom, and I had a heated confrontation with my parents over it; with mother in particular, who thought that the CWS was the final word in security. . . . I was young and restless; I wanted to go and blaze trails in Nigeria or whatever. I backed down to please my mother and agreed to stay at the CWS, but this time as an apprentice electrician. It was to prove a grave error of judgement: I was to that employ what the Pope is to brothel management. But the die was cast; off I sallied in a set of overalls to learn the trade. . . .

One day a week they sent me to the Openshaw Technical School, but I couldn't take in the dreary data and I used to sneak out to a pub that turned a blind eye to age regulations. I was sent to various sites and I hated the early risings in mid-winter, the chilled bus journeys and the bleak buildings that we had to rewire: I hated the cold impersonal lengths of conduit and miles of cable that always knotted themselves at my feet; the endless whine of the power drill into girders, and I loathed most of all the humiliation that an apprentice had to endure at the hands of so called "tradesmen" who were quite often totally inept. I learned very little, so little, in fact, that my lack of expertise nearly led to my life being terminated before it had really begun. For some reason which I have never fathomed out, I instructed a vast red Irishman in the art of wiring up a plug socket. After listening solemnly to my words of constructive advice, he went home and dutifully carried out my instructions to the letter. . . . The following day, he came to work minus his eyebrows and a forelock of hair, plus a set of blackened nostrils. It took the combined strength of four engineers to prevent him from braining me with a lump hammer, and after a heated conference twixt all the workforce from diverse trades, I was sent back to Manchester and on to another site for my own safety.

By the time I was seventeen, I had been "sent off" several sites because of my total inadequacy as an apprentice electrician. The list of my bunglings read like a chilling indictment, more dreadful than any Nuremberg war crime:

1. That he did cock up so many lengths of galvanised conduit at the Sun Flour Mills, Old Trafford, whilst trying to bend them, and in an effort to hide his blundering, did creep into the night and throw said conduit into the waters of the Manchester Ship Canal, thus creating a hazard to shipping.

2. That he did fully wire a dining room in Balloon Street and cause a small conflagration in the confines of the Buttery.

3. That he did cheat his workmates of twopence per person by buying meat pies cheaper from another shop. A kangaroo court was held in an MK switch depot, and the foreman kicked his (Dawson's) arse via the application of a steel-tipped collier's boot.

4. That he did spill hot solder down the overall frontispiece of an elderly electrician's bib and brace causing grave injuries to the artisan's crutch.

The list was endless, the mere mention of my name was sufficient to send a man packing to other types of employment.

My social life was as any other spotty teenager's: constantly trying for sex, constantly gazing at one's spotty visage and drinking beer illegally. Being seventeen meant experiencing the ups and downs of confusion . . . and for me, it meant the end of my virginity.

One night, on a number sixty-one bus that was empty save for myself, the omnibus conductress, a formidable matron of generous proportion, laid me back on a vandalised seat, removed her trousers and mine, and guided my organ into hers.

That uniformed harridan rode me as if I was a mustang: she thrust her hips at me like a battering ram; she snorted, sweated, moaned; she clutched my buttocks and clawed my testicles and she climaxed with a series of bellows.

I lay there on the seat as she hurriedly dressed herself, and I felt utterly dirty and disgusted. Thus ended my innocence, and my vision of God-like femininity.

At best, adolescence is bewildering, and I hated those formative years . . . but I have never forgotten them. I had started drinking heavily, I smoked like a bush fire and became a pub pianist and singer. As is often the case, I mixed with young men of dubious character: through some of them, I got into fights and on one occasion, a brawl with knives. At the tender age of fifteen I fell in love with a comely maiden in Wales: it was a holiday affair and when it ended, I wanted to die. . . . I was to fall in love many times in my life, but that first bitter-sweet encounter is one that I will cherish forever.

At sixteen, I became the North Manchester jitterbug champion, and I realised that being in the limelight was the stimulus I needed to combat the feeling of inferiority that haunted me. So many fleeting memories of painful growth to manhood. . . . A group of husky lads queuing in a wooded glade for the favours of a young prostitute, and when eventually seeing her lying on the grass, legs apart and displaying the vast pubic region, all fleeing in horror. My relationship with girls was, to say the least, odd. I took a dark beauty to a cinema, and found to my dismay that I had forgotten my money so she paid. I needed to visit the lavatory, but thought that if I excused myself to do so, she would "go off" me. Throughout the film I squirmed and twisted my nether limbs in a feeble effort to ease my brimming bladder. When we left the picture house, I ambled at her side like Quasimodo, and upon reaching her front door, I could contain myself no more, and I peed up the wall of her house. She stormed indoors, and her father threw me into a thicket.

So many memories of times passed. . . . Trying to join the Royal Navy, and being hustled into the street by a marine and beaten up for giving cheek. . . . The hot dance halls and the lurid lights pressing down on perspiring competitors; the gangs, the girls, the drink, would there ever be a tomorrow?

There was a frenetic feel about the late forties, the war over but unrest still in Europe, as the Russians tightened their grip. We still had shortages, in fact it would be 1953 before rationing ended in Britain. The cinemas were booming in those days, films that were purely escapist in content. . . . I'd spend hours in front of a mirror trying to comb my hair like Alan Ladd, pulling my face in an effort to look like Robert Mitchum or Turhan Bey. I masturbated over Rita Hayworth and Veronica Lake, I tried to drink like John Wayne, and there is many a back street in Manchester where my vomit has lain. The attitude to life was "To Hell with tomorrow." Good times were around the corner. . . .Television would soon rivet our attention; washing machines were on the way, the Good Life was shortly to be upon us all.

So there I stood at seventeen. In my short span of existence, I had known poverty and despair, I had been a war victim; an evacuee from the holocaust; I had grown up with violence and the knowledge of death; I was confused and lonely; was I doomed to become yet another statistic?

My father and I could not communicate; his absence during the war had pulled us apart. . . . I couldn't confide in him. My mother's good sense of humour held the family together, but I was so restless, I hated my job. . . . Surely there was more to living than copper wire and fuse boxes? So, when National Service time arrived, I did not ask for exemption in order to finish off my apprenticeship – I joined the army to get away from my frustration. The night before I was due to report to Catterick Camp, I did the inevitable – I managed to get roaring drunk with my cronies as we stumbled from one low pub to another. Prostitutes embraced us and we brawled with anyone who even looked at us. . . . Growing into manhood.

I stood on the doorstep of our little council house and bade my parents goodbye. I remember that it was a grey morning with a watery sun dripping its rays over the conformist housing estate. The sky held little promise for a bright day, and my iron resolve not to be emotive soon melted when I saw the tears in my mother's eyes. She looked so small and helpless. . . . She'd known great loneliness and I had not been a very attentive son. I held her close and I too cried. My father stammered, "Good luck, son." I smiled wanly at him, shook his hand firmly and walked away. I did not look back.

Some friends waited with me at the bus stop; waiting for the bus that would take me to a new life. I was young for eighteen, there was no hint of maturity in me at all. . . . But within a very short space of time, the army would put an end to that gauche persona.

The bus trundled into the heart of Manchester, and I alighted at Victoria Station to catch the train for Catterick Camp in Yorkshire. The station was awash with other con-scripts and we smiled shyly at one another. . . . It took me back to the days of the war when I was evacuated to Blackpool . . . a little kid with a gas mask and a small case, being herded along the platform to a hopeful sanctuary away from the screams of destruction.

One last long look at Manchester, and off I went to play my part in military matters. What lay in store? I honestly, at that point, didn't give a damn.

FIRST REHEARSAL

Catterick Camp, bastion of army brutality; the transit area designed to turn boys into men. Catterick.

We striplings stumbled off the truck that had been used to load us from the railway station at Richmond, and we received our first taste of the army. Uniformed louts shouting at us, screaming at us, abusing us. Men marching up and down the horizon of the parade ground; bright boots drumming a disciplined tattoo; weapons glinting in the shaft of sunlight. . . . Conscription.

A thickset sergeant with battle ribbons confronts the latest intake and he mutters oaths at us. . . . Stupidly I make some remark, and he overhears me. He puts his swarthy face close to mine: "Little bastard, shut up . . . what's your name, hey? Dawson is it? Comical bleeder, are you? I'm going to take a personal interest in you, son." He almost whispered the words, but the venom was there. Catterick, 1949. . . . Heads shaved, ill-fitting uniforms that smell of age thrown at you by a sullen quartermaster. . . . The constant shouting, the indoctrination of new pride in your regiment, the Eighth Tanks.

My sergeant does take an interest in me; for three days I pound around the perimeter of the parade square with an Enfield rifle above my head, and the sun drags the sweat from every one of my pores.

For a minor diversion, he puts stones in my pack. He makes me do press ups, and all the time he watches for my breaking point. After three days, I refuse to submit to any more of this and he smiles tightly and paints a portrait of the "glasshouse", the detention centre to which I will surely go, if I don't do as I'm ordered. I do as I'm told, and resume the punishment.

Abruptly, my ordeal ends and he seems to lose interest in me, yet he has achieved his aim. . . . My ego is now submerged. Training, training, marching, marching, boots nightly gleamed; boy sleeping fitfully in the one blanket provided, waiting for the dawn, to shave in cold water and stand rigid for the minute inspection: should one speck of dust be revealed, the nearest bed will be strewn on the floor and detention given for the whole hut. The tension leads to fights in the billet, and muffled sobs can be heard in the darkness. Some nights, a drunken NCO will lurch into the billet and try to bugger one of the weaker conscripts. . . . One listens to the moans of the victim, and one shuts one's eyes tight. Catterick Camp, 1949.

Then a miracle occurred. After six weeks of humiliation, I found myself actually looking like a soldier, or, more to the point, a man. I began to learn the art of surviving in a military jungle. . . . When my kit was stolen I went out and stole somebody else's. When any NCO appeared, I made myself look busy. I learnt never to volunteer for anything, and older hands taught me how to creep out of camp for a night's booze in Richmond. I became a gunner, wireless operator in a Comet tank, a sort of tank which was used solely for training purposes, and the time came for me to be posted to a serving regiment. I was given a week's leave prior to the posting and when I arrived home my mother wept at the spectacle of her son . . . thin, hard, head cropped like a convicted felon and distant to her. The week flew past in beery nights with my friends and visiting relatives, one of whom now resided in HM Prisons. When I looked at some of my contemporaries, I silently blessed National Service, for a lot of them now had police records, and indeed two of my old companions were in Borstal. I was glad to go back to army life, and I found myself in the Dale Barracks, Chester. I was a trooper now in the Queen's Bays 2nd Dragoon Guards. The life there was much easier and I found I could cope with all the irritants that the army seems to enjoy. The days were spent on pistol drill and training in the new tanks, Centurions. I soon became familiar with the great giants of destruction and was earmarked for promotion, until an MP arrested me in an "out of bounds" inn, which led to that remarkable mode of punishment known to all serving men as "jankers". A month later, the queen inspected the regiment, and two days after, we embarked for service to Germany.

Germany in those days was still a defeated nation and its major cities were merely heaps of rubble. As yet, the Iron Curtain hadn't fallen and our chief task was to patrol the uneasy border, and assist Displaced Persons into our sector. These pathetic men, women and children were the true indictment of war: in their faces, one could read the emptiness of their existence, and it had a profound effect on me. Our barracks at Fallingbostel had once housed a fanatical SS division, and the presence of those accursed men could still be felt. To the north, a few kilometres away, was a place whose name will be forever etched in the annals of ignominy: Belsen. No birds ever sang in the trees that encircled the shrine to man's inhumanity to man, and the chill of horror was a constant ghost. Many a time our tanks ploughed up the bones of those who perished in that concentration camp.

The Cold War twixt the Allies and Russia commenced in earnest, and we now stood a round-the-clock watch. Some of my fellow soldiers succumbed to the propaganda that was nightly churned out from Radio Moscow, and they went across to the Russians. I recall one such man, a corporal, who kept me spellbound with his philosophical adulation for the diatribe of Marxism. I was on guard duty the night he slipped away into the shadows for the Russian lines: I remember his face, shining with his fevered desire. . . . He gripped my arm: "Don't try to stop me or raise the alarm." His voice was that of a man possessed. "All my life I've looked for an ideal, I know I will find it over there." He stared at me and his eyes were wild. Dumbly I nodded and walked away from the fringe of conifers that lay at the edge of the camp perimeter. I turned only to watch his figure vanish into the rolling mist which skirted the forest that yawned between two opposing ideologies.

A week later, I heard his voice on Radio Moscow. He was extolling the virtues of life with the Soviets, but his tone was that of a man fully duped. I never heard of him again.

It was now a time of war games: tanks crashing through

thick woods; infantry sidling in ditches; planes bombing all movements with mock explosives. . . . The smell of petrol clinging to clothing. . . . The cold chill biting into the very marrow. . . . The tiredness that was a constant companion to Britain's conscript army, the Young Lions. Once on such a foray into darkling plains, a soldier was crushed under the tracks of a tank; his pathetic remains were scooped up and placed in an army blanket. Once on such a foray, my tank commander, a son of a famous general, ordered me to instruct the driver to plough through a field of corn. Still in my mind to this present day, I can see the faces of that German farmer and his wife and child as they watched us destroy his labour. The officer turned to me after our squadron had wiped out the crop, and as he removed his goggles, he crowed, "That should teach the Nazi bastard, what?" I simply stared at him with anger churning my gut. He lowered his gaze and lit a cigarette self-consciously. Germany 1950.

In that month, through foul map reading, I managed to deliver a scout car into the hands of a Russian patrol. I had taken the wrong path down a valley, and we had strayed into alien territory. Within seconds, hard, drably dressed Russian soldiers had surrounded us with a ring of bayonets. . . . The Dawson cowardice was to hit an all time record during the interrogation, which took place in a large, ill-lit tent. A chain-smoking Russian officer faced us from behind a rough hewn trestle table, and despite a warning from my sergeant to give nothing but my name, rank and number, I blabbed everything: not only did I relate the name of our regiment and situation, I damn near told them what I'd had for breakfast. No, never would I be the stuff of heroism, and after twenty-four hours, when we were allowed to go, my fellow troopers were quick to point out my basic inadequacy.

I did not like the army. I tried everything to get out of it. After listening to old soldiers' tales, I spent hours rubbing blanco into my skin in order to create a rash that was supposed to be a sure fire winner for a discharge. . . . Nothing happened, not even a blemish. I wrote home to my parents asking them to write to my commanding officer, saying that my mother's health was so bad, my presence at home was necessary: hardly the handiwork of a man. That didn't work. . . . I stayed in the ruins of the Third Reich.

To avoid the dreaded guard duty, on which one could get knifed by prowling gangs of German fanatics, I went to Hanover for a medical examination of my feet, and managed to get excused boots. The night I returned gleefully with the news was a bitterly cold one; cold as only Europe can be. Snow had drifted over all the barracks, and an incensed wind blew the snow flakes into a white fandango of fury. As some of my hut mates dressed for sentry duty, I snuggled under my blanket and bade them a fond farewell . . . I awoke with ice pelmets crusting my vision. I could not breathe; snow packed my mouth. I sat up and gaped: whilst I had been asleep, my bed had been carried out and placed in the middle of the parade ground.

We young braves constantly yearned for sexual gratification, and when you get six hundred immature bulls milling about inside an encampment, the very air reeks of physical lust. There was one main stumbling block to our quest for women: venereal disease at the time was running at something like ninety per cent, and to nullify our desires, films that displayed the penalties of sexual intercourse were shown to us in grim abundance. For me, it was akin to a cold douche of water and I indulged in chronic masturbation. But the need grew, of course, for the solace of a female, and one night in Hanover I met a girl called Erica, who assured me that she was "safe". For the sum of a hundred cigarettes she led me to a heap of rubble that had once been a house and we lay on a battered mattress and began to fondle each other. For some reason, a spark of sanity penetrated my frenzy, and as I gazed at her naked flesh, something told me not to go any further. . . . She whispered a sentence of query in German, and put my hand on to her vagina. . . . Suddenly there was a sound of an army truck coming close to where we lay. I rose to my feet, nude from the waist down, and, to my horror, saw a bunch of military policemen. They were obviously combing the area, because I saw dishevelled soldiers pulling their pants up and loping off into the dusk. My companion began to tremble and she looked so frightened, I almost felt a wave of tenderness for her, until I saw scores of sores on her buttocks and thighs. That did it. . . . Off I darted through the ruins only to rush into the waiting arms of a sallow man with a knife in his hand. I didn't ask if he was Erica's "pimp" or a scavenging derelict, I simply kneed him in the groin and ran like a dervish.

Germany 1950. A full scale exercise is in progress throughout the Fatherland, and my regiment is in the thick of it. For days we trundle through forest and more forest; our eyes are thick with fatigue and we smell of tank fuel; we eat iron rations when we can and we watch the infantry trudge at our side through a vision of listlessness. One night I am ordered to keep radio watch, because tomorrow all the armoured regiments are to attack at dawn and it is my task to see that the Queen's Bays are alerted when the signal is delivered. It is nearly eight o'clock before I awake. Suffice it to say there is the father and mother of a row and I am placed under arrest, prior to a court martial.

I can still hear the drum of heels as the military escort took me before my commanding officer. My heart pounded with open fear of the punishment that was awaiting me and it took an effort of will to stay my bladder from performing its function. In vain I pleaded that nobody had awakened me as was promised by the guard picket commander, but the corporal who was supposed to have done so said that he had made sure I was alert. I knew that he was lying. His face was shiny with sweat as he gave his evidence, but the court tribunal seemed to believe him. I was placed under open arrest until a court martial could be convened, and marched out in disgrace. For two nerve-racking days, I was followed everywhere by a military camp policeman, then abruptly the charge against me was dropped. I never found out what happened, but my squadron sergeant winked at me and the corporal became a trooper once more. . . .

A month later, for being drunk and disorderly, I was thrown into the guard house, and Destiny took a hand in the somewhat sordid affairs of Trooper Leslie Dawson. It came in the shape of an event that is eulogised in the history of the Tank Corps: Cambrai Day, commemorating the time when tanks were first used in World War One. Traditionally, it is a time for all tank men to get well and truly pissed, and to do so with gusto under the benign eye of the officers, but on this occasion there was turmoil – there was nobody to play the piano in the sergeants' mess! It was a tragedy of limitless proportions, until someone remembered that a certain dumpy trooper called Dawson could knock a tune out, and often did for his mates in the NAAFI. So it was to be. I was marched out under heavy guard and piloted to the beer-soaked piano and I played and sang dirty songs and ditties for the hardened NCO's throughout the night. I never went back to the guard house and I heard no more about my crime. From then on, I played and sang whenever needed and life became quite tolerable. Demob was on the horizon for my intake and I couldn't contain myself for that great day. . . . Then my dreams of getting out of uniform took a dire tumble. While I was on tank duty in a wooded area close to the roving Russian patrols, the voice of Clement Attlee, the then Prime Minister, droned eerily through the pine forest. He spoke sadly about the situation in Korea, and informed us that because of our commitment to the Americans, we were to be totally involved in South East Asia, and therefore, six extra months would be added to the two years we were all serving as conscripts.

I didn't cry. I wanted to, but I didn't. . . . I took myself off with a bottle of cheap Schnapps and drank myself into a sullen stupor. Many of my friends fell in that futile struggle. As for myself, I was convinced that I would never leave the army alive.

It seemed that the world was deranged: Korea, the Iron Curtain, Palestine, Malaya; death was on the rampage again. In Germany our tanks were stoned and neo-Nazi groups set on soldiers who strayed from busy centres and beat them to a pulp. Our lads often retaliated and a blind eye was turned by the authorities. Incidents happened for which there was no excuse. I witnessed a rape in our barrack block. A photographer looking for business brought a young German girl with him into the camp. Many of the lads were drunk after a bout in the bar and frankly, many of them were out for trouble. The girl had no chance; she was stripped and ravaged before my eyes by a bunch of otherwise ordinary young men. I tried to protest but I was knocked to the floor by a drink-maddened Scot, and I had to crawl away from the scene. The girl was allowed to lurch out and as we heard no more, I can only assume the rape was not reported.

Time hung heavy and to speed the six months on, I took

to writing bits for *The Soldier* magazine. It was a thrill to see my name in print. One education officer urged me to take up a correspondence course with London University, which I did, and I began to aspire to a career in journalism. At last my demob came around. There was no trace of the callow youth who had first entered Catterick. Instead there stood a man, a somewhat cynical man who had learnt to survive with cunning and deceit. The army may have turned me into a passable warrior, but it had forced me to emerge from the larva of childhood far too soon.

It was a cold morning when I left Fallingbostel. We shook hands with those left and for the last time gazed at the grey blocks which had been our home for what seemed an eternity. The trucks taking us off to the railway station grunted into life and we left Germany for good. No trace of regret on my part. . . . Not for me the uniformity of army discipline. The burden of regimentation was a manacle to my soul, and I unshackled it with a burning relief.

SECOND REHEARSAL

I left Bovington Camp in my civilian clothes and mentally blew a raspberry to my defunct army service. I was leaving behind the idiotic passion for conforming to witless orders; behind me lay the constant bullshine of boot and brass, and NCO's whose brain energy was that of a retarded pit pony. Stuff it. . . . No regrets, right? Well, there was a sweet girl in the picturebook hamlet of Wool who had tarried with me in the hay wain. . . . I knew I'd miss some of the lads – my capacity for strong drink had given me quite a standing among the sots of the NAAFI – but that was all.

I spent the three weeks after demob in a haze of alcohol and pitiful self-indulgence, but I had to get back to work, and to please my mother, who believed that "having a trade" was a passport to security, I reapplied to the Co-operative Society in Balloon Street, Manchester and was accepted back as an electrician pro-temp. I still had to finish my apprenticeship and I was placed under the heading "Improver". Wrong. I was still as useless as ever, I hated the job and blew up several installations with gusto. The end was, of course, inevitable. . . . I was summoned before a gentleman who rejoiced in the name Birtwhistle, a grey thin man who carried the burden of inept tradesmen upon his shoulders, and I was summarily dismissed from the CWS.

I wasn't too bothered. In those days there were always jobs of sorts, most of them dead end occupations, but jobs for all that. My trouble was, I simply could not settle down. I even began to miss the life of the army; I was restless, and when I celebrated my twenty-first birthday, I wallowed in self-pity and depression during the festivities of my coming of age, which were held in a pub called the Old Loom. My life was one of pub crawling and trying to worm the pants off any female who appeared half willing for bed sports. My parents were more than irritated with me, and when I started to write poetry, I'm sure they were fully convinced that they had an imbecile on their hands; but write I had to, I don't know why. I still have a positive alp of rejection slips from sundry magazines to prove it. Finally, the words of my old teacher, Bill Hetherington, "You have the ability to be a fine writer," drove me to plunge willy nilly into one of the more stupid acts of my life. I went to Paris.

Paris, was there ever such a city? With less than thirty pounds in my pocket, I wandered from the Sacré Cœur to the Bastille, and from Odeon to Madeleine: the city drew me into its maw of enchantment. . . . Paris is a woman; a spoilt saucy minx of a woman, who steals your heart away. Paris, city of smells: cheap perfume, exotic tobaccos, pissoirs, heady aromatic wines. . . . Paris is pavement cafés and dark glasses, Pernod and bistros. . . . She is history and avenues of trees, she is panting traffic and starving artists, she is the turgid Seine and strolling lovers. . . . She is magnificent: if you have money.

I rented a flat that was so small, when I turned the light off, I was in bed before it was dark. The flat was situated in a winding street called Monsieur Le Prince. I eagerly began to write my essays, which wasn't easy for a red-blooded young man, there were too many distractions: noisy cafés, beautiful women who drifted by and played merry hell with my libido. Within two weeks, I was a pauper, and my landlady, a voluble, heavy-set, bad-tempered virago, was demanding the rent. . . . I didn't need to understand French to get the message that soon I would be pitchforked on to the streets. My diet consisted of a length of dry bread and wine so cheap, it was probably fermented for a shilling a gallon. The landlady one night grabbed my collar and propelled me to the stairs. In abject despair, I pleaded with her for time to pay. . . . Something happened, maybe I struck a chord deep within her, anyway, the upshot was, she lent me ten thousand francs, about ten pounds in English currency. France in the fifties was experiencing dire inflation, but the ten pounds was a life line and a breathing space.

I was alone, and yet I did not feel alone in Paris; the magic of the metropolis gripped me, and with my ill-shod feet and sprouting beard, I looked the part of what was referred to as an "existentialist", the forerunner of the modern "hippie". They were to be found everywhere, those existentialists: in jazz cellars, pavement cafés and smoky bistros; talking about Life and the need to relinquish all the fetters of responsibility that manacled mankind. But it was apparent that if I didn't get a job, I would finish up a mouldering bundle of rags in a charity ward. . . . I had to earn money. One night I met two English lads who were on holiday, and they took me for a drink, which led to many more. I toured them around the Left Bank and I felt Parisian. We finished up in a small, dimly lit club called the Al Romance. The place seemed empty, vacant bar stools and a huge grand piano . . . but no people, save an Algerian barman. My new friends ordered the drinks and I played the piano. The tune I played was the haunting theme from the Charles Chaplin film *Limelight*. A blowsy woman in a tight red dress came down some stairs, lit a small cigar, and listened to me play the instrument. When I'd finished, she patted me on the shoulder and spoke to me in rapid French. Then, as now, I didn't speak a word of the language.

The woman was the owner of the night club and her name was Eva. The upshot of that meeting was that she employed me to play the piano nightly, from midnight until three a.m. One catch, and a strange one: she only wanted me to play *Limelight*. I was to find out why later.

My two newly acquired friends had nowhere to stay for the night so we crept up the rickety stairs to my flat and threw ourselves on the floor to sleep off the drink . . . A smell roused me from my dormant state, and again, a new fact of life entered into my existence for the first time. My companions were smoking "pot". Just what the concoction consisted of I'll never know, but it must have been quite remarkable because one of them was crowing like a rooster with an inane grin on his face and the other one, to my intense dismay, was attempting to climb through the window of my cramped quarters. As the room was a few storeys up, not unnaturally I was panic stricken.

I pulled the would-be aviator down from the ledge where

he was now perched, and as we fell in a heap, I saw to my horror that the other one had removed his trousers and was showing his pink rump to my landlady, whose face was something out of Hogarth. . . . She screamed, and kicked his naked backside with her formidable sabot. This caused him to hurtle into the room and he cannoned into his friend, who in retaliation bit me on the foot. It was a nightmarish scene which ended its comic run when the landlady's soul mate, upon hearing the rumpus, chased us all out with a cavalry sabre. Needless to say, I spent the rest of that night sleeping on the banks of the Seine. I never saw my two would-be chums again, but the mere mention of drugs or usage of can immediately conjure up the scene that took place that night.

Broke and nowhere to stay. I sat throwing stones into the turgid waters of the River Seine, with Notre Dame glaring down at me with a religious fervour and passers-by glancing tentatively at my forlorn figure. A rather well-to-do man approached me, and spoke in voluble French. When he discovered I was English, he asked, haltingly, had I nowhere to go? Was I hungry? Oh sod it, thought I, "que será." If he wants my bum he can have it. . . . I was famished. We set off and we ate a delightful steak in a steamy bistro that was wedged on the Saint Germain Des Prés. Later he ushered me into a nicely furnished flat and bade me stay until I wanted to leave of my own accord . . . and that was that. The bed looked inviting and I undressed. The door opened and a bold looking girl came in and simply smiled and took her clothes off. Well, what does one do? It was all satisfactory until I heard a whirring sound coming from behind a closet door. We were being filmed . . . I was out of that room like a Polaris missile, leaping about as I dragged my pants on. . . . I went back to plead with my ex-landlady, and mercy of mercies, she took me back.

The piano-playing job helped me to pay back my snorting landlady, but it was an engagement of madness. Every night I would sit playing *Limelight* over and over again, and there wouldn't be a soul in the place. Eva seemed satisfied with me and she would stand with her hand on my shoulder, humming the tune and pouring drinks into me. I'd been there a week

before the penny finally dropped: the club was a brothel. . . .
The clients entered the club by a rear door and bounded up
the stairs to cubicles, where five girls plied their trade. I was
merely a front for the place.

One of the prostitutes, a coloured woman called, somewhat
exotically, Emerald, took a liking to me and looked after me
in more ways than one. She was highly intelligent despite the
way she lived, and we would talk away the hours, then stroll
down to Les Halles and rub shoulders with every strata of
society who went to Les Halles for one thing: the onion
soup. . . . Ah, that soup! In the smoke-wreathed, dimly lit
cafés, we sat and slurped that most delicious concoction, with
its raft of strong cheese and spices. Later she would lead me
to bed and use my body with her professional expertise. . . .

It couldn't last, and it didn't. Riots in the Algerian quarter
led to increased police activity, Eva was arrested and the club
closed down. I tiptoed out of my lodgings, still owing two
thousand francs, and I went home by train and boat. I arrived
at my parents' council house with twopence in my pocket,
but a wealth of memories. To keep the wolf away, I took a
job selling insurance for the Liverpool Victoria, whose offices
were situated in a poor area of Manchester. My first task was
to post two thousand francs to my landlady in Paris, and a
thank you note.

That insurance job opened my eyes to a lot of things:
the way some people eked out a living in such depressing
circumstances. I saw hovels where children had rat bites on
their pale, thin bodies; I saw dampness running down walls
where large families had to sleep, and I vowed that one day
I would try to make something of myself. . . . I would escape
from a class who seemed to have lost all incentive. I have
always maintained that a slum is a state of mind, not a physical
thing. I had been raised in poverty; cleanliness costs nothing.
These people wore their dirt like a badge, and didn't want
anything better. . . . It was poverty of the spirit, not circum-
stance.

It was a rotten job. The insurance monies were counted in
pennies, policies taken out for the purchase of a black coat
for attendance at funerals; enough to buy a tie or a wreath. . . .
Within a month, I owed the insurance company money: it

was pointed out politely that I was no longer an asset to the firm, and once again, I was fired. For pride's sake, and to save her son from becoming infamous as an embezzler, my mother paid back the money to the Liverpool Victoria, and the shred of Dawson self-esteem was salvaged.

I was playing the piano in pubs professionally now: low sleazy inns full of thugs and prostitutes. For three hours' work they paid me the princely sum of ten shillings, and I put that wage back over the bar in bills for my drink. I was in a twilight zone of my life: no work, not respectable work that is, frequently drunk and waking up in a harlot's bed, I was clinging to the bottom of the ladder all right.

Whilst I was performing in an inn called the Alliance I met and fell in love with the daughter of an Italian ice cream manufacturer, and she swept me off my scuffed shoes. She was dark and lovely with a soft olive-coloured body, and we decamped to London, to a drab hotel in Islington, and stayed in bed for two days of bliss. I took her home to meet my parents and my mother detested her on sight. I could see no flaws in my Beloved, but Mother could and my little Italian knew she'd never get round Ma. She gave me an ultimatum . . . her or Mother. I decided she was too precious to lose, and we made plans to elope.

I had two pounds in my wallet and a parcel of sandwiches when I crept out of the house to join my sweetheart. I waited her coming in a park, which was near where she lived. I waited and waited. . . . She never came, so I ate the sandwiches, went into a pub, spent my two pounds and got drunk in the process. I picked up a red-haired girl and made love to her in a cemetery.

Slowly I was enlarging my entertaining. I started singing as well as playing the piano, and my wages went up to twelve shillings. About this time I joined a traditional jazz band. The Cotton City Slickers was the name we rejoiced in, and we were so bad, we actually got paid off on a charity show. Auditions were being held at the Hulme Hippodrome for a show called Top Town Stars. The idea was for two areas to vie with each other to see who had the best entertainers. I duly auditioned to an ill-shaven impresario with nicotine-stained fingers and I was chosen to represent Manchester against

Stockport. The fee was to be eight pounds . . . a fortune. The show was a disaster, the audience was thin, in fact it became a gag that the Dress Circle was so empty, someone shot a stag in it. My act was awful. I played the piano and I wore a ginger wig and imitated Quasimodo. . . . Nobody laughed, and the compère came on stage to halt my efforts and spare the audience from more punishment. My parents were present that night but went home before me, because we amateur artistes had a rough idea that we wouldn't get paid, and in that assumption we were correct. The so-called impresario was found trying to get through a dressing-room window with the loot. He was dragged back in and we took what money he had and spent it in a pub.

I was so cocksure of myself, I really thought I'd done well, and I couldn't wait to see my parents. When I knocked on the front door, my mother opened it and pulled me in, saying as she did so, "Get in before any bugger sees you. . . . You were bloody awful." I swayed with hurt dignity and replied by vomiting on the rug.

I applied for, and got, a job as a sales representative with Hoover Limited, the vacuum cleaner people. The wage was seven pounds a week plus commission, and to get the wage, one had to service cleaners and washing machines. I couldn't drive a car, I'd never bothered getting a licence, but it was imperative that I had a vehicle of sorts, and Mother, bless her, lent me a hundred pounds to buy a van. I had a few lessons off a pal of mine, then got a friend to get me an Irish licence. Some fool told me that a Southern Irish licence was legal: it wasn't, of course, but I was clutching at straws. I had only taken possession of that wretched van a week, when I overturned it after a drinking bout. I had a girl in the van at the time but luckily she was unharmed. The van was a total mess, but I had to get home, so several brawny men righted the van and I lurched off in a limping slanting motion. Reluctantly the insurance company agreed to pay for it to be repaired, and it was. The same day I retrieved it from the garage, I crashed it into the back of a lorry. I went back to the insurance office and when I told them of my mishap, they paled. I was going out with a sultry girl who enjoyed sex to the full; little did I realise, that everytime we made love in the back of my recently repaired van, her mother would be watching every writhing movement through the window on the back door of the pantechnicon. . . . I found out that the old lady got her kicks that way, and encouraged her daughter to get herself pregnant. I got out of that absurd dalliance in the nick of time, and she eventually contracted a bun in the oven from a simple-minded stoker from Glasson Docks.

As a salesman I again proved the truth of the old adage: "If at first you don't succeed, fail, fail again." Within a year as a Hoover representative, I managed to sell a washing machine to an elderly couple who were still on gas, no electricity. . . . I demonstrated a vacuum cleaner to a rather impatient lady, and in my frantic desire to sell one of the damn things, got my necktie caught in the agitator roller and nearly strangled myself. The Hoover company despaired of me and relegated me to an area of tight slumland called Moss Side. My superiors left me severely alone.

In Moss Side, which teemed with a rich polygot stream of humanity, from Irish to Dyak head-hunters, I serviced machines in cellars where mouse droppings abounded, where frightened Indians lay on rush mats, where children actually played with rats. I saw myself haunted by failure, and every night wandered into various pubs, got drunk and played the piano and sang, and sometimes the publicans would pass the hat round for me. At the age of twenty-three, I was a mess. One day, as I drove past the Manchester Hippodrome, I saw a billboard asking for acts to audition for Max Wall, then a big variety name. Almost without thinking, I went into the now defunct theatre, played the piano and sang for Mr Wall. He said he'd let me know, and that was that.

Although by now I was actually selling a few cleaners and washing machines, I was restless and couldn't apply myself to the job in hand. Most nights I was out with the boys, drinking far too much and playing the piano wherever I could find one. One night, I telephoned an agent in Scotland, the William Galt Agency in Glasgow, and arranged an audition for a brilliant pianist called Bernard Collins, a comedy singer named Val and myself. I took time off work and we drove to Edinburgh to the theatre for an audition. A bored pair of impresarios listened to us, liked Bernard and Val, and told me they might let me know if anything came up.

On the way home the lads were thrilled with the prospect of professional work, whilst I slumped in the back of the car dejected and depressed. I kept asking myself over and over again was there anything I could do right? Was I destined to be a failure all my life? It was a low point in my existence.

Three days later, I received a letter from Max Wall saying that I had passed the audition, and would I consider moving to London in order for him to promote me? It was the spur I needed. My mother cried a little when I told her I was leaving Hoover and going away, and my father said I was an idiot, but it was my life and I must do what I thought was right. Bernard and Val were despondent, they'd heard nothing from Scotland, and my news didn't lighten their spirits one iota. Frank Thompson, my Hoover chief, accepted my resignation with barely concealed glee, and I went out to work my last week as a salesman. On the Friday of that week a letter arrived from the William Galt Agency offering me work on a touring variety bill, but I was already committed. My friends took me out for some rather grand binges, and with their good wishes ringing in my ears, I set out to conquer the metropolis. On the train, a small paragraph in the newspaper caught my eye: "Max Wall cited for divorce." I shrugged my shoulders. What the hell . . . Dawson was on the way.

IMAGES

After the Royal Command Performance of 1973 was over, Her Majesty the Queen would leave the Royal Box, accompanied by Sir Bernard Delfont and Reg Swinson, and she would be presented to all the artistes who had appeared in the show. She would shake hands with Duke Ellington and Nureyev, the singing duo Peters and Lee. She would speak to the violinist Francis Van Dyke and the comedian Dick Emery.

Eventually she would see an overweight little man with baggy eyes and a downcast expression. His name, she would be reminded, was Les Dawson. What she wouldn't see was the nine-year-old evacuee with a safety pin fastening his frayed cardigan together. She would never know the anguish of that smut-faced child, as kiddie after kiddie was chosen by the adults living in the evacuation area, leaving him alone on the pavement with a shabby holdall. That little boy was too much of a slum dweller to be permitted in a decent home, and so he waited alone for someone to take pity on him. Eventually a policeman and a grim faced official almost bullied a couple into taking him along to a grey council house. The couple's two children sniggered at the waif and held their noses in mock horror. The slum lad was stripped and scrubbed, given a piece of bread and sent to a trundle bed in a small attic. He lay trembling, unable to sleep. . . . He was frightened and without love. . . .

THIRD REHEARSAL

London in the early fifties. Truly a place of enchantment to a raw provincial young man with but thirty pounds in his wallet. . . . London in the early fifties: well dressed throngs in the West End; garish signs wavering atop the roaring traffic; theatres and clubs; pubs and cafés haunting the imagination with sight and smell. Towering buildings and the tree-lined Mall; the palpitating view of Buckingham Palace and the sweep of history seen in Whitehall. . . . I was going to conquer this curio of a city . . . . But before that happened, I was to know loneliness that only London can inflict on the solitary ego.

My first "digs" were in Battersea above a sort of sinister looking café that catered for the homeless and the defeated. The accommodation had been recommended to me by a variety act in Manchester called the Mull Brothers: how they had chanced across this most awful of watering holes is a mystery worthy of Agatha Christie.

For a start, there were simply no decent toilet facilities: one stood to evacuate, if one was sensible enough, over the ghastly lavatory bowl. To have sat down on the discoloured seat would have been tantamount to exposing the buttocks to the Black Death. A large tin was provided in which to wash and the water had to be carried from a tap stand in the rear yard, and trundled up three flights of rotting stairs. I lay in a ramshackle bed in a room with three other men in it. One, an elderly alcoholic, kept me awake on my first night there by fighting off some dreadful creature from his drink-sodden mind. Another man kept calling out somebody's name, and the third boarder, a heavily bearded ex-sailor, snored like a bronchial moose. Holding on tightly to my wallet, I eventually drifted into a troubled slumber, only to be roughly aroused by a hamlike fist that tugged at my single blanket. Startled, I awoke to find an enormous man and a blowsy, gum-chewing woman glaring at me. "Get up, kid, you're in my bleedin' bed," the male apparition growled. I assure you, I lost no time in complying with his demand. Framed in the doorway was my landlady, who trumpeted, "Sorry, love, I forgot 'Arry was due in tonight. . . . You'll have to kip on my couch." I muttered something and even before I had finished trousering my nether limbs, 'Arry had the woman on the bed and was nuzzling her throat. I shall never forget the feel of the springs in the small of my back as I tried to get back into the arms of Morpheus on that confounded settee. London in the early fifties: Les Dawson's introduction into that polyglot society.

The following day, to save money, I walked from Battersea to the office in the West End which Max Wall had leased for his company, "Wall Wall Enterprises". In those days Max Wall was enjoying a huge success as the foreman, Hymie, in a stage musical called *The Pyjama Game*. The show was the hit of London's theatreland and Max was the star of the production.

The famous old comic with his inimitable vocal delivery welcomed me warmly, then sat me down and forgot about me as he drooled over a beautiful girl. Her name was Jennifer Chimes and she was to be the instrument of his decline in popularity and his banishment to obscurity for many years. In those days, morality was much stricter than it is today, and for a comedian to go off the rails, especially one as beloved as Max Wall, meant certain *fini* to his career.

It was to be one of the oddest periods of my life. Max didn't know what the hell to do with me, and the press were persecuting him over the breakup of his marriage. Many times he pleaded with me to take Jennifer out and away from the Fleet Street hounds who pursued them both. He managed to get me to a recording studio where my singing aptitude was tested, and he decided to send me back home in order to study vocal technique with a world famous teacher, Madam Styles Allen, who had a studio in Leeds. Two days later, I left Battersea with just enough money for my train fare, and returned home with mixed feelings.

For some three weeks I journeyed across the Pennines to warble for Madam Allen, occasionally bumping into a young student there, also undergoing training for a singing career: she was a sweet thing, did all right for herself, actually . . . Julie Andrews. Madam Allen was a vast lady with a great deal of aplomb. She liked my baritone voice and telephoned Max to say that in her opinion, all that could be done, had been. The following night, after that telephone conversation, I went back to London and the squalor of my Battersea lodgings. From the outset, the situation was dire. Max was under great stress from the glare of publicity, and the bookings for the show were dropping off. He gave me five pounds a week for the job of ostensibly understudying the other male star of the *Pyjama Game* Edmund Hockridge. . . . As Mr Hockridge stood about six feet four inches, there was an element of farce about it all, but luckily I never had to stand in for Edmund. After I had discovered some items missing from the locker at the side of my bed, I decided to escape from Battersea, and I launched out on a hunt for a small flat. It was a search that will be forever etched in my memory. After scanning the newspaper ads, I picked one out which read "Young man in need of strong discipline, requires someone to share apartment in Earl's Court and go halves with the rent." I should have realised what it entailed, after all I'd been about and had observed the peculiarities of the human condition, but on this occasion, I sallied forth wreathed in innocence.

I found the flat with some difficulty; Earl's Court in those days was a crowded transit camp for expatriate Australians and all that was missing was the odd wombat leaping about. I knocked on the ill-painted door of the apartment which was situated on the third floor of a neo-slum dwelling, and when it opened, I was confronted with a slender, pouting youth who reeked of perfume. After showing me around the cramped quarters he groped my backside and tried to kiss me. I pushed him against a wall that had posters of body builders festooned on it and I bolted to safety.

During the days that followed, I visited many flats and, to assuage the loneliness of my existence, I compiled a dossier on the near idiots I encountered: pouffes by the score; madmen and perverts; crooks and tricky bleeders; Lesbian wrestlers and elderly matrons brimming with lust. I began to take a dim view of life in the Metropolis, and seriously thought of returning home with my tail between my legs. I was alone and going nowhere. I possessed one suit that was so old, every time a band played *The Lancers* the trousers broke into a gallop. One day when I was at my lowest ebb, a telephone call came which caused my spirits to soar like a falcon . . . . Max Wall wanted to see me urgently.

Like an eager pup, I loped across London, through to Garrick Street where Max Wall's office was to be found. The comedian looked haggard and drawn, but he mustered a smile when I shook his hand. "Look, son," he said, "there's a musicians' strike on, and the guest star on my new TV series, Edmund Hockridge, has been advised to pull out of the programme . . . I'm taking a chance on you . . . Les, you're going to replace Hockridge on this Saturday's show." I rose to my shaky feet and trembled, aspen-like. . . . Me, on television; I couldn't grasp it.

Max Wall's television show for the BBC was a "live" one, and the comic saw it as an opportunity to bolster up his tottering career. On the Wednesday of that week, I met Max Wall's producer, George Innes. I sang for him and he recorded me on a tape recorder and seemed genuinely pleased with the result. All that week I spent hours sat in the auditorium of the television theatre in Shepherd's Bush, watching the old maestro rehearse; the technical crew fixing monitors into position; the scenic hands working on the rostrum and "flats". . . . It was a wonderful world to be part of. For the first time, I came face to face with the national press. They interviewed me and photographed me, and on the Friday morning all the newspapers carried the story about my "big break" into show business. . . . I recall one such banner line: "NON-UNION UNKNOWN LES DAWSON GETS BIG SHOW BIZ CHANCE." Telegrams from my family and friends, well-wishers and current girl friend poured into the theatre in a never ending stream: I was walking on air; people pumped my hand and London, dear old London was Disneyland after all.

Saturday went by in a semi-dream sequence: I rehearsed and rehearsed; make-up girls frowned over me; the wardrobe people minced round me and fussed and ironed and dressed me; I was a Star in the making. . . . An hour before the show was due to be televised, Edmund Hockridge walked into the theatre and announced that he was defying the union embargo, and that he would do the programme. . . . I was Out.

George Innes grimaced sympathetically, and I was given fifteen pounds by Max, as a sort of compensation. . . . Compensation? Fifteen pounds for a broken heart. I left the theatre numbed, and in my hand I held my telegrams. I walked from Shepherd's Bush all the way back to Battersea. Tears were very close that cold damp night, as I stumbled through the hungry, dispassionate carnivore they called a city. . . . I felt very much like ending it all, and the turgid waters of the Thames almost beckoned me. In a pub on the Battersea Park Road, I watched the show on the TV set in the bar, and I drank myself to a stupor. . . . I spent the night in the dreadful digs, lying on my thin blanket in a cocoon of despair.

The Max Wall show took a hammering from the public and critics alike. He left the *Pyjama Game* and I didn't see him for over three weeks. I managed to find a garret flat in Notting Hill Gate, a room so small the mice had to sellotape their whiskers to walk through it. . . . But it was only two pounds a week, and I was nearly broke. All that was in the room was a bed and a gas ring, there wasn't even a coat hanger, but after having spent over four days sleeping on a bench in Hyde Park, with a policeman threatening to arrest me for vagrancy, it was a refuge from a world that seemed determined to destroy me. For entertainment, I used to stand outside the big hotels just watching people pull up in cars and stroll in. I lived on chips, occasionally accompanied by a sliver of fish, and my shoes let water in.

I signed on for dole money at the Hammersmith Labour Exchange and sank into a depression. Whilst taking part in discussions regarding my future, Max had introduced me to a lady by the name of Betty Lawrence: she was a pianist who worked nightly in one of London's famous landmarks, The Players' Theatre, Villiers Street, off the Strand. It was she who had accompanied me on the piano during rehearsals. Betty lived with her husband, a fine man called Jack, and her two children, Nigel and Meryl. Their home was a basement

flat in Basset Road, Ladbroke Grove and from time to time
I had baby-sat for them. . . . They were the only friends I
had. It was she, that wonderful woman, who took me under
her wing, fed me and gave me confidence.

To keep body and soul together, I became a dish washer
in one of the Lyons Corner Houses; the wage was three
pounds a week and meals. From dawn to dusk I cleaned
greasy plates and was damn glad of it. On my odd day off,
I haunted the theatrical agencies, gave the odd audition, and
received the dampening response, "We'll let you know." Of
course they never did. I dashed off articles for magazines, and
the heap of rejection slips grew into a positive alp. Now and
again I managed to pick up a stray girl and would sneak her
into my hovel for a few moments of physical escapism. I was
losing my confidence by the passing hour; eventually I went
to see Max Wall but his office was empty. . . . His business
venture had failed, as did his television series. I did hear
from him by letter: it read simply, "Sorry about everything,
suggest you go home."

I decided on one last throw of the dice. . . . I auditioned
for an agent who was well known in the business: his name
was Al Heath, and in a strange way, he was to change the
course of my life.

He sat in the Max Rivers rehearsal room, toying with an
enormous cigar, and listened to me as I sang blues and played
fast tempo but inaccurate piano. When I had finished, he
remained silent for what seemed an eon, then: "Not bad,
son. . . . Tell you what I'll do," he rasped. "I'll give you a
week in Hull, you'll be playing the fishermen's clubs. . . .
How does eighteen pounds grab you?" I very nearly shook
the gold off his hands. . . . I had an engagement! True, the
engagement was four months away, but it was a date . . . I
couldn't wait to tell Betty and Jack, and they were warmly
enthusiastic for me. Jack gave me good advice: "Don't hang
around any longer, Les, go home to your parents. Don't feel
as though you are going back with cap in hand, God knows
you've tried, old boy, but luck hasn't been on your side, go
home now." I took his counsel and a week later, after a year
of struggling, I bade London a temporary farewell. But I
promised myself that one day I'd retrace my steps back to
this indifferent city, and I'd win through, I'd have this grey

old pile on her knees. . . . Because I had no money, I had to hitchhike home: I came back from my daydreams with a bang.

I sat in the seat of the lumbering lorry next to the taciturn driver who had picked me up off the edge of Staples Corner, and coughed as the fumes of the eccentric vehicle pervaded my breathing passages. The rain threw a curtain at the windscreen as we rolled along towards the north, and the lights of traffic coming towards us stung the vision with illuminated icicles. I went over the past events in my mind . . . I had achieved so little. . . . Fragmented scenes scampered briskly through the tired imagination: the hunger, the loneliness, the emptiness of despair. Self-pity, I confess, filled my aching being. What was I destined for? Before I discovered the answer to that question, many paths would I take, and many a challenge would I face.

In order to explain my respect for the power of television, I shall have to leap forward in time, with the reader's forgiveness, and recount a small incident. After the debacle over my debut on *The Max Wall Show*, I felt as if the world had closed its door on me; understandably my heart ached over what had transpired, but in fairness, not for the right reasons. I'd really wanted that television airing to demonstrate to the folks back home that I was a success. . . . My thinking was totally parochial, in no way was I thinking objectively about the future. In those inexperienced days, I took it for granted that once I'd been seen on the "box" that would be it: fame and fortune as a matter of course. Never once had I studied the impact that television possessed over our lives, until years later during a show in my series *The Dawson Watch*.

The programme that night was a discourse on family life, and in my opening patter I gave a large part of the script over to the role of the mother-in-law in our society. . . .

"My wife's mother tells people that I'm effeminate. I don't mind, because compared to her, I am.

We get on well, in all the years I've known her we've only had three fights . . . morning, noon and night.

I'm not saying that she is an unattractive woman, but British Rail have banned her from putting her head out of a carriage window in case passengers think it's a cattle truck.

When she tried to make an appointment at a beauty salon she was advised to write to *Jim'll Fix It*.

To give you some idea what she's like, she telephoned the Good Samaritans and they hung up.''

It was the last wisecrack that brought home to me the awesome duty we performers have to the public.

Three days later, a long buff envelope arrived in the morning post. Meg handed it to me and said, "Looks as if you've upset somebody."

On the front of the envelope was the printed legend "Society of the Good Samaritans". I opened the letter with trepidation. Then as I read contents, I felt as if I'd been struck across the forehead. . . . The letter read thus:

Dear Sir,
Regarding your remark concerning the work of the Good Samaritans on the programme *The Dawson Watch*. We thank you for the mention of our society, because that night we received many many calls for help from people in distress.

I sat in the kitchen, my breakfast untouched. Meg read that letter and she studied me. "That's nice," she said. "Aren't you pleased that it did some good?" How could I explain to her that the letter had frightened me? Supposing that I had said something that might have triggered off a different response from someone finding life too difficult to cope with? It appeared to me then that every artist who is engaged in television work has an enormous responsibility to his or her public. The performer's image flickers in the homes of people he will never see; people who are ill or lonely; people whose only lifeline to the outside world is the television set. The performer is there simply to entertain, not to set up a situation in which he or she uses the medium to put across personal ideas about politics and religion, or to assume a persona of being remote and untouchable.

In the days of the theatre, an artist was separated by the apron of the stage and the footlights. . . . Today, we are seen in the public's homes and we are part of their lives.

One old lady approached me not so long ago and said firmly, "Next time you are on television, don't forget to wave to me, otherwise I will switch you off." Was there ever such a power?

IMAGES

Her Majesty moved slowly down the line of the waiting artistes; she shook hands and smiled and the foyer of the Palladium was charged with adrenalin. She saw the performers standing in anticipation of the contact with the First Lady of the Realm. . . . What she could never see, was a small boy of eleven in a second hand Boy Scout's uniform, pedalling to the troop's annual camp on a bicycle with no lights or bell on it; with patched tyres and a rusty frame. The urchin panted as he wheeled the contraption across Belmont Moors in his effort to get to Morecambe. All the other lads had gone by train, but his parents couldn't afford such a luxury, so he had to cycle.

He had no money to spend on amusement but won the other scouts' respect by being able to get pennies out of machines by poking thin wire into the slots. His one friend, Ken Cowx, bought him lemonade, and the scout master, Reg Wereman, had the holes in his trouser seat sewn up. That week was the only holiday the boy had ever had . . . and it was the first time he had seen the sea. It was the thrill of his life, apart from the one Christmas when his dad had managed to buy him some second hand soldiers to go with the apple and orange in his stocking.

FOURTH REHEARSAL

I was glad to be home. London had excited me, but I knew that for all time, my heart would be in the north. The people, most of whom had experienced hardship, were more tolerant than the average southern dweller; they had a greater depth to their character than their London counterpart, and the north was changing. Gone now the "flat cap" image of a northern male, and there was an air of sophistication in Manchester, equal to anything I had seen in London. In St Anne's Square, the women were dressed in the latest fashions and the shops and department stores glowed with the new wave of prosperity that Britain was beginning to enjoy. . . . My mother made no secret of the fact that she was glad to have her only son home, and my father and I started on a new footing together, often going out for a drink in various pubs and clubs. The year was now 1956. I reviewed my life and decided that apart from the week's engagement in Hull for Al Heath, I would carry on in show business as a semi-pro. Much to my astonishment, Hoover took me back on as a sales service rep; and with mother's help, I bought myself a decent second hand car and plied my trade.

Hoover sent me back to cover the poor area of Moss Side. Its slums abounded with a seething mass of children who came in all sorts of colours and creeds, but somehow, I sold a lot of washing machines and cleaners. I now had money in the bank, and on occasion even received a smile off the bank manager. . . .

The week of my engagement at Hull finally dawned. To get time off from my job with Hoover, I had to tell a pack of lies to my area manager, one George Walker, a nice sort of chap who had once pleaded with the vacuum cleaner company not to sack me because of my falling sales figures.

I drove to the east coast, little knowing that the drama that would unfold in that coldest of cities would shape the future course of destiny for one Les Dawson.

Hull. Surely one of the windiest, chilliest sprawls in the northern hemisphere. . . . Hull. . . . It was so cold there, brass monkeys were lagging one another. I went straight to the first club on the circuit I was to play: inside it had all the radiant charm of Lenin's Tomb on half day closing. . . . Beer-soaked old tables; a blackened pattern of cigarette burns on the faded carpets; a sour reek of spirits and ale, and a ramshackle stage upon which sat a rickety piano and a set of well-battered drums over which was to found a seedy man with a balding head and a red nose who turned out to be the leader of the "band": two of them, known as the Downbeat Duo. The seedy man with the nose like a rail terminus played the percussion instruments as if he was beating a bull moose to death. The pianist, when he arrived, stalked over to the ageing pianoforte and virtually raped the yellow keys with fingers that vaguely resembled Fife bananas. . . . From the outset, I smelt disaster, and later, when I found my accommodation, the premonition became a reality: the house was appalling. It was so dirty, vandals broke in one night and decorated it. The landlady, Mrs .... (she might still be alive) possessed a face like a tin of condemned veal, and her legs were merely a trellis work for varicose veins. God knows when the house was last painted, but Rembrandt must have done the first coat. Several other thespians were sitting glooming over their fate in what passed for a living room, and when the landlady introduced me, they merely grunted and turned back into statues.

One of the "pro's" present that depressing day was the old timer, Randolph Sutton, whose hit song *On Mother Kelly's Doorstep* had made him a household name. . . . Frankly, throughout that week, he was to treat me like a lump of canine excrement. The gorgon of a landlady took me up to my bedroom, which was actually a box with a plug socket; the room held a narrow cot and a wardrobe so old, Hannibal probably hung his jerkin in it.

I sat on the edge of the lumpy mattress and a flood of depression came over me. It was to turn into an ocean of woe . . . .

I drank heavily out of fear as I watched the club fill up with
hard-faced fishermen and their blank-featured wives. My
co-artiste Jessie Jewell, a pleasant and very funny lady, was
making up in the cramped dressing room which we both
shared and I envied her composure. The room became noisy
and hot and cigarette smoke hung in the stifling air like
low-lying wisps of nimbus; waiters with lit cigarette ends
behind their ears scurried to and fro with glass mountains
of beer to damp tables where sat the salt-caked men of the
sea. . . . There was a smell of sweat and cheap perfume that
intermingled with the odour of ale and spirits, and hovering
behind like an invisible backcloth, a stench of latent violence.

The band wailed into a musical birth and the tempo of the
harmony seemed to increase the volume of the drinks traffic.
I had undergone the salutary band call for my one musical
number, *Hey There* from *The Pyjama Game*, and I knew that
the accompaniment from the trio would be only slightly less
disastrous than the sinking of the *Lusitania*. . . . The din by
now was a tribute to Babel, and the lavatories were in a state
of siege as the night ground into second gear. My stomach
was in a turmoil and my heart rate was going like a Gene
Krupa solo as I swept the scene with a jaundiced eyeball. Like
a cork from a wine bottle, a lithe man in a double-breasted
blazer flew on to the stage and with right leg banging up and
down on the floorboards, began to sing *I've Got You Under
My Skin*. This invoked a terse comment from a heavily built
lady with few teeth: "Crap."

After the murderous treatment of *I've Got You Under My
Skin*, the stricken compère went into a stream of filthy remarks that convulsed the audience and, in particular, the
heavily built lady with few teeth, who roared like a windy
drain and sprayed the immediate area with gobbets of saliva.

I had sunk so far into myself, I didn't hear the compère
announce me, and it was Jessie who prodded me into animation. With a mouth drier than the Gobi Desert, I mumbled
a very subdued "Good Evening" which apparently came out
as "Gurr Errerin' Lazies and Gendlemen" and I launched into
the song *Hey There*. At first there was a stunned silence amid
the swirling fag fug and a few pop-eyed denizens peered at
me, but within seconds the noise was akin to the Frank

Whittle prototype jet engine, and someone threw a beer mat at me. After the song, which was greeted with an audible raspberry, I sat at the piano and played and sang *Mamma Don't Allow No Music Playing 'Ere*. . . . Dear reader, the degradation was complete. . . . Not only did nobody listen to my effort, quite a few of the audience threw pennies, and the flop sweat rolled in riverlets.

I finished my act, if one can excuse the expression, stumbled off the stage to a chorus of jeers, and fled into the black night and returned to my digs. That night I sobbed myself to slumber. During the next three days, I wandered through the harsh streets and by night I "died" on stage. Friday, early evening I could take no more: cheerfully, I would have upped and stolen away from Hull, but I had no money for petrol, but with what money I did possess, I managed to lose myself in drink in a small pub in an area called, colourfully enough, the Land of Green Ginger. It was where the slave market used to be before Wilberforce ended the traffic in human souls. . . . But that night I would have traded my lot with any one of the benighted devils who had seen his future in commercial chains. When my money had evaporated, I lurched to the club in truculent mood, prepared to be humiliated once more but ready to curse back, and to hell with the consequences.

Because I was late arriving at the club, Jessie had gone on before me and I watched her go through her routine with an experienced smile, despite rough remarks from the crowded premises. Frankly I could hardly see a thing . . . booze had laid a mantle over my vision and my co-ordination was, to say the least, suspect.

The compère beckoned me to rise. I did so with great difficulty and made the short trek to the stage steps, as if I was a lame primate fumbling for a foothold on a hanging creeper. Somehow I managed to squat upon the piano stool to steel myself for the opening number, *Bim Bam Baby*. As was my wont, I used to perform that number first, then bound off the piano like an eager wombat and go into my patter. . . . As the compère shrieked my name to the uncaring aviary of an audience, I realised with alcoholic dismay that I couldn't focus on the keyboard. Three times I strove to plummet my wavering fingers on to the appropriate keys and three times they finished up my nostrils. It was when I fell off the stool and lay on my back like a stranded waterman beetle, that the boozy throng began to cease their uproar. After what seemed an age, I rose dizzily to my feet, dusted myself down, sat my buttocks back on to the stool and rested my aching head in my right hand. There I slumped. The silence was quite eerie, and suddenly all the depression I felt pumped out of my mouth:

"Thank you for that brief spatter of applause that greeted my appearance on the stage of this renovated fish crate. (Good God! I heard several titters.)

It's a great pleasure to be working here, in fact it's pleasure to be working anywhere. . . . I'm booked here tonight and I have a booking for next October. . . . Not just engagements, to me that's a career . . . (Laughs.)

What you are about to see is an act that has given a whole new meaning to the word "Crap".

I don't do this for a living, oh no . . . just for the luxuries in life . . . bread and shoes." (Hoots.)

I'm so far behind with the rent the arrears are ticked off in the Doomsday Book. . . . I used to sell furniture for a living, the trouble was it was my own.

This suit I've got on is my only one, I bought it on HP from a tailor. It's called a kangaroo suit, two payments and you hop it. . . .

Nothing goes right for me, I had a puncture last night and as I took the tyre off to mend it, a car drew up and a fellow opened my bonnet. I said what the hell are you doing? He said if you're having the tyres, I'm having the battery." (Solid laughs and attention.)

I must have appeared like something out of a circus that night in Hull, and yet, for the first time in a chequered career, I was hearing genuine laughter from one of the toughest audiences a comedian could face. . . . I went on with a renewed confidence that was finally emerging from behind the mist of the drunken, self-deprecating Dawson façade:

". . . Not the first time I've been in Hull, but last time I was here, it was shut.

I didn't believe you were a Yorkshire crowd, after all, you walk upright.

Yorkshire, that's a sort of Cumberland with a sneer."

I wobbled off the stage to a magnificent ovation: several pints of ale were proffered and accepted, and a thin middle-aged female caressed my thigh as I sat down.

How I got back to the digs I will never know. All I can recall is being bundled into a Morris Minor and a voice saying, " 'E's a funny little bleeder."

A watery morning sun glanced off my bruised eyeballs and surfaced me to a rude consciousness, made all the more harsh by the sight of the thin middle-aged female of the night before, lying in a foetal position next to my left flank. As I stirred in an effort to diminish the battalion of drummers in my head, the creature next to me also stirred and murmured, "Shove it up us."

Had the statement been delivered in a bell-like tone, I may have complied; however the sentence was expelled from the lady's lungs with a breath that on occasions one would associate with the rank snort of a dyspeptic pig. Eventually, after a sort of bedroom brawl, I disentangled myself from her perspiring embrace, and with the aid of a crumpled fiver, removed her from my sanctum with a whispered promise to "see her again". She simpered, nodded and went. I had only just thrown myself back on the bed, when the landlady drifted into the room like a bank of fog and said slyly, " 'Ad a bit o' crumpet, hey?" I shrugged in the manner of an experienced libertine, and then gaped in horror as the conical woman removed her knickers and got into bed with me. . . .

That was the pattern of my life in Hull for the next two days and nights. After a long hard look at the events of the Friday evening success, I decided to keep the insulting formula of the material I had used, to see if I had "found" a style that an audience would appreciate, or if it had just been a sheer fluke. As things turned out, it wasn't.

Saturday night, I didn't get too drunk, although in fairness, I consumed enough to knock out the average horse. I sat at the piano in my depressed posture and went once more into the cynical patter that had served me so well:

"Good evening, culture hunters . . . just by looking at you all out there I can tell if tonight's going to cruel . . . Well, I've gazed at the brutality etched on a lot of faces here, and all I can say is: Welcome to the show . . . and Heil Hitler.

Great club this, should be called Twiggy's chest because the beer is flat and warm.

Had an audience in here last night . . . Jesus! I've seen more life in a tramp's vest.

Food's great here, though, the kitchen is spotless . . . in fact you can eat off the floor; you have to, the tables are filthy. . . . No mice in there, the rats have ate them all."

How they roared, those hard-bitten men of the sea and their long-suffering wives: I held their attention until I reached the end of my performance, and under the circumstances, with drink and noise the absolute norm for these places, that was no mean feat.

I left Hull in a cloud of exhaust fumes on the Sunday morning, after having received many accolades and having, of course, sated the sexual appetites of the Thin Middle-Aged Lady, and the Conical-Shaped Landlady, whose bottom was so big, when she sat down she was taller than when she stood up. As I drove away towards Lancashire, I felt elated: was I at last establishing myself as an artiste? Worthy of rubbing shoulders alongside such clubland luminaries as Johnny Hackett, Dukes and Lee, Don Crockett, Dickie and Dottie Arnold?

There were in those days highly polished performers who deserved better venues than working men's clubs. The names come back: Johnny Leroy, Pat O'Hare, Jack Diamond, The Starr Brothers . . . each of them star potential.

We cannot leave the club scene without some mention of one that became infamous among the artistes of the day. Every battle-scarred pro has bitter-sweet memories of the venue: Greaseboro' Social Club. A long wooden tunnel of a place, it lay not far from Sheffield and was run by a concert secretary with a wall eye whose name was Les Booth. He was everyone's idea of the perfect northern club official: stubborn, not too bright and possessing not one idea of what show business was all about. The club became a major cabaret date after the committee found that it had quite a few bob in the kitty and so they embarked on a policy of booking star names to appear. One of the first giants of the day to be booked there was Johnnie Ray, the American singer. All over Rotherham and Sheffield, large posters proclaimed proudly: "All week, Greaseboro' presents: 'The sensational Johnnie Ray and his orchestra'." On the opening night, the club was jammed to capacity and on to the stage stalked the Delfont of the Northern Climes, Les Booth. This was his address:

> "Reet, let's have some 'ush for the turn. Now this feller has cost a lot of money so I for one want to 'ear 'im. This feller 'as worked with all the great names: Frank Sinatra, Perry Como. But before I bring 'im on, it 'as come to my attention as the car park 'as been used as a urinal, this practice must cease forthwith . . . . Any road 'ere is the star turn put thy hands together for none other than . . . Tommy Ray and 'is band."

Les Booth became a legend for putting his foot in it. Once, after a ventriloquist hadn't gone down well, Mr Booth said to him, "Tha was bloody awful, half the trouble was, people at the back couldn't hear thee, so next time you go on't stage for your second spot, put the dummy nearer the microphone."

He told me on one occasion, his face reddened with Tetley's Bitter, " 'Ad a good turn 'ere last week, Emily Pond." When I said I hadn't heard of the lady, he snorted with indignation and spluttered, "She's done reet well 'as the lass, she's got her own shop in Halifax."

He really was the most extraordinary man and he helped the club along very nicely to its eventual ruin.

Many big names appeared at northern clubs: Louis Armstrong was seen at Batley Variety Club, one of the more sophisticated watering holes. The club was run by Jimmy Corrigan who had great ambitions for his venue, and indeed rumour has it that he actually travelled to America, to see if he could book Elvis Presley. The story goes that he managed to be interviewed by "Colonel" Tom Parker, who guided Presley's career. With modest pride, Corrigan is reputed to have said that he was prepared to pay Elvis thirty-five thousand British pound notes for the singer's services, and in response Parker is supposed to have said, "Mr Corrigan, my boy wouldn't get out of the bath for a piss for that money."

I myself got embroiled in a curious situation at a miners' social club in Wales. I'd fought through a veritable blizzard to get to the place and my veteran Ford Popular saloon was in danger of having a sort of mechanical cardiac arrest. A large gentleman with a coal-seamed face shoved me into a chair, a pint of ale was dumped in front of me and I was left to my own devices. The premises badly needed restoration and they smelt like a charnel house. The place soon filled with hulking men and sullen women who cast odd glances at me. A pianist and drummer filed on to the stage and listlessly began to plough through a version of *Hello, Hello, Who's Your Lady Friend?* The first few bars sounded like a Piute rain dance with just the merest hint of a Serbian burial chant in it. They were cut off in mid strangle by a large man with a cigarette smouldering on his bottom lip. "Before we have the artist for tonight, we are going to play a game of Bingo." Before he could go any further, a chap sitting near my table jumped up and howled, "What the hell are we playing Bingo on a Saturday for? We always play that on a Sunday, boyo." The man on the stage glared at him and retorted, "We're playing Bingo so that we can pay this bloody comic." I didn't know where to look as he went on, "That is why we're playing just one house." The man in the audience still stood, obviously not satisfied with the answer, and he shouted, "How much money is this comic getting, Evans?" The man on stage, Mr Evans, shouted back, "Nine pounds." To which the chap on his feet replied in a chilling tone, "That is bloody stupid money to pay, I don't get that for a bloody shift." A stout woman, glass of something in hand, stood at the back of the club and screamed, "You're a bloody liar, Thomas, you get more than my 'Arry does." Within seconds my meagre fee was forgotten and a full scale row broke out with politics thrown in as well as a few shoves and threatening gestures.

Eventually, amid deep breathing and scattered snarls, a sort of armistice was established. The concert secretary remembered my existence and indicated that I should do my "turn". Without any introduction or musical snatch to herald my arrival on to the podium, I went into my patter:

> "What a pleasure to be here in this chapel of rest. In my time I have played to near idiots and imbeciles but for progressive asininity you are beyond recall."

That was as far as I got. I was given three pounds and shown the door.

Many a comedian today will relate stories of concert secretaries to an audience and they may laugh, but I doubt if they realise that the comic is probably giving a true account of an incident. Many years ago, I overheard two burly concert chairmen talking about the quality of the "turns" they had booked. One said, "I booked that lass you mentioned, Arthur, tha were reet, what a good turn, she did sweat." If that wasn't bad enough, the other suet-faced impresario painted a more chilling picture. "Last neet, we 'ad a reet bleedin' artist, an escapologist or summat. He got some lads up out of the audience and they chained him up, that were at half seven. Silly bugger were still in chains when Queen were played."

My favourite story, and I vouchsafe that it's true, concerns the booking of a well known London impressionist into a club in Halifax. The mimic "died" and the concert secretary told the artist that he was being paid off and would therefore receive only a fraction of his fee. The impressionist was made of sterner stuff than bethought, and demanded that he put his case before the committee, which he did upstairs in a private bar. In no uncertain terms he told the beery assembly that (a) His act was sophisticated, (b) There was no control over the audience to make them listen whilst the cabaret was on and finally (c) His act was far too clever and had gone above the audience's heads. Apparently there was a short silence and then one member sighed and remarked, "Feller's got a point there tha knows . . . 'bout his act going over the heads of the audience, I allus said them loud speakers on't wall were too high."

Slowly, ever so slowly, I began to get known on the Manchester club circuit. The style of delivery; the "woeful" formula
gleaned from the engagement in Hull, didn't always go down
as well as it had, but at least concert secretaries knew of me,
and that, in a city that abounded with excellent performers,
was a tribute in itself.

My life away from the club scene remained the same: I plied
my profession with Hoover, trying to sell my merchandise in
the crowded streets of Moss Side and Hulme, with little
success. . . . The only reason Hoover kept me on, and of this
I am certain, is that no one in their right mind would have
wanted to work that most unsalubrious area. Yet I found the
occasional soul who left a lasting impression on me. There
was a lady who lived in what appeared from the outside to
be a rotting tenement, but once you went inside the roughly
painted portals, you entered a time warp of an age of elegance
long dead: a hallway with magnificent paintings and busts of
Homer and Socrates escorted the visitor to an oak-panelled
reception salon with velvet drapes at the high arched windows
and Hepplewhite furniture sedately at ease upon thick piled
carpeting. The lady of the house was a matron of considerable
dignity and she gestured a welcome with a hand whose long
and attractive fingers many bejewelled rings adorned. Her
features were finely chiselled and her hair was iron grey and
swept back from her face. She spoke in a well-modulated
tone and her speech was punctuated with foreign expressions.
As a girl she had lived in Moss Side, when the houses had
been the gracious dwellings of Mancunian cotton barons;
although she had lived in many countries, she had flatly
refused to abandon Moss Side, despite the dereliction of the
area. Her life had been a full one: she had been the mistress
of the Kaiser Wilhelm; she had known the glory of Vienna
before the First World War; the grand balls of Berlin and
Paris. . . . As she talked to a most attentive audience, the
shadows of the past engulfed me. She left a lasting impression
on me; years later I heard that she had died after being attacked
during a burglary attempt on her home.

It may seem incongruous that my mundane job as a Hoover
representative should be a veritable fount of experience, but
going into divers homes was just that. I recall a house in

Firswood, South Manchester, where there lived three spinster sisters, one of whom was simple-minded. When I was summonsed to the address to see the occupants about the possible sale of a washing machine, I walked down a crumbling pathway between rows of enormous sunflowers that seemed to glare at me like triffids. After I had knocked a large pitted brass replica of a lion against a faded door, it opened slightly and a pair of bright eyes surveyed me in a burning fashion. I held my card towards the apparition and heard a girlish giggle as the door swung open and I was admitted. Once in the musty dark hall, I was just in time to see a figure with pigtails, ankle-length socks and a short dress cantering up the stairs. Two elderly ladies approached me and bade me follow them into a small living room. Theirs was an enchanted realm. After the death of their parents, the three daughters had shut the door on the outside world and had become virtual recluses, but they were charming and the one who had admitted me, simple she may have been, but she looked and behaved like a young woman of thirty, not sixty-eight as she turned out to be. Frequently I would visit them for a chat and it was an oasis in a society of greed and encroaching ignorance.

My social pattern during these days was still drinking and whoring with the "lads". It was 1957, I was nearly twenty-six with money in my pocket and the devil take the rest. . . . Then my world collapsed. It started when my mother's eyesight became impaired almost overnight. At first, we thought little of it until I took her to the Manchester eye hospital and learned that she had thrombosis behind the right cornea. She sat alone in the hospital corridor, her hands toying with the straps of her handbag, her sweet face pale and expressionless. I went into the gents' toilet, locked myself in a cubicle and wept for that little woman who had gone through so much.

The nights I'd caused her heartache with my drinking; my neglect of her through the lonely war years when my father had been away; the way I had taken her for granted. . . .

IMAGES

Her Majesty came slowly down the line of waiting artistes and I stood nervously aware of my inadequacy before the regal presence. The Queen was shaking hands with Dick Emery and I saw her glance towards where I was standing. What Her Majesty would not see was a frightened boy of twelve being forced to look at his grandfather lying in his coffin, with black-draped relatives drinking noisily around his remains. She would not see the sobbing lad of fourteen at the funeral of his friend Billy, who had died from spinal meningitis . . . . Billy, who had told me such wonderful stories about his parents: only when he died did we find out that he was an orphan and homeless. Little Billy, who never knew any love, only hunger and want . . . . My friend Billy, and they were lowering him down into a pauper's grave. The rain fell that day in Philip's Park Cemetery as they laid the pathetic lad to rest, and I had brushed shoulders with Death.

FIFTH REHEARSAL

Saturday night, and the taxi drivers' South Manchester Social Club was full to capacity. The armpits of the Liverpool soprano were awash with perspiration; the droplets of sweat were clearly visible as she flung her arms high in the air to the last bars of her finishing number, *Answer Me*. The audience roared their approval, mainly in relief that she'd actually concluded her performance. Frankly, her voice was like a parrot urinating on a tin roof, but she'd found favour with the florid-faced concert secretary who was by now groping her considerable backside with gusto. I followed the obese songstress and did a "bomb", as they say . . . I could do nothing wrong that night:

"Good evening, ladies and gentlemen . . . there that's my first joke.

I've never played this club before, but I knew my luck couldn't hold.

I just loved that singer, didn't you? What a figure, in India she'd be sacred. She's so fat she had to lose weight to model maternity frocks.

Mind you, I'm putting weight on, I used to have broad shoulders and a deep chest but that's all behind me now.

I knew I was playing for taxi drivers tonight, the concert secretary deducted commission and a tip."

The patter went very well and I played and sang dirty ditties and they went a storm. . . . I shudder now, but here was an example of an early Dawson ditty (to the tune of *Molly Malone*):

"There was a young woman from Hitchen, who was scratching her arse in the kitchen.

Her mother said "Rose? It's the crabs, I suppose. . . ."
She said, 'Bollocks, get on with your knitting.'"

Hardly the material of a budding Noel Coward, but on the
level I was, it was sophisticated. After completing my act, I
was feted and I was soon well in the grasp of Bacchus, sexual
desire being fanned by the embrace of a blonde woman with
more teeth in her mouth than a basking shark. The world was
my oyster as I rolled about the heaving, smoke-choked concert-
room. It was, by any of my standards, a damn good night.

How I drove my van home I'll never really be sure. I
remember being sick down the front of my suit at some traffic
lights, but the remainder of the journey to Blackley is a blank
now as it was then. The house was in darkness, my parents
were in bed. I dragged myself up the narrow staircase, un-
draped on the landing, leaving my reeking clothes in a pile,
and lurched into bed.

I was dreaming that a giant hand was pulling me upright and
lights, sparkling little lights were helping the tom toms in
my head; my vision swam into a befuddled focus: Dad . . .
what was he doing? His face was contorted with grief; creases
of pain dug into his features. . . . What was he saying?
Mother, was something wrong with my mother?

I stumbled out of bed, trembling. Oh no, God, leave her
be. I followed my father into their bedroom. My mother was
lying on her back; she seemed to have shrunk in stature . . .
Oh no, God. . . . I tried to shake her into animation as Dad
knelt by the side of the bed, his shoulders shaking with
torment. "Mother," I cried, *Mother*." Her mouth hung
agape and her deep brown eyes, once so full of warmth and
fun, were now clouded and bereft of life. I held her close and
I screamed and cried out to God. I babbled on and on. . . .
My father had telephoned the doctor and when he arrived,
he had to prise me away from her as he went through a
perfunctory examination, the result of which we already
knew. Julie Dawson, slum child and mother, was dead. No
more would she wait up until the early hours for her errant
son, no more would she, who had known only hardship,
look at me with love in those oh so brown eyes . . .

Dad and I buried my mother in St Joseph's cemetery and over two hundred of her friends attended the funeral. That little lady, who could be one moment as kind and as gentle as a deer, the next volcanic in temper, had touched all these people's lives . . . In their faces I saw genuine sorrow, and I knew, that, like mine, their lives would never be the same without Julie.

The weeks that followed the death of my mother were in every sense sombre ones. My father was lost and deep down I knew that he had made his mind up to join her. For the first time in our lives, we were close and between us, we strove to keep the family together. He and I would go out with my mates on drinking sessions that helped to bury our pain for that moment. I started to do the cooking and he the house-work, and between the two of us, we coped. My father began to go out at least three times a week with his cronies, and they swapped yarns, drank and played bingo.

During this period, I played clubs and pubs all over the north of England. The names flood back in a rill of nostalgia. The Mersey Hotel, Didsbury. The Gorton Loco Club, the Russell Club, the Cromford Club, Blackley British Legion, Frascati's, Dino's, Stretford Trades and Labour, the Salvage Inn, the Derby Inn, the Forrester's. . . . The names of the club and pub circuit acts: Jimmy Ryder, comic; Al Auguste, singer; Renee Rhythm, jazz pianist. Talented people abounded in the lively night life of Manchester in those days: Pat O'Hare, Tony Hulme, Jimmy Higginson, Jack Grice, Al Garner, Barney Blake, Jack Diamond. . . . Up and coming acts: Johnny Hackett, a brash Jimmy Tarbuck, Barbara Law. . . . Amid the talent there were the strange theatrical agencies, like the Ace Agency in Salford. Nobody ever met the lady who ran it: you telephoned her in the afternoon and for the grand sum of a fiver or, at best, eight pounds, she would despatch you to pulse-pounding places such as the Tavern or the Cornbrook Hotel. If a comic got a laugh in those places, he usually got a fortnight's holiday in Malta. Hard times . . . but always learning. Manchester was Ham-burg and Soho rolled into one; it was the axis on which the wheel of bawdy entertainment revolved. There were the prostitutes and the strippers and the "drag" queens of the night. We drank and we had women and in the intervals between these events, I mended vacuum cleaners and washing machines. I was still attempting to write, particularly essay compositions, and the pile of rejection slips grew and grew. Britain in the late fifties was a good place to live: two car families no longer raised an eyebrow; there was full employment and the Good Life and always good time girls to appease the male groin.

I had a succession of old cars, mostly two tone – black and rust – and my mates, Harold and Terry and Jimmy and Gordon, not forgetting stoic Fred – who, upon reaching the ancient Forum in Rome, remarked mournfully, "All this way to see a bloody ruin" – would roar about the streets in a cloud of smoke.

We toured Europe in a battered van. . . . In Rome, the police raided a brothel where I was performing nature's finest emotion with a sultry professional when the law burst the door in. Naked I stood with passport aloft, a few pounds changed hands and I resumed the performance. In Sweden, I was chased by an outraged husband, and in Barcelona, I made love to a cool beauty under a shower, watched by her "uncle".

I had applied for several auditions with BBC Radio in Manchester and I had failed every one, until a man who was to launch me in a small way, on my last desperate attempt for a show business career, gave Fate a push. The man's name was Bill Scott Coomer, the producer of a radio show called *Aim At The Top*. He decided to use me as a second spot comic, and despite shaking knees I did well and the studio audience were most appreciative. From him, Bill Scott Coomer, came a chance to work in Filey in a small theatre in a two day revue.

"Hi, my name's Les Dawson and frankly, I'm about as well known as the mating habits of the Polynesian hermit crab. . . . In fact, I'm the only one on this bill I've never heard of.

But what a thrill to be in Filey. . . . Filey, that's a sort of borstal with sand.

I'm not saying that my act is boring, but last night a man in the front row was firing off a distress signal.

I've got nice digs here in Filey, well not really digs, more like a monsoon ditch. I'm not saying the place is dirty, but you have to spray the kitchen with DDT before the flies will come in.

There's one thing about it, the digs remind me of home . . . filthy and full of strangers. The window cleaner doesn't use a leather on the glass, he uses a Brillo pad.''

The act was well received and I felt that Bill was pleased with my effort, but from my point of view, what made me feel a sense of satisfaction was that I was gaining confidence and not having to get drunk before I faced an audience.

I was getting bored with Hoover, and one incident which occurred in Moss Side whilst I was canvassing for business was almost too much for me. . . . What happened was like something out of an early Ben Travers farce. I knocked on a door that was warped and damp in a street of houses so small the landlord probably had the occupants evicted with a ferret. The door opened with a protest, and an elderly chap with braces dangling down his stained trousers peered at me myopically and grunted, "What the f. . . do you want?" I straightened with injured dignity and replied tartly: "A little civility, sir, if you please." He struck a vaguely pugilistic posture and retorted, "Piss off" and with that, the churl slammed the door in my face. Outraged, I knocked on the door yet again. The old loon threw it open but before he spoke, a female voice yelled out from the dark cavern of the hall, "What's up, Cyril?" The old man turned and snarled, "A young fellow at the door, he's threatening me." I was opening my mouth to defend myself when suddenly a floor mop sailed from the gloom and struck me in the face. I had scarcely begun to reel, when a bucket of soapy water soaked me to the skin, accompanied by a cry that was reminiscent of a dervish with piles. This attracted the attention of other residents of the street and two burly thugs chased me around the corner with the result that I was forced to hide in an outside lavatory until the coast was clear.

I was restless and the future seemed bleak. At this time I was courting a blonde girl who stirred me physically, but I was having trouble getting her in the mood. I was drinking far too much and spending too much of the day in billiard halls. In despair, I did an audition for a certain Mr Arthur Fox, the Manchester king of strip shows which then were all the rage in the rapidly dying world of the old music hall theatres. . . . Ah! the names of those shows: "She Stoops to Concur", "Bare Way To The Stars", "If You Nude Susie". . . . Frankly they were dreadful and did indeed help to kill off variety. Television was a new toy and apart from dirty old masturbators who haunted the stalls, theatres were empty. Much to my surprise, Fox signed me up as a singer for a new revue going out called "The Pauline Penny Peep Show", featuring a raddled elderly lady with a heart of gold – named, of course, Miss Pauline Penny.

The show was awful; to me, however, it spelled out SHOW BIZ, and when I walked out on to the grimy stage and knelt on one knee singing *It's Witchcraft* to naked girls dancing around me, I knew that this was what I wanted to do with my life.

After the opening night, I drove to the Piccadilly Club to celebrate, to drink and listen to Jerry Harris, a very funny Jewish comic, and oblivious of the company I was sitting with, I looked back in retrospect. . . . The failures, the low troughs, the idiotic conduct of my life, had I put it all behind me at last?

The strip show went to Manchester, to the old Hulme Hippodrome. During the tour I had gone "sick" so that I could steal time away from Hoover in order to further my stage craft, but I felt safe being at the Hulme Hippodrome, because nobody from Hoover would ever sink so low as to grace the old dump. . . . Oh capricious Fate.

On the Monday morning our sales team were summoned to meet a new branch manager, his name escapes me now, but he was by his very appearance "a new broom". He shook my hand and said he would be looking forward to my sales expertise, and that was that, or so I thought.

I stole away from the Hoover meeting and went straight to the Hippodrome for two reasons: (1) To go through my four numbers with the pit orchestra . . . orchestra! That band was so bad, it was a pleasant change when they played out of tune. Reason (2) I was having an affair with one of the strippers. It was our custom to sate our desire in a dressing room, and we did that often. She was a good looking girl with quite a superb figure, and her aim, I feel sure, was to co-habit with every male in Christendom. Monday night dawned, I peeped through the faded curtains and there they were: small bald men in raincoats, licking their lips in anticipation of naked flesh. Backstage, electric razors were humming as the girls shaved their pubic bushes off before placing lengths of sellotape across their genitals; this moment was known amongst the stage hands as "the six o'clock shadow". The lights dimmed and some popped into oblivion; the band struck up in a banshee wail of despair, and the girls, discarding their chewing gum, swayed on to the podium to the sound of a heavily beaten big drum. I made my entrance with a hand microphone, and sang *That Old Black Magic* on my knees, looking up the powdered crotches of les femmes. I went off to a mild spatter of applause, then Pauline, dressed in a red ball gown, sauntered on singing in a voice that would have been capable of shattering the mortar in the walls of Jericho. The song was called *Sugar In The Morning, Sugar In The Evening, And Sugar At Suppertime.* As the sound filtered through her adenoids, Pauline took off the dress in a tantalising fashion, followed by the black stockings, saucy garters and French laced panties. The old men in the raincoats moaned audibly as she thrust out her naked bottom over the footlights and caused the ample cheeks to quiver as the light dimmed, followed by a total blackout which enabled Pauline to get off stage whilst the stage crew set up the props for the sketch. The sketch featured Pauline's husband, Barry Piddock, the revue comic, Jimmy Edmundson and yours truly. The sketch was a simple one: a girl stood on stage naked apart from three bowler hats; one on each breast and one covering her vagina. All that happened was: I walked on first, and took a hat from her left breast; Barry came on next and took one from her right breast; then Jimmy came on, pulled a set of leering faces with suitable gestures, made as if to take the bowler hat from her mound of pleasure, and she very swiftly gave him one which was hanging on her backside. It may sound a trite piece of business, but the hard-breathing customers loved it. As I waited in the wings to go on, I peered through the front cloth and nearly had a cardiac arrest: for sitting in the front row of the stalls, was my new branch manager, the one I'd met only that morning. I had to be pushed on to the stage and unintentionally got a laugh when I stumbled against the girl and nearly pulled her over. I stole a quick glance at my Hoover boss and his face looked like a bag of spanners. I pulled the bowler hat away from the girl's breast and nearly took her nipple off with the action. She screamed and shouted, "What the bleedin' hell are you doing?" I muttered an apology and again struggled with the hat which seemed reluctant to leave the damsel's mammary. The thin audience roared as I wrestled with the headgear, and when it finally came away, I almost fell into the orchestra pit.

In my dressing room, I drank a large Scotch and thought, "This is it, son, unemployment yet again."

Tuesday morning dawned and there was no summons from the Hoover office, but that night the show was raided by the police. One of the strippers was cutely named Virginia 'Ding Dong' Bell – so called, one must presume, on account of the fact that Dame Nature had entrusted her with a forty-six inch bust. The highlight of the act she performed was known to her many admirers as "The Dance Of The Frustrated Banana". Need I go on? Suffice to say she did things with that object undreamt of in the imagination of your average pervert. At the hearing in court on Wednesday morning, the stolid policeman said that he and his colleagues had been "painstakingly watching the lady's performance with the fruit for a considerable period". The magistrate, who couldn't take his eyes off Virginia's legs, said in a sarcastic manner, "It's refreshing to know that our policemen are forever vigilant in the pursuit of the transgressor." He then dismissed the charge, and we trooped off for a drink.

On Friday, I was ordered by my unit sales manager, George Walker, to go before my branch overseer. This is it, I thought, out. Oddly enough, although he upbraided me mightily, he didn't fire me, but I knew that from now on I was under close scrutiny. I promised that I would never take part in any show business activities again; that I would pledge myself to the God of Hoover to the exclusion of all other things. . . . That night I went to do a small cabaret act in a Crumpsall Labour Club for a private party, and little did I know that my life was about to change through that engagement. Looking back, I wonder if there isn't some Power that dictates one's existence. The club was quite a change from the slums I normally played in and as an added bonus, a table groaned with food and I was told to help myself, which I did, because frankly, my father and I weren't eating too well – in fact if it hadn't been for an old lady next door who cooked meals for us both, we would probably have taken out a ground rent at a chip shop. As I happily devoured a meat pie, a slimly built girl came across with her boy friend, one Peter Oscar who had, if memory serves me well, booked me for the night. Her attractive features puckered in an expression of disapproval as she watched me gorge the Dawson frame with savoury fodder. She introduced herself as Miss Margaret Plant and asked me if I wanted to use a thing called a clavoline, which was fastened to the piano and could reproduce the sound of an organ. I replied twixt mouthfuls that I didn't want to use the clavoline, I'd already been. Instead of smiling, she sniffed in distaste and stalked away. "Sod you," I muttered and swilled the food down with an amplitude of strong ales. That evening was a disaster, the microphone didn't work, nobody laughed and I was clearly pissed. On my way out from the infernal mess, the haughty lass called Margaret Plant threw a gleam of malice from her grey green eyes, and I thought, "God help the guy who marries that one."

A week later dawned the date for the big Hoover dance that was to be held in Sale, a suburb of Manchester. Sale was a sort of nose in the air place where they didn't believe the working class deserved sex. My plans were drawn up; I was going to take my blonde lady to it; she was going to be plied with drink and by the beard of the prophet, I would get in her bloomers afterwards. . . . It was not to be. As with most things in my life, Someone Up There cocked it all up, and I never found admittance to her knickers and the delights therein. When we sat in my car after a session of thrust and parry, she said sadly that she couldn't accompany me to the dance, as she had to attend a hairdressing class.

The night before the Hoover dance, I went with the "lads" to the Northern Sporting Club, where for a trifling sum, one could see top class performers, wrestling bouts and boxing matches. Alas, that sort of venue is no longer with us and night life is the poorer for it. It was a good night, but I was depressed at the thought of attending the dance on my own, so I sat through the entertainment and drank heavily and moodily. At the end of the evening's jollities, the lads and I left to go to an Indian restaurant – they were springing up all over the city then and were gaining popularity. A hand tapped me on the shoulder, and I turned to find Miss Margaret Plant standing there. "Excuse me," she said. "Aren't you the comedian who was at the Labour Club last week?" Modestly I answered in the affirmative and weighed her up. She was small and very slim and resembled the actress Jean Simmons, a famous screen beauty of the day. On impulse, I asked her if she would care to accompany me to a Hoover dance tomorrow evening? My simper turned to a scowl when she said flatly, "No." It was obvious I wasn't her type at all, and looking back I really couldn't blame her. My dress sense still leaves a lot to be desired, but then it was appalling; ragged jackets and cravats that quite often hung like a heap of bandages around my neck. I tried to talk her into going with me and finished up pleading with her – all to no avail, until her sister, Elsie, who wanted to head for home said, "Oh go on, our Margaret, it's only for one night." I nodded in agreement: one night, thought I, would be more than enough, but as the ticket had cost me thirty bob, I would have quite cheerfully taken the Elephant Man with me. Finally, but with a trace of reluctance in her tone, she agreed to come with me and that was that. . . .

In those days I owned, through the courtesy of a HP company, a green Ford van, which had, for the benefit of passengers, an old bus seat in the rear. Although I never bothered to clean the vehicle, it was nevertheless my pride and joy and had atop the dash panel tiny dolls glued in a row, memories of trips to various countries. That van had witnessed drunken revels and love making and it had a truly glorious aroma of decadence about it that easily matched any that Ancient Rome had inhaled. I was late in picking up my date for the evening and when I finally drew up outside her house in Chattaway Road, both Miss Plant and her mother were standing on the front door stoop gazing at the apparition before them. I bounded out of the van, conscious that my evening suit was too tight and that my dress shirt was badly ironed. Gaily, as Margaret introduced me to her mother, I cried, "Hello love" to the grim-faced parent, who pursed her mouth into an even grimmer contour. My date's father, a small stocky man with twinkling eyes, was also introduced to me, and having heard my cheerful greeting, grinned and said to his daughter, "That's a good start with your mother, he's right in the shit now."

. How was I to know that nobody but nobody, ever said "Hello love" to Mrs Plant, especially on a first introduction? I thought, "This is going to be a bloody night to remember." I backed away from the steely eyes of the mother, ushered Margaret into the van and off we sped to the city centre. I stole a glance in the rear view mirror to find Mrs Plant looking at the departing van as if she'd just had an encounter with some sort of ill-shod alien.

The journey was uneventful. I kept repeating that I was glad she'd accepted my invitation to the ball, and the weather and things, and how nice she looked . . . and she did. She became animated when I told her I worked as a Hoover representative, and she told me in return that on Saturdays she helped out in an electrical shop and that in her opinion, Hoover was rubbish and that she much preferred Morphy Richards. I rose like an idiot to the challenge and we got rather hot under the collar. The argument heated to boiling point and at a set of traffic lights on Corporation Street I opened her door and told her to get out if she wanted. She flushed angrily, and I couldn't help thinking how lovely the flush was. She made to get out of the van, but just at that moment the lights changed to green and, spurred on by an impatient horn behind me, I drove on, with silence a wall between us. Slowly we both cooled down, we lit cigarettes and, almost timidly, I asked her what her weekday employ-met was. When she told me, I began to sense that Fate was using my life as a jigsaw, as piece after piece fell into a pattern. Margaret worked as a secretary in Crumpsall village for a company that made ropes. The astonishing thing was that my mother, for some time prior to her death, had worked for the same company, James Austin and Sons. Margaret had known my mother only slightly, but she was well aware of the legends that had surrounded her. As Margaret talked, now in a softer tone, I saw again those sparkling brown Irish eyes, once so full of fun and mischief. . . . Whatever talent for comedy I possess, I inherited from Julie Dawson.

By the time we arrived at the Sale Assembly Room, where the ball was being held, Margaret and I were on amiable terms, and the prospect of a good time was in evidence. We sat with other Hoover employees and Margaret delighted in "ripping off" the pride of Hoover. As we danced, I began to realise that I could very easily fall in love with this girl. During one dance, I said flippantly that if we met again in five years time, and she still wasn't married, I would wed her. It was a wonderful night and I insisted on calling her Meg. She told me she'd often wanted to be called by that shortened name and on we danced and I didn't want the night to end. Forgotten now was my blonde lady, only the lass in my arms mattered, and on we danced. As usual I was asked to perform, and I sang the only song I've ever really known, *Bye Bye Blackbird*. I sang it for just one person, the girl I was halfway in love with, the one night only date, Meg Plant.

It was with sadness that I drove her to her front door, thanked her, and tentatively asked to see her on the Sunday. She said no, she had a previous engagement, but indicated that she was free the following weekend. Like a teenager or a recently fed puppy, I nodded eagerly and then drove the rest of the way home in a seventh heaven.

I couldn't get the girl off my mind, the lads sensed it and of course I was given a ribbing over it. I tried to look at things in a dispassionate way, but for the first time in my life, I knew with a certainty that I was really in love. I told my father in one of his rare moments of sobriety about Meg, and when he heard the name Plant, it turned out that he knew her father, Arthur Plant: they had worked together once at ICI in Blackley Village. . . . Fate put another piece in the jigsaw of my existence.

I was made welcome in the Plant household, because – dare one say anything about Fate's interference yet again? But Mrs Plant, that formidable matron, had worked with my mother at Austin's and that really thawed any ice in our relationship. I felt that Julie's Ka was working overtime for her son's happiness.

I seldom went out with the boys again. My every breathing

moment was spent with Meg and her family, and I often enjoyed the company of her father. It was so pleasant to anticipate the possibility of being a part of a large family. Meg had three sisters, Alma, Elsie and Ann, and a brother, Walter, and I wanted so badly to be one of them. I never really succeeded in that endeavour; being an only child does breed a solitary ego and no matter how one tries, acceptance to a conformative family pattern is difficult to obtain. Frankly, I was tolerated.

If only one could recapture the joy of courtship! The nights spent in friendly inns, the long wonderful plans laid out for the future: I had made my mind up, I wanted to marry Meg. But what could I offer her? My job was in jeopardy, I didn't seem to be getting far in show business, and what I'd earned, I had spent on drink and women. Physically, I was not the stuff of a young girl's dreams; I was short and wide across the shoulders and with a tendency to run to fat. I was convinced that Meg didn't feel for me what I felt for her, but after a short weekend spent with friends in a caravan in Wales, when, after attempting to get physical with her on the sands, an attempt that was made impotent by a freak whirlwind that blinded me like a latter-day Samson, she led me to safety, I believe it was then that she realised that beneath the sturdy exterior of her potential swain, there lay a child, who needed to be loved.

Meg changed my life and gave me a direction at long last; she also gave me the will to succeed. Where I was often devious and hypocritical in my dealings with people, she was honest, plain spoken and as straight as a die. We were married in Saint Thomas's church on June 25th 1960. My father's wedding present was a honeymoon in Austria and after our reception in The Woodlands Hotel that is where we consummated our marriage. Was there ever such a honeymoon as that one? The soaring Alps and the crowns of snow atop the frowning peaks; the tinkle of the bells on the necks of the lowing cattle; the delicious exploration of the warm inns on the Maria Teresa Strasse in old Innsbruck. . . . The knowing glances of people as they saw the young couple go past, oblivious of all others. . . . The nights spent in bodily harmony and the sense of belonging to each other. Learned men talk loftily today of the power of the atom, but there never has been anything as powerful as the love between two segments of humanity.

We couldn't afford to set up home when the honeymoon was over, but there was room at my father's house, and Meg agreed to live there until such time as we could afford a place of our own. We both knew it wouldn't be easy. In retrospect, despite the fact that through sheer luck I had won the major selling prize at Hoover, mainly the Derby Dinner and visit to the race itself, I knew my position was precarious and I would have to leave the job soon. Meg took over the running of Dad's little council house and we became a family once more. My father was eating properly and although I knew that inside, he mourned for Julie, at least on the outside, he looked healthy enough. Meg refurbished the house and the woman's touch was to be seen and felt everywhere.

Well, here I stood, a married man with a history of partial failures and disappointments; a self-deprecating individual, yet to make anything of himself and, more important by far, yet to prove himself to his wife. I felt that I was entering a new phase in my travels through life and I was jubilant and looking forward to new challenges. . . . If I could have foreseen what was in store for both Meg and me, it is quite possible, knowing my craven make-up, that I would have leapt on to a passing lugger and fled to the tropics. The show hadn't even begun to take shape. . . .

IMAGES

The atmosphere in the Palladium foyer was electric as Her Majesty, smiling radiantly, spoke to each artiste. She would see the pride on the faces of the performers, happy that they had been included in the glittering gala. When she eventually spoke to Les Dawson, she would see the same glow of pride on his crumpled features; she would probably not catch what he said, owing to his thick, flat, guttural Manucian accent; what she wouldn't realise was that that accent once saved him from an angry mob.

I was working as a labourer in Clitheroe. . . . The little market town was full of men, hard men, who were building the Hawsewater Tunnel Scheme to supply Manchester with Lakeland water. The public houses were packed nightly and prostitutes flocked to relieve the working crews of their hard earned wages. I used to finish up playing the piano in a pub called the Craven Heifer, one of the noisiest places in the town. There were frequent fist fights and it was a common sight to see bodies strewn about the streets. One night I took a gum-chewing paint-daubed lady to a club. I remember I was wearing a leather jacket at the time, and the garment plays a big part in the drama that was to follow. There was an odd atmosphere in the club; the girl noticed that every eye was upon me as we sat drinking in the smoke-wreathed room. At the end of the evening, even I became uneasy as the crowd blocked the exit when I rose to go. Some men had picked up empty bottles and violence was in the air. "That's the bastard," I heard a woman say. "It's him all right. I recognise that jacket." They backed me into a corner and formed a circle around me. I pushed the girl away and grabbed a fistful of coins, determined to hurt one of them as much as possible. My heart beat a sickening tattoo as angry men came closer.

"He'll not rape another girl in this town," one huge bearded man said in a low whisper. "He's got a bloody nerve coming back here, the filthy bleeder," spoke another. Rape? What the hell were they talking about? I blurted out, "What the hell is this all about? I've done nowt." The crowd stopped in their tracks. "It isn't him, he's not the one," said a lady with a cigarette in her mouth. "The one who did it was a Pole." "Sorry, lad," one man muttered, "but bloody hell, you're a dead ringer for him." They all apologised and they even opened the bar up again; trembling with fear I downed a few pints, it had been a close call. . . . As I was leaving, an elderly man in a cloth cap, puffing heavily on his pipe, tapped me on the shoulder and said, "It's a damn good job tha said summat, lad, in't it?"

SIXTH REHEARSAL

Many things happened in 1960, and all would have a bearing on the future. Meg had a miscarriage. We had both been in a seventh heaven when it was confirmed that she was with child. She had bought baby clothes in anticipation of the event, and now our joy was soured by the loss. As we hadn't been married long, it was clear that we had conceived on our honeymoon, and when we happily told her parents, her mother's face displayed disapproval. After the miscarriage, I held Meg in my arms and we wept for our lost life, and I vowed to her that one day we'd have a family. For some time I had sent what I hoped were funny letters to the head of BBC Manchester radio, Jim Casey, the son of that great old music hall comic, Jimmy James. I kept bombarding him for work, and eventually he gave me a chance on the big show of the times, *Workers' Playtime*, a radio programme that launched many a famous name. I did well on the show, and Jim and I struck up a friendship that is still strong to this day. Jim was a great help in my career, and it was he who opened the door for me on the radio, which is still, to this very day, my first love. In 1960, I left Hoover with mixed feelings; I had come to enjoy the job, but I sensed that the good years were over for the company, and in that respect I was correct, as shortly afterwards, the parent American company took over and altered the structure of the firm. I took a job as sales representative with a plastics manufacturer called Plysu and I was doomed from the start. They sold plastic trays and lavatory holders and tea strainers, and I couldn't get enthusiastic when trying to sell the damn things because frankly I hate bloody plastic. On one occasion, I managed to sell a slightly peculiar hardware shop owner in Giggleswick three gross of plastic lavatory brush holders, and upon revisiting him three months later I was appalled to find he hadn't sold one. They were everywhere: in his windows, up his windows, outside his windows; ranks of them, platoons of them in tiers. I put my head round the door and said brightly, "Good morning, how's things?" He threw a holder at me and thundered, "Piss off!"

For months I tried to sell my wares to a dreadful little man in Kendal. One day, as I sat at home moodily thinking that it was a good job the wife was working, the telephone rang and I was amazed to hear the voice of the dreadful retail dwarf from Kendal on the line. "Get thee up here, lad, I've got an order for thee." Overjoyed, I motored north, thinking that the order I would get would be worth hundreds of pounds, and I would thus avoid the possibility of being sacked. The dreadful little man shook my hand and out came my order form. "Now, lad, this is what I want . . . six tea strainers." I paled. The tea strainers retailed at one and threepence, in pre-decimalisation money, so on today's reckoning, a dozen would have cost 75 pence, and the order he had given me was worth 37½ pence. In vain I tried to sell him other of the ranges. . . . No. Six bloody tea strainers was all he wanted and the vista of unemployment loomed ahead. I put the order into the mail and waited. The reply duly came from head office.

Dear Mr Dawson
We thank you for the esteemed order for the six tea strainers. Rest assured that the factory is in full production to fulfil this most lucrative order,

Most Sincerely,
Mr Atkinson, sales manager.

P.S: Return the Ford Anglia car at once, you're fired.

So it was written that Dawson must move to other fields. After all, wasn't that the Dawson motto: "If at first you don't succeed, fail, fail again"?

I was taken on by a very reputable company who manufactured lighting equipment. The name of the company was Benjamin Electric, and I was employed to sell their new range of fluorescent fittings. They supplied me with a car and I had carte blanche permission to wander anywhere in the north of England to sell my product, which I didn't. Of all the jobs I've had, that was the most unusual: for a start, the fitting I had been employed to sell was by far the most expensive one on the market. . . . It was an excellent product, but in a hugely competitive market, it had no chance. But at least I had a good car to get me around on the club bookings. I had acquired a manager, himself a retired performer from a well known group called the Cordites. Kevin Kent became a friend and did his best to promote me, but the big clubs still eluded me, and in all fairness, I hated the club scene and would often turn engagements down. We met in a musicians' hang out, an untidy shop that sold musical instruments and was owned by one of the country's top saxophone players, Johnny Roadhouse.

One windswept morning, Kevin met me and excitedly informed me that he had got me a week's engagement as comedian compère on the Billy Cotton Band Show being staged at the Manchester Opera House. I was thrilled! The Big Time at last. . . . Hurriedly I got myself measured for a stage suit, bought new shoes and a bow tie, and three weeks later I turned up at the Opera House and was given a cordial welcome by the old maestro, Billy Cotton, himself. On the week's bill were the full Billy Cotton Orchestra, of course; a gloomy tightrope walker; and Gilbert and Partner, a chimpanzee act, whose primate's main interest in life was to feel chorus girls' backsides with gusto. . . . Opening night arrived; I waited for the overture to finish, then I would bound on to the stage, and slay 'em. . . . The overture ended and on I sprang. . . . I managed to say "Good evening, ladies and gentlemen", then realised that there was hardly any audience, just a few white blobs scattered around. I "died" the most awesome of theatrical deaths. . . .

> "Well, there's not many of us . . . ha ha ha . . . looks like the Moscow Conservative Club . . . ha ha ha. I'd like to thank the management for letting me work here, and also to thank the wife for making it necessary. . . . I'm not saying things are bad, but the mice in our kitchen are setting traps for us . . . . I'm not used to playing to a furniture exhibition. . . . Shall we hold hands and try and contact the living?"

There was a silence like a forgotten grave in a disused cemetery, and I hastily introduced the dancers, who looked as if they'd just had treatment for chilblains. Billy Cotton asked me to go into his dressing room. "What's the house like, son?" he queried. "Er, it's not full," I stammered, "but what's in are very nice, Mr Cotton." He looked at me. "Bloody awful, I'll bet, the box office said it was a poor advance."

After the dancers I introduced the tightrope walker, and he fell off the wire halfway along it, I wasn't surprised, you could have smelt his breath in Denmark: the only time he didn't have a bottle in his hand was when it was in his mouth. Gilbert and Partner went on, and the drummer in the pit thought he'd be funny and blew a raspberry at the chimpanzee, who got enraged, climbed up the curtains and crapped on the footlights.

It was a nightmare of a week. . . . Hardly anyone came to see the show; on a good night I've seen more people in a telephone kiosk. The chimp tried to rape a dancer, Billy Cotton's feet were bad, and the tightrope walker didn't know where he was, but on the final night, Saturday, he came out with an ad-lib line that I have used myself, it had me on the floor when he said it. He was walking across the wire with his pole and suddenly, halfway through his act, he turned to the audience, what there was of them, and breathed, "You can walk along here some days and never see a soul." For myself, if anybody laughed at my patter, it threw my timing. . . . Here's an example of the material I was using:

"I used to be a private eye . . . the right one's a pupil. Not everyone can be a detective, not every Tom or Harry can be a Dick.

I used to work in the Bank of England at Christmas as a secret agent. . . . Yeah, I was a Mint spy. (Mince pie, get it?)

One day I was sat in my office, the curtains were drawn but the rest of the furniture was real.

A letter came through the door and it brought tears to my eyes . . . it was written on an onion."

To this day, that show holds the record for the worst

business in the history of the Opera House. Nothing went
right for me that year: I took part on a local BBC TV show,
that I knew Jim Casey had set up with me in mind. Johnny
Hackett and I shared top billing and I did well, but it was
Johnny who took the honours, and I was shunted out. That
year I played the Shakespeare Club in Liverpool, a number
one date, and I stormed them. On the Thursday of that week
in the morning, I received a phone call from the Delfont office
in London, saying that someone was coming up to see me
work at the club. The Delfonts, well, need I say more? Meg
made me an early meal that Thursday night, because I wanted
to get to the venue with plenty of time to work on my
routine. I opened the evening paper and the first headline I
saw read: "Famous Liverpool Night Club Burnt To The
Ground". During the early hours of Thursday morning the
Shakespeare had been engulfed in flames, and with it my stage
clothes, music, the lot. I began to feel totally and utterly sorry
for myself.

Three days later, I was dismissed from Benjamin Electric
and I couldn't blame them one iota. I had been sent to the
site of the Piccadilly Hotel, a new project, with plans for
Benjamin to light the whole edifice. The job was worth at
least a quarter of a million to the company and I started off
well, got to know the foreman and electrician and bought
them drinks and things, but again, our product proved too
expensive and I finished up with an order for six lighting
shades for the boiler house. Total value? Ten pounds.

Here I was again, out of work and to make matters worse,
things at home were not smooth: my father was drinking
heavily and it was upsetting Meg, who desperately wanted
her own home. I did a couple of *Workers' Playtimes* for Jim
Casey, but at fifteen pounds a programme, it was hardly
likely that a building society would take me on. Kevin had
me signed up with a very well known agent from London
called Dave Forrester, of the agency Forrester George. We
had lunch with him at the Midland Hotel, and as he had
Ken Dodd on his books, not to mention the rising star
impressionist, Mike Yarwood, I was most impressed.

At the time, I had always managed to book myself into
Blackpool venues such as Jenk's Bar, a crowded seasonal place
where the artiste was merely a backcloth for the noise and

booze. In those days we played four venues a night for the princely sum of forty-five pounds the week. Dave Forrester's first engagement for me was, yes you've guessed, Jenk's Bar in Blackpool plus three other venues, and all for the fee of . . . thirty-five pounds a week. London had entered my life once more and I was down ten quid.

Meg lost another baby through a miscarriage, and one night the poor lass offered me a divorce as she felt she'd never have any children and she knew I wanted a family. Meg was my life and I told her so; divorce, never. I didn't know where I was going, nothing seemed to go right and I was tippling too heavily for my own good. ABC Television gave me three stand up spots on shows with Mike and Bernie Winters, and although I did well, nothing came from that. Money was short and I was driven to take yet another job as a salesman with a firm that made refrigerators. It was awful, and to make matters worse I started in the winter, one of the worst we'd had. Just try selling a fridge to a butcher who's standing behind his block, holding a frozen sirloin in his reddened hands. . . . At least they supplied a van of questionable vintage and that enabled me to work a few low clubs and pubs for five pounds the night.

In 1961 the refrigerator manufacturer decided that they and I had better part company, before my expenses bankrupted them; in all the time I had been with the firm, I hadn't sold one damn thing, in fact I had damaged two freezer cabinets during demonstrations. They were quite civilised about it all. . . . The boss pointed out that the mileage on the van's clock didn't warrant my appalling sales record. With a slightly trembling hand he ushered me out of the office and back I went to the ranks of the unemployed.

Meg wasn't working at the time because yet again she'd suffered a miscarriage, and the effect on her was traumatic: every night she would wander into the small room we'd hoped would become a nursery, and I would find her weeping over a cradle cot she'd bought in anticipation. . . . Relations between Meg and my father were strained, too, in fact they were becoming impossible.

We seemed to spend the entire time at hospitals. Meg went in after every miscarriage for a D and C operation. If ever a little lady had guts it was my wife and I often wept to see the pain in her eyes. She'd had enough miscarriages and I began to think that perhaps it was my fault; was my sperm count low? Was there something wrong genetically with me and was Nature aborting? I lashed myself into fits of self pity. . . . I was only one fraction ahead of extreme penury, everything I did seemed destined for failure, and I felt I had let Meg down badly. Her other sisters had children and bitterness was creeping into my every waking thought.

Finally, I decided that I should consult a doctor in order to see if there was anything wrong with me. I was asked to take home a bottle and produce a sample of my semen. I lay on the bed with my trousers around my ankles and started to masturbate, but shame overtook me. . . . I tried again, and the telephone rang; again . . . the milkman knocked for his money and I fell off the bed. In disgust, with cheeks aflame, I drove to the hospital and sat in a toilet and tried to do it . . . . Even the vision of Raquel Welch, nude, lying in my arms couldn't effect an ejaculation. . . . Finally I achieved an orgasm with someone pounding on the lavatory door shouting, "What the bleedin' 'ell are you doing in there? Having a wank?" If only the irate person knew how right he was. I placed a tissue paper carefully over my specimen bottle and opened the door to admit a red-faced man, presumably the same one who'd banged on the door. I shrugged past him and gave a nurse the small phial; in front of other patients, she whipped off the tissue and said loudly, "That's a grand amount." I paced the corridor of the hospital until a nurse, not the same one as before, came across to tell me that my sperm count was very high and that I had nothing to worry about. . . . At least, I now knew it wasn't my fault we couldn't have children.

Something had to be done. Meg was becoming increasingly depressed and I was worried about her mental condition. I borrowed some money from the bank, and I paid for her to see a specialist in St John's Street, Manchester. Her mother came with Meg and me one drab grey morning. The clock ticked away the hours as we waited while the specialist examined Meg. Finally he invited her mother and me to join him in his office. Meg was there, pale and tearful. The specialist sat behind his roll top desk, cleared his throat and spoke in an unemotional manner: "Mr Dawson, I'm afraid that you'll have to be a man about this. . . . You can never be a father, and your wife tells me you want to be one. Your wife can never see a pregnancy through, she will be forever without child. May I suggest adoption at a later stage? I really am very sorry about this." We left in silence and it wasn't only my dear wife who was blinded with tears.

She went back to work and seemed resigned to our lot; I carried on doing clubs and looking for a job during the day. I got one, with Rima Limited, a company that sold cooker hoods and electric fires. Once again, a vehicle was provided, this time, an Austin Mini and a poor wage to go with it. . . . What can I say? The only defence I can proffer, is that I started selling their appliances during one of the hottest summers we'd ever experienced. . . . So down went the sales of fires to a very low zero. The sales manager wrote to me saying that I was to be fired, but he didn't believe in dismissing a man until he'd spoken to him personally. In the letter was a photograph of the sales manager, one Mr Monks, and would I meet him at Exchange Station, Manchester? I did. He was a large, broad-shouldered military looking man with a "no nonsense" air about him. He wanted a coffee. I took him to a hotel, they had no coffee. The waiter suggested a beer? He said yes, we had several beers which brought us to lunch time. By now, he was calling me Les and telling me ribald jokes. Lunch was held at a pub in Heywood near Manchester . . . . More beers and chased with spirits. . . . He lost his umbrella and hat. At closing time, he wanted more and began to sing *Bladen Races*. I was a member of a club called Beechhill, so I took him there and more ale made conduits down his throat. His speech was now that of a spastic parrot and to add yet more mortification to the farce, he ripped the cloth on a snooker table and threw up in the club steward's lap. It took three burly men to shove him back in my mini, he wasn't able to stand and it was as though his bones had become elastic. I was frantic to get him back to his hotel, but it was an exercise in Cumberland wrestling to stop him grabbing the wheel one minute and to prevent him urinating through the car window the next. With the aid of a waiter and a taciturn porter, we somehow heaved him into his hotel bed, and I left hurriedly, ignoring the strains of *Bye Bye Blues* floating down the stairs.

The following morning, I picked him up at the hotel and drove him to the railway station. The journey sped by in silence. As we waited for the train, he gripped my upper arm and whispered, "How bad was I?" I saw a chance to blackmail him for my job: "Pretty awful sir," I replied mournfully. Then added brightly, "But don't worry, I wouldn't dream of saying to anyone what happened." He glanced at me with a sharp and knowing look. He coughed and shook my hand warmly. "Listen, Dawson, er Les" – I simply gazed at him with radiant virtue – "don't worry about your position with Rima, do you understand?" I nodded modestly as he intoned with suffering, "I'm not going to sack you, oh no my dear fellow, just carry on." He scuttled on to the train and off he chugged . . . . Three weeks later, Rima fired him.

In 1963, Kevin my manager procured a television show for me, it was a programme called *Comedy Bandbox*. The series was not fully networked, merely northern, but it had good viewing figures. I sat in the auditorium fidgeting with my briefcase as I waited to go before the cameras to rehearse, and my confidence had gone completely. I was trembling with nerves and I yearned for a drink; around me was the usual bustle of a television crew but I was oblivious to all that was happening. . . . I just wanted to go away. Top of the bill was that great northern comedian, Norman Evans, and as he stood on stage, it was as though my pitiful vibrations tuned in to him, because for no reason that I can fathom, he trundled off the stage and lumbered towards me. His health was poor and he had trouble getting his breath as he neared me in the seat where I sat rigid. He shook my hand and said gently, "Hello, lad, I don't know you, but I hope you have a good show, just relax and enjoy it, treat it like a concert."

Norman Evans was one of nature's gentlemen, and he talked to me, drew out my doubts and fears and stiffened my resolve. I never forgot his kindness, and in later years, after his death, I tried to carry on his character comedy so well defined in his "Over the Garden Wall" sketch, only I portrayed it as "Cissie And Ada". I couldn't think of a better tribute.

That superb magician and illusionist, David Nixon, was the compère and the show went well. I was, naturally enough, the bottom of the bill but all the cast and crew rooted for me and I did well with this sort of patter:

"Hello, my name's Les Dawson, nobody knows me now, but one day I'll be a household name. . . . I'm changing it to Domestos.

I said to the producer, he's the one with the red handbag, thanks for having me on the show, after all there isn't much work for comedians . . . . He said there you go again, Les, worrying about other people.

Since I arrived this morning the studio simply couldn't do enough for me, so they haven't bothered. I'm not worried . . . . I can always fall back on the wife . . . she looks like an unmade bed. I'm not saying she's ugly, but when she sucks a lemon, the lemon pulls a face.

Trouble with the wife is, she's bone idle. . . . I have to wake her up in the morning with jump leads.

I'm going to play the piano for you and what a bargain. . . . Winifred Atwell gets a thousand pounds for one tune . . . with me you get a thousand tunes for a pound."

The producer, Peter Dulay, was pleased with my five minute spot and I was rebooked three weeks later; a date that was to become infamous in the brutal annals of Man's inhumanity to Man. But before that, I found myself once again, un-employed: this time, dear thunderstruck reader, I resigned from Rima, after my mini was stolen and they wouldn't give me another one. Temporarily, I became an electrical goods rep for an old established company of wholesalers, Beardsall's by name and reputation. I hated it, but there was a Vehicle Supplied.

On the night that I appeared in the second of my *Comedy Bandbox* programmes, President John F. Kennedy was killed in Dallas, and the world entered the next phase in its crawl towards anarchy and destruction. The whole television layout for the night was cancelled, except for the Saturday news and a shortened version of *Comedy Bandbox*. One act, Syd and Max Harrison, were taken out of the show altogether, because one of their sketches had included the use of firearms. I

remember being stunned at the news of the American President's death. . . . It was as though we'd reached the end of
sanity. The sixties were the years of retarded civilisation.
Vietnam had split America and would drain the will of its
youth; there was Flower Power and Hari Krishna; we had the
Cold War and the Beatles; it looked as if the Anti-Christ had
arisen to lead us to Armageddon with bigotry and rock and
roll. . . . In the Deep South of the USA they threw blacks
into prison for riding in the wrong section of a bus, and
Martin Luther King marched on Washington. The Second
World War, the Korean War, the hell of Indo-China, Malaya,
Palestine, Cyprus. . . . It seemed to me, that my whole life
had been attuned to violence and death. Had the crucible of
Goodness emptied forever?

Meg was expecting. The doctors told us so. "Don't worry,"
they said, "this time she will be fine." Happiness flows between
us, the Miracle has arrived. . . . We buy clothes again for the
baby, I watch her knitting things for the new life. . . . Meg
looks fine, no they haven't given her an internal examination
at the hospital; they think, with her history, it could be
dangerous. "Don't worry. There's a heartbeat, all is well and
after six months, what is there to worry about?" Time for a
check up at the hospital. I sit in the car smoking and wondering who the baby will resemble. . . . Routine check up. I see
two nurses supporting my wife as she staggers through the
door. . . . I have a dry throat. . . . No, God . . . . Not again,
please. . . . Meg is crying and from her lungs comes a scream
of pure torment. "*In Christ's name what's gone wrong this time?*"
I shout at the nurse. . . . A doctor holds me at bay as I make
a lunge for the nurses. . . . Meg looks at me with empty
sockets and her lips move. . . . What's she saying? There isn't
any baby? No baby? The doctor leads me to one side and
explains that my wife has had a phantom pregnancy . . . there
never was a child in the womb . . . she had willed it there.
No baby? But I saw it move as she sat knitting. . . .
    For a long period Meg was ill, both physically and mentally,
and I hadn't the heart to tell her that I had lost my job with
the electrical goods company. No, I wasn't sacked, this time
I had been made redundant. We were broke.
    I drank what money we had left and it didn't help to ease

1. My father of the same Christian name, Les, during the war looking for deserters. When he found them he ran off with them

2. My mother Julia – a great lady. Tragically her life was cut short

3. Yes, I was such a handsome boy – Mother had me kidnapped to get my photo in the papers

5. Dawson the boxer – I was on the canvas so often I was known as the battling Rembrandt

4. Les Dawson aged 14. No hint then of the obese twit to come. Also the suit was my first one. It was called the 'kangaroo' style – two payments, then you hopped it!

6. Beware all England's foes! Me on the left – I don't know who last wore my uniform, but it could have been John o' Gaunt!

7. Early days as pub pianist in Manchester. Those pianos were so out of tune, if you struck a right note you were given a brewer's citation

8. My first date with Meg, my future wife – she'd taken her bike clips off

9. Our wedding day. Can you blame Meg for looking so radiant? The car was paid for

10. My first protégé for TV – Syd Lawrence, creator of the Big Band revival. I still haven't had my commission

11. Shaking hands with my sovereign at the 1973 Royal Command Performance

12. A sketch for YTV's series *Sez Les* with John Cleese and Roy Barraclough and the magnificent profile of the author with his own chins

13. The opening set for *Sez Les*. The girls wouldn't leave me alone, or was it the other way around?

14. Signing my first novel, *A Card for the Clubs*, in Bristol. I think we sold three

15. Queen's Theatre, Blackpool. In bed with Dora Bryan and getting paid for it

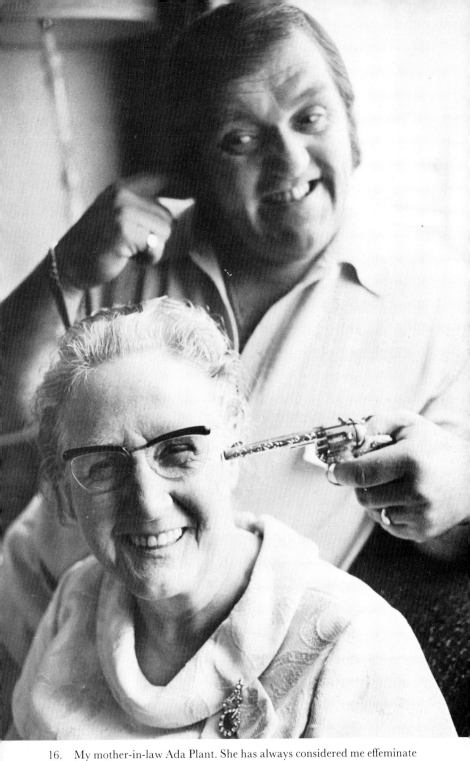

16. My mother-in-law Ada Plant. She has always considered me effeminate and next to her I am

17.   The dreadful Cosmo Smallpiece, typifying the inner Dawson libido — but not getting enough

the pain. Never have I been a religious man, but one night I entered a church and I sat alone in the echoing stone edifice, and I asked God what use was I in the great Scheme of Things . . . if any. Christ gazed back at me from the Cross of Martyrdom, but I found no solace or guidance in the anguished sculpture.

What was I? A dreamer or a fool? My past record was not an uplifting one – the only thing I seemed to excel at was failure. I longed for satisfaction, I wanted only happiness for my wife. . . . Fragments of my life kept wavering before me; a disjointed picture show of farcical inadequacy. Meg was asleep when I got back home, and I sat down on our old settee and sobbed with self pity and despair.

1963 died and 1964 was born and we raised optimistic glasses to the new epoch, hoping, like Micawber, that "something would turn up". I found that Kevin, my manager, wanted to break away, and I didn't blame him, why hitch your wagon to a mule that can't progress? Dave Forrester and I parted company, there wasn't any work from him, so I was alone. Jim Casey, bless him, gave me radio work: *Midday Music Hall,* with artistes the like of Ken Dodd, Max Bygraves, John Hanson, Rosemary Squires, Harry Bailey, Des O'Connor, and always, I was the bottom of the bill, but grateful for the experience. I was now a counter manager in an electrical wholesalers, Sun Electric in Trafford Park, Manchester. . . . It wasn't a job with much of a future, but at least some money was coming in. Meg was back at work; we had agreed to look into the possibility of adoption, and this kept her spirits up. Meg went into St Mary's Hospital for one last D and C to make sure all was healthy with her, and whilst we were there, a young doctor suggested we had one last throw of the dice in an effort to reproduce. I was against it, but not Meg . . . . She agreed to undergo the "thermometer test". That simply means that when the thermometer indicated that the ovum was at its most vulnerable for the sperm, we had to make love. It didn't matter what time of day it was or what one was doing at the time. . . . One had to cohabit. It did have its funny side: once as I sat on the loo, she rushed me into the bedroom and off we went; another time I was trying to mend my old wreck of a car, one I'll never forget:

a 1932 Standard. She pulled my legs from under the car and virtually raped me in the hallway. . . . Of course, all to no avail.

I was still playing clubs, doing well in some, dying in others. I still longed to write and back came the rejection slips. One night, I was watching *Sunday Night At The Palladium* on our tiny television set, and every time Jimmy Tarbuck got a laugh, I became more morose. Finally Meg put her inevitable knitting down and she fixed me with her grey eyes: "You want to be on there, don't you? No, love, don't lie. . . . You've got to get it out of your system . . . . Why don't you write off for an audition to *Opportunity Knocks*?" I drew myself up to my five foot six and a half inches of quivering indignation. "Me . . . audition for a talent show. . . . Never," I cried in ringing tones. "Why not?" my wife replied quietly. "A lot of stars started their careers on that show, at least have a go."

I wrote off to Hughie Green and was accepted for an audition which was to be held in Manchester. Looking back now, it's a shame that shows like *Opportunity Knocks* are no longer on our screens; they gave people a real chance in flamboyant sets, and I mourn the passing of those talent shows.

I didn't realise, that wet damp morning that I auditioned, that I had a friend at court, so to speak. His name was Royston Mayoh and I had known him at ABC Television when I had appeared with Mike and Bernie Winters. In those pioneer days, he had been a floor manager; now, he was the producer of *Opportunity Knocks* and I found out later that he had persuaded Hughie Green to give me a real hearing. I hate auditions: I always feel as if I am begging for work. This one looked like the whole of show business crammed in one room. . . . There was a pop group, fire-eaters, comedians by the shoal, singers and dancers. . . . Old men with mouth organs and small kids in pink tights. They broke for lunch just before I was due to show my paces, and I spent the hour in a pub, alone and depressed.

After the break, I followed a fat soprano who kept clicking her dentures and twice she broke wind on a high note. I was called.

I sat at the piano . . . I played three notes, then:

"That's enough for the money I'm getting.

What a day to audition, it's so damp outside they've got lifeboat drill on the buses.

Nearly didn't get here. I was struck in a traffic jam, don't know how long it had been there, but a car in front had a sticker on the window which read 'Just Married' and on the back seat I saw three kids.

Mine's an old car, I don't have a hand brake . . . it's a pike staff.

It's got leaf springs, they fall off in autumn. The man who sold it me, said I'd get a lot of pleasure out of it . . . . He was right, it's a pleasure to get out of it.

I took it to a garage, the mechanic suggested I tried Lourdes."

I passed the audition.

At last events began to move. In that year Meg and I put a deposit on a small bungalow in Unsworth, Bury; it was only a two bedroomed house, but we reasoned that we couldn't have any children, so it would be sufficient for our needs, and the other bedroom would do for my father, if he decided to come and live with us. . . . I hoped he would, his health was worrying me slightly; he'd never recovered from my mother's early death at the age of forty-three, and he wasn't looking after himself.

DRESS REHEARSAL

I took part in a radio show in London, at the Old Camden Theatre. The show, *Light Up The Night*, was compèred by Don Arrol, who was to die tragically young; on the bill were Johnny Pearson and his Galaxy Orchestra, Mrs Shufflewick and Charlie Chester, not forgetting a rising young lady, Anita Harris. It was an instant hit, and I felt happy with my short spot. I was sitting in a pub, alone as usual, when an agent strolled across and introduced himself as Norman Murray from Foster's Agency. He asked me if I was represented and I said no, apart from Dave Forrester who still kept in touch. Murray seemed thoughtful, suggested I send a letter finally terminating my agreement with Forrester George, and when I had done that he would see what he could do for me . . . I thought, "Why not?" and that was that. Murray shook my hand and I watched his stout, arrogant figure leave the pub.

I investigated my Post Office account, and found that I had two hundred pounds in it, my total savings after the deposit on the bungalow. "Sod it," I said to Meg, "you deserve a rest from it all, have a week off work and I'll take you to Paris."

As the aeroplane taxied to a halt on French soil, it was like returning home for me. The smell of Paris is enchanting; the smell of the wine, the pissoirs, there is only Paris. Meg and I checked into a small hotel in the Latin Quarter, and during the day, I walked her all over that wonderful city. By night we made love like abandoned Apaches. Like newly weds, we held hands in Les Halles; we kissed under the trees in the Bois, and we drank cheap wine in the Boulevard St Michel. It was a wrench to fly home to the confined atmosphere of our dreary council house, and it took a while to settle down.

Clubs and pubs by night, serving retailers by day. . . .
Monte Cristo had it made compared to my futile existence.
Meg complained of stomach cramp once or twice and I tried
to reassure her by saying it was probably something to do with
French plumbing. Meanwhile ABC television summoned me
to appear on *Opportunity Knocks*. I worked on my script all
the week before, honing it and getting it down to a sharp five
minutes, no more. Meg came with me to the Didsbury studios
to keep an eye on me, but I still managed to slip away from
her to gulp back a few large ones.

Although I didn't win the talent show on a national level
through votes, I received the highest number of votes with
the studio audience, and this is the act that did it. . . my first
success:

(Seated at piano) "Tonight, I should like to play something from Chopin, but I won't . . . he never plays any
of mine. Then I toyed with the idea of playing Ravel's
Pavane Pour Un Infante Defunct, but I can't remember
if it is a tune or a Latin prescription for piles.

Anyway . . . before anyone slides into a coma, I'll play
a song that was written by Bach as he lay dying. (Played
and sang one note.) Then he died.

The neighbours love it when I play the piano, they often
break my windows to hear me better.

My father was musical, he collected old instruments.
The police often asked him if he'd still got the loot (lute).
Dad spent so much time in prison, when they did finally
release him, the governor asked him to go back part-
time. Mother used to sit me on her knee, and I'd whisper:
'Mummy, Mummy, sing me a lullaby do,' she'd say,
'Certainly, my angel, my wee bundle of happiness, hold
my beer while I fetch me banjo.'"

When I ended the act, there was a storm of applause from
both my fellow artistes and the audience, and I knew that this
was where I could find myself.

A month later I took Meg to the hospital, she was having
a lot of abdominal aches and she vomited a lot. I drove to the
hospital in dread of what they'd find. I remained in the
corridor whilst she went in to see the doctor. Against the

regulations, I smoked cigarette after cigarette, and inwardly
I begged God not to hurt her any more. Meg emerged from
the examination cubicle and she was crying her heart out, and
I sank to the floor on one knee. "Get up, old man," the doctor
said cheerfully. "You'll need all your strength, old chap,
especially now, you're going to be a father." I looked at Meg,
she nodded through her tears and we flew into each other's
arms and cried together. "Thank you, God," I mumbled.
"Thank you." Meg took great care of herself and I went
through hell. . . . How could a specialist be so wrong? His
words came back: "You'll have to be a man about this. . . .
You will never be a father." On May 9th 1965, in St Mary's
Hospital in Manchester, a baby daughter was born. Her
name was Julie Helen Dawson, born to Mrs Margaret Rose
Dawson, whose husband Les just happened to be the happiest
little man on the entire planet. I was due in Newcastle to play
a club, La Dolce Vita, but before I left, I just had time to gaze
at my little scrap of life in the cot. . . . Her damp hair hung
over long lashes; so long to make my little one, so long. . . .
Surely she was a chosen child?

On the train going to Newcastle, I got into conversation with
a commercial traveller. "Nice to get away from the old
woman for a bit, hey?" he chuckled jovially. "By the way,
are you married?" "Oh yes I am," I answered. "I have a
family too. . . . A daughter."
    I have never uttered such lovely words as those since.

INTERLUDE

People often ask me, are clowns born or can anyone develop their personality in order to become a comedian?

My answer is simply: "I don't know." In my case there were certain factors that would seem to indicate that it was my destiny to become what I am.

During the end of my short career as a pro boxer, an opponent smashed my jaw with a juddering right cross, and ever since, I have been able to pull my chin over my nose with superlative ease and create the most grotesque grimace; having a face like that is of immeasurable value. My figure is a signal for people to have near hysteria when they see me in a bathing suit: I had the bathroom mirror taken out some time ago, because every time I rose from the water, I looked in the nude rather like a badly tapped keg. My legs are mere stumps, and clothes hang on me like a sale of work stall.

Also, to be a clown, one must have the ability to be unable to cope with the merest trivia. . . .

When I won the Hoover sales contest in 1960, the prize was a visit to the Derby horse race and afterwards, a swish reception and dinner dance in Kensington. The Hoover moguls insisted that the winners from each branch wear the full evening dress with tails. Now as I have already indicated, my portly, sawn-off hulk is not one to inspire the poets, and in that sort of regalia, the spectacle is absurd.

The suit of tails was hired from Moss Bros; and I had to endure the sight of that emporium's assistants shivering with ill-concealed mirth as I tried the damn thing on. At the reception, the rear end or tip of the tails stuck out like a set of dorsals on a predatory fish; when I attempted to smooth them down, the shirt cuffs became disentangled from the shirt sleeves proper, and they enveloped the whole of my hands. When I sat at the table, the top four shirt buttons flew off and one landed in the farmhouse soup, closely followed by the imitation collar stud. In every sense of the word, I was a mess, and I spent the entire night hiding behind a potted fern.

The true clown cannot cope with anything remotely mechanical.

There was an occasion when I tried to get twenty cigarettes from a machine outside a newsagent's shop. Other people placed the requisite coins in it, and out sprang the packet. . . . I did precisely the same, and lo! Nothing. I banged the side of the infernal contraption and money spilled out all over the pavement and the newsagent lifted up his living quarter's window, and blew a whistle for the police. They duly arrived with an insane dog who proceeded to take the sleeve off my sports jacket.

In my murky past I may have done some loutish things, but I have always prided myself on good manners, and so, whilst on a bus which was full, I proffered my seat to a matron of fair proportions, who it turned out was an ardent sexually equal female. She berated me and my sex for having kept women down for centuries, and in a loud voice, demanded to know if I was some kind of pervert. The omnibus conductor ordered me off the vehicle, and when I protested, a tiny pensioner tweaked my nose and angrily maintained that "Burks like 'im should be castrated."

The first day of our holiday in the West Indies, I lined the children up and instructed them on how to use a surf board. The waves were quite substantial and I pointed out sternly the perils of not heeding the words of their august parent. Just at that most inappropriate moment, a regular twelve foot column of water flicked me atop its foaming crest, dashed me down with utter contempt, and I lay inert at the mercy of the current, with two cracked ribs. Suffice to say, the fruits of my loins cried with impassioned delight.

During one of my television series, I had occasion to take a charming lady to dinner. She was a freelance journalist of considerable power, and many performers ached for her interest. I recall with pain, that she rammed a cigarette into a long holder and asked me archly for a light. My battered old Dunhill refused to function, so I picked up the candle that stood on the table between us, and leaned across to ignite the weed. Just then somebody called my name out and as I turned my head to see who it was, I lunged further out and the flame of the candle burnt her nose. As she leapt to her dainty feet she knocked over the bottle of wine and it cascaded over my trousers, which was just as well, because the candle was burning the trousers in an area most sensitive in men.

I am totally inept at house parties. I am still reminded by certain friends of the time the wife and I were invited to a Sunday cocktail party. Nobody spoke to me apart from asking me where the lavatory was. In an effort to break the ice, I hove on to a small group of well-groomed gentry, and offered them each one of my cigarettes. There was a stunned silence, and a large woman wrapped in angora, snorted disdainfully, "We do not indulge." I felt like a social leper, and I couldn't find an ashtray. Eventually, I stubbed the cigarette end out in a waste paper basket, which then to my alarm started to smoulder. Totally ignored, I picked up the basket and, blinded by smoke, I rushed into the kitchen and sprawled my length over a ginger tom cat. The basket flew in a parabola towards a collection of gardening magazines, and flames spluttered to life. By now, in a state of near collapse, I filled a small pail with water and threw it over the magazines, and as I swung the bucket, the lady whose house it was drifted into the kitchen just in time to receive some of the water in her outraged face. . . . I was asked to leave.

The awesome part of these stories is that if I attempted to do them in a sketch, nobody would find them credible, but in reality, they happen all the time.

Ordinary men and women in the street can be capable of using humour to mask tragedy. Many years ago whilst working as an electrician, I used a local train service, and I always travelled on the seven forty-five in company with the same set of passengers. It seemed as if we gravitated to the same carriage unaware that we were doing it. We never spoke; it was heads down and bury oneself in the newspaper. One morning a dumpy little woman joined us for the first time and she never stopped chatting about her husband, Bill. . . . The affection she had for her spouse was obvious, but to a man, we ignored her, although it was impossible to shut out the torrent of words that she uttered. Finally, one of the passengers threw down his newspaper and shouted, "For God's sake, woman, shut up!" She merely smiled and replied, "I do go on a bit, don't I? Bill's always telling me to belt up, but I mean no harm, sir." She stopped, cocked her greying head on one side and said shyly to the angry passenger, "Am I forgiven?" Somehow that remark opened a flood tide of conversation. . . . The passenger laughed and said of course she was forgiven. He in return made a remark about himself, and soon we were introducing ourselves to one another and from that moment on the journey became something to look forward to. The woman began to bring a flask of tea, and I then brought forth some biscuits. . . . Then one day she didn't turn up . . . nor the next day; in fact we never saw her again. Urged by my travelling companions, I went to see if she was all right; I knew where she lived because she had told us all her address. It was a pretty little house and I knocked on the bright yellow front door, and when it opened a man stood there and he looked very sad. "Excuse me," I said. "I'm a friend of Mrs W..... and with not having seen her for a long time, I wondered if everything was all right with her?" He shook his head and asked me inside. The room was airy and clean and on the mantelpiece was a large framed photograph of a handsome smiling man in uniform. "I'm sorry to tell you that Mrs W.... is dead. She took an overdose a week ago, poor woman, she was my wife's best friend," the sad-faced man said. I stammered out, "But what could have made her do such a thing? She was such a happy lady." He looked at me curiously and said, "Amy, happy? My dear chap she was so lonely, she never got over the death of her husband Bill."

So that was it, her beloved Bill must have died recently and she had found that she couldn't live without him. "I'm so sorry," I said. "She was always talking about her husband on the train we caught every morning." The sad-faced man glanced at me sharply. "What are you talking about?" he said curtly. "Bill was killed during the war at Arnhem."

All those lonely years. . . . Our little lady had kept his memory alive: to her he was still with her; a defence against a world that had died when he perished. I made my goodbyes to the sad man, and I left hurriedly.

That's the trouble about a book like this – as you put it down on paper, so many things from the past begin to haunt you; the people you have known who left an indelible impression on your life. There are so many things experienced that words can never recapture: the smell of old theatres and countless dressing rooms; faded stills of long dead performers in empty foyers staring from walls that retain their energy force for all time. So many memories. . . . The child beggars in Calcutta, tugging your arm fiercely and the defiance and brashness made impotent by the helplessness in the huge pleading eyes. . . . The poor of Rome outside the Vatican Walls with shining faith and empty bellies, unnoticed by the prelates in their cardinal red.

Comedy and tragedy are twin companions, and as any artist will testify, we see both. Once, after having been received by Prince Philip at a Variety Club dinner, I then went on to present a cheque to a home for deprived children, and the diversity of both occasions was an object lesson to me. Some years ago at a matinée, we had a hundred spastic children in the theatre, and after the performance, all the artistes stayed in their respective costumes and we invited the kids up on stage. For them and for us it was enchantment, until one of the artistes, the girl who played the bride in the finale, came out in her full bridal trimmings. I was holding a small, badly disabled girl in my arms, and at the sight of the shimmering bride she said loudly, "Will I ever be one of those?" What does one say at a time like that? I had to put her back in her wheelchair and walk away.

There's a lot of hot air talked about the evils of television, but it also helps enormously to give happiness, however brief. To see a child's face gazing in awe at his or her favourite performer is a treat for cynical eyes. Come on, Dawson . . . pull yourself together, the human spirit will always defy shabby reality . . . it even worked for you, despite your-self. . . .

With a large portion of one's life now just a piece of the past, looking back can be very tempting. . . . If one could change the course of events, would one? Frankly, I'd like to alter a lot of it, because on reflection I was, and still am, an idiot.

I can cringe still at the memory of the time I brashly accepted an engagement and "died" for over an hour, only to discover at the end of the ordeal that I had just performed for three hundred German policemen on a convention in Blackpool. . . . A shudder runs through me when I think back to the summer show when, after a long drinking bout, I fell off the stage and into the orchestra pit, first breaking my descent by landing and breaking the skins on the drummer's percussion set, and in attempting to clamber back on the stage, fusing the footlights with a frantic kick.

I recoil at the memory of being in attendance at a function to raise money for charity in the company of Prince Charles, and being chagrined to find that the seat of my pants was rent asunder to reveal my new bright Marks and Spencer underpants in full sail; a sight which one hysterical person said, "looked rather like one of Jupiter's moons peering through a 'J' cloth."

Was that really me, all those years ago, crawling naked on hands and knees with an alsatian dog clinging to one trembling buttock via the application of canine molars, after refusing to pay a certain lady for favours in the bedroom? As I rolled over, trying to disentangle myself from the infernal animal, the lady in question went calmly through my wallet for the sum required before ordering the dog to release me. . . . I had to dress behind the stump of a tree with the harridan at the door cackling in a frenzy.

My young manhood. . . . Dignity, always Dignity. Even when I tried to elevate myself there was always somebody to put my dreams to the sword. For a short time (fifteen days to be exact), I was gainfully employed as a junior reporter for a local newspaper, whose circulation was about as vast as the blood supply of the average gnat. I was sent off to cover the funeral of an ex deputy mayor, and I was thrilled with my description of the interment:

> "Gone now, that common clay that once so noble strode his purpose. What price now, endeavour? The casket lowered and only memory left as the mourners filed away with bitter grief from that mound of earth."

The sub editor looked at it, finally stopped laughing and thundered to all in earshot, "What a load of bull shit." The account in the paper read: "Councillor .... was buried today."

BOOK TWO

1965–1985

OVERTURE AND BEGINNERS

I entered a blissful stage in my life, and it was little Julie who was responsible for it. After all the heartaches Meg and I had experienced in trying for a family, we felt as if God had relented, and whatever sin we had committed, was finally forgiven. There was never a baby so loved and wanted as Julie Helen Dawson. Meg and I would spend hours with her, playing, cuddling, loving her. I "wet her head" in every pub in the northern hemisphere; I had joyous hangovers and a depleted wallet, but even the spectre of poverty failed to diminish my sheer happiness, and after returning from her christening, a telephone call from the agent Norman Murray put a seal on my state of Nirvana. . . . An offer of a summer season in the Isle of Man.

Julie was only three weeks old when Meg and I flew off to the Isle of Man for the summer season at the big theatre there: the Palace Coliseum, where I was to be bottom of the bill on which Val Doonican was the star attraction. . . . It was my first taste of the 'Big Time'. I stood outside the theatre, and pride flushed within as I studied the playbill: Val Doonican, Jackie Trent, The Jones Boys, Don Dwight, a clever young comedian who was to die tragically young of cancer. . . . Where was I? Yes, yes, there I am on the bill at just about the height where dogs find it easy to urinate. . . . Les Dawson, bill matter, this and that.

Meg and I found nice digs with a couple who became firm friends, and I eagerly awaited opening night. My salary was only sixty pounds a week, but Norman Murray, who was to be my agent for many years, wouldn't take any commission from me which was a help.

The show was an instant success. I received nice if some-what cautious reviews, and I was delirious with happiness.

During the day, I would perambulate my daughter all over Douglas, pushing her trolley with the sort of stern and regal dignity that one associates with a general who's thrown back an invader.

Looking back on that season at the Isle of Man, I realise now that it was a turning point in my life: not so much the show business side, but in me personally. . . . I was growing up and maturing. I liked being a father, I relished the responsibility and all that went with it. The time flew by all too quickly for me, and it saddened my heart when the summer season ended its run. As the cast finished the last night with a company party, the demolishers were trundling into position for the destruction of the old theatre.

Meg, Julie and I flew back to Blackpool Airport, and then on to Manchester. My father looked thin and it was obvious by now that he was not caring for himself, the house felt dead and frankly I wasn't sorry when we were informed that our little bungalow in Unsworth was ready for occupancy. I implored Dad to come and live with us, but he was adamant: "Son, you need to be just yourself and Meg, you'll have enough problems bringing up a family, and I would only be in the way," he said firmly, and I knew there and then, that he was preparing to join my mother. So many heartaches, so many sad things in our lives.

We moved into Number 2 Bradley Drive with a few sticks of furniture and eager dreams, and from the moment we walked through the door of that tiny bit of heaven, Dame Fortune embraced my life. I have often pondered since on the possibility of Chance allied with the energy for Goodness. Can it be found in a small plot of land? Was there once on the site of that bungalow a moment of radiant happiness? All I know is that the feeling of "something special" hung in the very atmosphere of that dwelling. Materially we still had nothing: a bed, a fireside carpet, three chairs and a settee. Our first Christmas in Unsworth made Oliver Twist look like a blatant capitalist. We couldn't afford a budgie for Christmas dinner, let alone a turkey: what we set before us were two boiled eggs and a slightly peculiar mound of sliced bread. Meg and I sat opposite each other across the rough hewn slab that passed as a dining room table, and we surveyed the eggs, studied each other's faces for an expression appropriate to our pauperised celebration, and instead we broke into roars of laughter and hugged each other, became silly and woke Julie up and hugged her as well. The door bell rang, and our neighbour who lived across the drive stood on the stoop. He invited Meg and me, with baby of course, he added with a smile, to join him and his family for Christmas dinner. . . . Buck Rogers couldn't have sped more swiftly than my little brood, and the day was saved. Our neighbours had realised the predicament we were in and, bless their hearts, had held out the hand of Christian friendship to us.

When we returned home in the early hours of Boxing Day morning, Meg put Julie, who had slept throughout the festivities, back into her cot, and I went into the weed-infested back garden and stood in silence, remembering those who I had loved who were no longer a part of my existence. Mother, with her great zest for life; my grandmother whose wild Irish eyes had utterly captivated me. . . . I saw again, as if I were watching a moving picture, my grandmother fighting off the police when they came to arrest my cousin Tommy for armed robbery. He had been hiding in her flat in Blackley, and worthless though he undoubtedly was, she loved him sins and all. I drew heavily on a cigarette as dawn commenced to rinse the sky, and I saw that wonderful old lady lying on her bed, with a face creased with satisfaction as she ruffled my hair and said softly, "It won't be long now, young Les, before I go. . . . David (my grandfather dead for many years) was here last night and sure he needs me so." Two days later she was gone. I threw away the cigarette butt and whispered a prayer of thanks to God for our daughter and for the blessing of having Meg for a wife.

Norman Murray tried very hard to get me engagements, but despite my small success in the summer season, bookings were slow. I managed to get some radio work thanks to Jim Casey, and I was still employed by Sun Electric, but I was bored with the job and spent a lot of time writing down script ideas. Then the magic of the bungalow began to work. . . . Norman Murray was sitting in his office one day and the telephone rang. "Hello, Norman, Iris Fredericks here." Now

Iris Fredericks was the booker for ABC Television, as it was then, and she was a powerful and shrewd lady, well respected and in some cases feared. "How's things, Iris?" replied Norman. What followed I can only assume was the usual show business conversation, then: "One reason I'm ringing you up, Norman, is this: do you know of any comedian who's available, cheap and willing to stand in for a television try out? ABC are putting on a follow up to the *Sunday Night At The London Palladium* at Blackpool; the show will be called *Summer Night Out* and we want to put a bill together in order for the technical crew to prepare for the actual start of the transmission." Norman pondered. Could he suggest Les Dawson? Up to now people had shied away from him. . . . "Iris, I have one comic on my books." Norman paused. "His name is Les Dawson." There was a silence like a forgotten tomb from the other end of the line. Iris answered, "I see, well I haven't heard of him, but I'll let you know later." That, thought Norman, is that. Meanwhile, dear old Jim Casey booked me through Norman for the radio show *Midday Music Hall*. It was a popular programme that was transmitted from a studio that lay on top of a Co-op hall in Blackpool. The money for doing it was only fifteen pounds, but to me it was a fortune. Julie was growing fast and that, coupled with the mortgage, never allowed me to save a penny; luckily, Meg was an incredible schemer, and somehow she always managed to feed us all and clothe the baby. We still had bare floorboards and the place needed decorating, but after a lifetime of strange rooms and awful digs, to me, the bungalow was Valhalla.

The bill for the radio show was a strong one: Harry Bailey, the Irish comedian was the headliner. Rosemary Squires, a popular singer and personality. Jimmy Gaye, a very funny man but labelled as a "pro's" comic. This meant that he appealed to fellow professionals more than the general public, but he was one of the funniest men I have ever had the privilege of working with. The Northern Dance Orchestra was the musical backing and they were the musicians of the day. The show opened up with a singing duo, and then it was my turn to be announced by Roger Moffat. On I went into the glare of the lights. . . .

"Nice to be here in this Co-op loft. The last time I played here, the act in front of me was so bad, the audience were still booing him whilst I was on.

I'm not saying my act is bad, but the night variety died they held my script for questioning.

It's been a poor year for me. At Christmas I played in a theatre that was so small, the only panto they could put on was 'Robin Hood and His Merry Man'.

Business was so rotten, the girl in the box office had been dead three months and nobody knew.

Things didn't used to be so bad, but alas, the wife lost her job, she got rheumatism in her arm and couldn't throw the harpoon properly."

I finished my act and walked off to polite applause; granted, I'd made them laugh in parts, but I felt depression wash over me when I heard Jimmy Gaye get roars from both the audience and the orchestra. Jimmy ended with a parody that had the audience in stitches, and after Rosemary Squires had charmed them, Harry Bailey had them in the palm of his hand with marvellous material. After the programme, Jimmy Gaye walked over to me. I was sat on a box feeling miserable and sorry for myself. "What's the matter, lad?" smiled Jimmy. "You were very good, and, what's more . . . different." I thanked him morosely and said how much I admired him, and that I would never be a true pro as he was, and so on. He gestured to me. "Come with me, son," he said somewhat sharply. He walked me to the doors where the audience was filing out and making comments about the programme. Jimmy and myself stood behind one of the doors as the audience passed through. "Now listen," said Jimmy. One couple remarked, "Bloody good show that. I loved that joke about the tortoise." "Which one was that?" asked his companion. "The one that comic told . . . what was his name? Anyway it was a good 'un." The man's companion retorted, "I didn't reckon much to that young comic . . . trying to be flamin' clever. . . . Bloody upstart, Les Dawson he were called."

This sort of critique was echoed by many others. . . . All talked about the jokes Jimmy and Harry had told, but never mentioned them by name, but all of them, despite not liking me very much, knew my name.

Jimmy and I went into a pub, and after taking a deep draught, he turned to me and said quietly, "You see now why you must keep on, son? They all remembered your name . . . not what you said. And that is what makes a star, not his material, but himself." He was silent for a moment and when we made to leave the pub at closing time, Jimmy paused, shook my hand and whispered, "Best of luck, lad, and just remember this: be nice to people on the way up, because you'll meet them on the way down." Dear Jimmy Gaye, I hope that I've never forgotten those words.

Jimmy Gaye died some years later in a hospital in Leeds. I went to see him but he didn't know who I was. As I stood at the bedside looking at his emaciated form, I felt angry that the ultimate winner in life was Death. . . . But then I thought back to all the enjoyment Jimmy had given to people of all ages, and I realised that he had created something that surpasses any demise; that Jimmy Gaye would never die in people's hearts.

Thanks to what was called "Two Years Interest Free Credit" which the Co-operative Society ran twice a year, Meg and I furnished the bungalow with carpets and new furniture. The place began to look like a home, and the magic of that dwelling rekindled.

Iris Fredericks rang my agent Norman three weeks later and said that she'd heard good reports about my debut on *Opportunity Knocks* and was therefore prepared to book me for the TV tryout at Blackpool in the ABC Theatre. The fee was thirty-five pounds, and although the show would not be shown on the screens, it was felt that the experience was invaluable.

I still had some club work in the book which I had gleaned from a Liverpool agency, Mike Hughes, so some money was coming in as well as my wage from Sun Electric. As the summer commenced, I became more and more agitated as the date for the TV programme loomed near: the show had been renamed *Blackpool Night Out* and the cast included Dickie Henderson as compère, a speciality act, a singer and, as top of the bill for the try-out, a well-established variety act indeed,

Pearl Carr and Teddy Johnson. Sunday dawned, the date of the Blackpool show. . . . I hadn't slept at all the night before; I couldn't, my mind was in a turmoil. Supposing I flopped? What then? Word would go around the business like a bush fire and I would be for all time dead. The hours ticked by, I lit cigarette after cigarette; the Sabbath morning washed away the dusk and I watched it from the kitchen window. Over and over again I checked that my one decent dress suit was clean and pressed. . . . Were the buttons on? The crease in the trousers? Yes, fine. . . . Briefcase with script in for final scrutiny? Yes, yes, it's all there, you fool.

Breakfast with a sick gut, small talk with Meg, both feeling the tension mount. . . . At the front door, I kissed Julie and embraced Meg. She looked me straight in the eye and she said in a strong voice, "You'll kill 'em, love, you'll see." I managed a weak smile, threw the briefcase on to the back seat of my battered second hand Ford Prefect, and without a glance backwards, I drove off to Blackpool, and, hopefully . . . Destiny.

I was in a dream when I reached Blackpool. I parked the car and floated off to the theatre with jokes spinning around in my head. The stage door keeper wished me well and gave me a key to a dressing room, which was already in use for the summer season currently playing there. Frankly, I forget whose dressing room I used, because my whole being was atremble with dire forebodings and doubts about my ability. . . . I started to recall the nights when the club audiences had booed me off; I remembered the time bottles were thrown at me; the times when I'd stood on a rostrum in a smoke-wreathed venue with sweat dripping down my suit as I battled to be heard above the din. . . . And then there were the lonely times, the bitter times. Could there be a future for me?

As per usual, inside the theatre chaos ruled supreme. Even now after all the years and experience, I still wonder how a show is born from the apparent debris of rehearsals. I watched the scurrying call boys and the harassed floor manager at work; the cameramen squinting down the fish eye lenses; the producer pleading and bullying in alternating moods. Chaos. Dickie Henderson worked through his paces with skill and verve; he was a pleasure to watch, and my spirits slumped even further down. Pearl and Teddy, expertise personified, made it all seem so easy.

Finally, someone spotted me cowering in my seat, and I was beckoned to the stage to run through my act. I stood where I was directed and I stumbled with the words of my script, which now seemed about as funny as a burnt crutch. Dickie Henderson, sensing my obvious uneasiness, came across, put his arm around my shoulder and urged me to take it easy. I muttered something to him through lips which appeared to have increased in size to that of the average German frankfurter. After the initial rehearsals, time sped as if tired of the trivia, and we were within an hour of the programme's commencement. A bevy of good-looking girls shaved me, powdered me, painted me, adjusted my hair style, fussed over me and propelled me out of the make up room, and I was taken in hand by some of the TV crew whom I had known from my local television work at the studios in Didsbury. They, bless them, escorted me to the theatre bar, and there in that most hallowed of places, I poured Dutch courage down my taut gullet. By this time, the audience were filing in and I looked for any sign of tolerance or kindness in their faces: none. They all looked grim and with rain whipping up a damp frenzy over the resort, I'm sure that any enthusiasm that might have survived was now in full retreat. One last drink, Dawson. . . . The time is nigh.

I stood backstage taking deep breaths as the lights went up and the producer started his "warm up". It went well, all augured fair. Now Dickie Henderson is standing there, he tells a few jokes. . . . Yes, the audience is laughing. He smiles, steps into his position; the orchestra strikes up. . . . This is It. . . . Dickie takes his cue as the cameras roll the film; he's funny, too damn funny I say to myself. . . . Now he's introducing the first act. . . . What, over already? What name is he calling out? Dawson? Who the hell is he? . . . I'm on. . . .

"Good evening, ladies and gentlemen . . . I only said that in fun.

I love Blackpool, it's a sort of Bournemouth with chips.

Blackpool is a sun trap, the only way you'll get the sun here is to trap it.

I've got nice digs here, just like home . . . filthy and full of strangers.

Great place Blackpool, you can eat rock, candy floss, fish and chips on the Golden Mile, then throw up in Fleetwood.

We often come to see the wife's mother here, she lives in Birmingham but looks better from Blackpool.

Before I came on I said to the producer that I felt a bit funny, he said get out there before it wears off.

I'm really enjoying this show, it's the first time I've played to a hung jury."

In show business parlance, that night I "murdered" them. They roared at every gag and I was in my seventh heaven. I finished my spot to a storm of applause, and as I was leaving the stage, an executive shook my hand and said, "Great kid, and what's more the show is going so well, we'll use it on the network." I beamed at him. . . . At last. Just as I began to mount the stairs back to the dressing room, I heard a loud crash onstage. I ran back and gazed in horror at the scene. A lighting tower had fallen over and it had pinned a member of the stage crew underneath its twisted metal. Blood was everywhere. . . . It was carnage.

White-faced, Dickie Henderson informed the audience that the show could not go on as the man appeared to be seriously injured. The curtains dropped and we strove to release the chap from the wreckage.

Thanks be to God, the crewman was not seriously hurt. The most he had sustained in terms of injury were superficial cuts. For myself, frankly I had nothing but pity and frustration in my soul. Again Fate had decreed that success was not to be gained easily, if at all. I drove home in a trough of dark depression and even Meg's unflinching belief in me could not lift the mantle from my beaten frame.

Sun Electric and I parted company on good terms and once more, dear reader, the spectre of the dole hovered like an incestuous moth. Because of the latest set back in my attempt

to crack show business, I was so intent in going round like a
ruined earl and muttering to myself, I forgot the magic of the
bungalow, which manifested its power two weeks later when
Iris Fredericks telephoned my agent Norman to say that
because I had done so well on the tragic try out at Blackpool,
ABC Television were going to put me in their first transmission of the series.

Once again I found myself rehearsing for *Blackpool Night
Out*. This time, however, I was more confident. I had burnt
the midnight oil over my script and now it was crisp and
funny. . . . I had no qualms whatsoever. . . . Oh how the
Gods must have sniggered at my complacency. *Blackpool
Night Out* was in every sense of the word a big show with
big stars as headliners. The viewing figures for the programme were high and acts vied to appear on it. Television
doesn't have the same impact today, but then, in 1966, it
could make or break an artist. On the show that night,
the one and only Cliff Richard and the Shadows, the usual
speciality act for which I still retain the greatest admiration –
in this case it was the now famous Johnny Hart, a superb
magician. Once again, Dickie Henderson was the compère
and the stage was set for a magnificent show. I couldn't wait
to get on under those lights and I paced the dressing room
like a caged puma as I listened for Dickie Henderson to
complete the "warm up". As he went into his patter, no
laughter came from over the tannoy. Nothing. Even I could
sense the desperation in Dickie's voice as he tried to rally the
packed house into amused anticipation. . . . But nothing was
forthcoming. I stood stock still with heart pounding; what
the hell. . . ? Just then Dickie's writer came into the dressing
room with sympathy written all over his face. "Bloody rotten
audience, son," he grimaced. "Of all the times to get your
break, you had to choose this one. . . . Jesus, they're tough."
He shrugged and left me alone with my thoughts. Two acts
went on and came off to desultory applause, then came the
commercial break, after which it was my turn to enter the
arena. There was a bottle of Scotch on the dressing room
table and I drank the contents straight from the bottle. I
looked long and hard at myself in the mirror, and I exclaimed
with a sort of bitter calmness, "So here we are again, kid,
well sod them all." I shook a fist skywards and trumpeted,

"Balls to life, if I'm going to be a failure, then I'm going to be a bloody good one." I emptied the cylinder of amber ambrosia, and tottered forth determined to "die" magnificently.

As I stood in the wings, swaying slightly, I saw Dickie Henderson mop his brow and his expression alone told me that the show was not faring well. Somehow, all the years of frustration gave me strength, and when the show recommenced and Dickie introduced me as a "promising new comedian", I strolled on and couldn't have cared less. The first thing that happened was I totally forgot my script, I simply could not remember one word of it, so I glared at the unfeeling audience, and I went on glaring at them with something akin to hatred. After what seemed an eon, somebody chuckled, and then somebody else. I made as if to see who was at the back of me and I rasped, "Who the hell's come on?" The laughter began to grow.

"Dawson's the name, I'm about as famous as Lord Godiva. In fact, I'm the only one on this show I've never heard of.

If you're popular in show business they give you a dressing room on the ground floor, if you're not so good, they put you on the first floor and so on. To give you some idea what they think of me, my room's full of falcon droppings, and the mice have blackouts.

Do you think I care? If things get bad I can always fall back on the wife, she's got a face like a camp bed. I'm not saying she's ugly but everytime she puts make up on, the lipstick backs into the tube. . . . Even the milkman flirts with me.

Nothing goes bloody right for me, we had North Sea Gas put in, now we can only light the stove when the tide's in."

I had them where I wanted them. . . . It was my night, and I grabbed it greedily. The laughter soared and grew in volume everytime I opened my mouth. I was one of them. Fed up, sick of society, I belonged to them.

The floor manager frantically waved to me; I was overrunning like hell but I couldn't stop. Then a germ of common sense wormed into my besotted ego, and I ended by saying, "Well that's enough for the money I'm getting, don't think it hasn't been fun meeting you . . . because it hasn't."

I walked off to an ovation; people were standing, actually standing and crying for more. . . . I walked up the now familiar stairs in a whirl . . . the applause was still sustaining . . . I threw myself into the dressing room and over the tannoy, the roars were still there. . . . A girl came running in. "Go back on the stage, Les," she said in a series of breathless pants. "They won't stop." As I walked back on to the stage the shrieks increased in volume and I stood with a beaming Dickie Henderson, who was holding my hand. . . . "Your time has come, kid," he said delightedly. Together we introduced Cliff and the Shadows and they couldn't follow me. . . .

The remainder of the night passed in a sea of alcohol. . . . People kept pumping my hand and slapping my back, and I was delirious. I phoned Meg and blurted out the news. She merely replied, "I knew you'd do it, love, now come home." I don't recall driving home at all, but I do remember stopping once on the moorland road that straddled Belmont, getting out of the car, urinating into a bush and shouting, "I bloody did it."

The lights were on in our bungalow. I peered through the window and saw Meg quietly knitting by the fireside, and my heart overflowed. Unashamedly, I wept. She held me close as if I were a small child who's seen Father Christmas for the first time. She smiled proudly at me and then, in her usual brisk no-nonsense fashion, went to put the kettle on. As she went into the kitchen to do so, she remarked in a very off-hand way, "Oh, love, I forgot to tell you, I'm expecting."

Open-mouthed, I found no words to utter, but a crop of grunts sufficed to express what I felt.

Was there ever such a night? Even today, after several successes, that night is a memory that remains tangible to me. The scene is still there in my recollection: sitting by the fire, mug of tea in hand, senses still reeling and now the prospect of another child to love.

Dear Meg, she'd stuck by me through the rotten days, and

now with God's help, she would be able to share the fruits
of triumph with me. We talked the whole night through; of
dreams and hopes, and as a finale we crept into Julie's bedroom
and held hands as our first born slept, unaware of what had
happened.

I awoke the following morning to the insistent clamour of
the telephone. Call after call, from the national newspapers
wanting interviews to friends and neighbours showering
congratulations. Was I a star? Gingerly I felt my crown, what,
no tiara? Should I feel different? Meg was bustling about,
Julie was sat in her high chair frowning in concentration as
she poured a cup of warm milk over her head, everything
seemed the same; was this what I had toiled for? But things
had changed. Norman rang to say that bookings were pouring
in for radio and TV, clubs (the better ones!) and cabaret dates
for conferences. Producers who wouldn't have given me the
time of day before, now almost pleaded for my services, and
this was all heady wine indeed.

Other things had changed as well. People who I had looked
upon as friends now seemed disgruntled with my small success;
on a shopping expedition to Woolworth's where Meg and I
had often gone for value, customers in the store nudged each
other and I overheard one woman say, "Fancy 'im shopping
'ere." Her companion screwed her eyes up at me and demanded, "Who is 'e?" " 'Im off the telly last night, get thousands of pounds on telly," her friend replied. It was there and
then that I learnt a vital lesson. Within the structure of a class,
your peers are with you as you struggle to attain whatever it
is you seek, but once you have secured it, they feel resentful
that you've moved up a notch. I was to find quite early on, that
it's the people who criticise your attempts who are the true
friends: they at least, by being critics, show true interest.

But I digress. I travelled to London and was interviewed by
the press on the roof of a leading West End hotel. During a
lull in the photographic session, the interviewer, in a voice
that clearly indicated that he was talking to a rank provincial,
said, "How does it feel to be above London, drinking champagne at a first class hotel?" I lit a cigarette and blew smoke
towards his condescending face. "I've been here before, old
chap," I replied in my flat Mancunian tone. He seemed

startled. "Really?" he said. "Oh yes," I drawled. "I used to come up here in my lunch break. . . . I was the head pot washer in the kitchens here, you know." With that, I sauntered away and tried to engage a charming lady reporter in a bout of flirtatious chat.

Forgive me if I appear hesitant in setting down an accurate record of the maelstrom of events at this time, but the sheer rapidity of things that happened was confusing. I was wanted on every variety show on the air; the national newspapers carried headlines like "SAD SACK IS OVERNIGHT SUCCESS" or "LES DAWSON UNKNOWN LAST WEEK HITS SHOW BIZ BONANZA". Overnight success, that was a goodie. But first, I had to face the biggest challenge of my new-found career . . . ABC Television had re-booked me for *Blackpool Night Out* and if I failed on this one, then the fresh recruit to the big time comedy ranks would be a has-been before he was a was-one. . . . It was a sobering thought, and of course the newspapers were quick to latch on to it.

Once again, Blackpool, only a fortnight after my triumph there. This time I was given a dresser to help me change and run errands for me, and his first errand was to mince away and buy a bottle of Scotch. Top of the bill was Frankie Vaughan and his "V" men. Despite the friendliness of the crew and producer alike, the old nerves became taut and I found that the quantity of liquid in the bottle of Scotch was going down quickly. I had to pull myself together and I did. If anything I went better than I had done the first time:

> "The ashen-faced mourners hunched closer together as the cold grey fog embraced them in its clammy shroud. The wind howled like a lost soul in dire torment, and from behind the bleak rain sodden hills, a demented dwarf strangled his pet racoon . . . 1, 2, 3. Sing together, "On A Wonderful Day Like Today."

> Thank you, there's nothing like a warm round of applause and what I just got was nothing like it.

> Since my success on this show a fortnight ago, I can now afford decent digs. . . . I'm staying in Lytham St Anne's.

It's posh there. . . . They don't have rates, just mice. It's the only place I know where they have grapes on the table and nobody ill. . . .

The woman I'm staying with thinks sex is something you put coal in. She said when my cat does anything in the garden he fills the hole in straight away. I said all cats do that, she said what, with a shovel?

I've brought the wife with me again, well it saves kissing her goodbye. Don't get me wrong, I'm not saying she's ugly, but I keep her photograph over the mantelpiece, it keeps the kids away from the fire.

I have three kids, one of each.

I can now afford a better car, the one I've got now is two tone . . . black and rust. The tyres on it are so shredded, every time I knock a pedestrian down, he gets twenty lashes as he falls."

My act was a repeat of last time; I stormed the audience, and I knew there and then, I had arrived.

I saw little of my family now. In quick succession I appeared on the *Billy Cotton Bandshow*, a very popular television show; I worked with Cilla Black and Val Doonican once more on their respective TV programmes, and I was still learning my craft. Star names that once I had merely gaped at, now shook my hand, and I confess that it was all a bit too much for me to cope with. I still had to fulfil some club engagements in the north east and there, my head was brought down with a bang. Clubs in the north east were plentiful in those days but a lot of them were tough to play; it wasn't surprising really, the hardy folk on Tyneside have only known hard work when they could get it and hard times in abundance. The people up there are the salt of the earth, but they don't suffer fools gladly and they can spot a phony a furlong away. Some of those venues were excellent in both decor and service: the Marimba Club, Middlesbrough; La Strada, Sunderland; Contessa Club, the Fiesta Club, Tito's, Franchi's. . . . All of those clubs would have graced the West End. However at the other end of the spectrum we had the South Bank Sporting Club and the Riviera Club. In my somewhat jaundiced view, if a criminal was sentenced to do a week's cabaret in either of those two horrors, you would have soon discovered that the crime rate was falling. . . . For my sins, I had to play a week at the South Bank Sporting Club, which was a sort of cross between Lenin's tomb and an Arab urinal. The people who drank in that place were so far down on the intellectual plain, it was a miracle that they'd learned to walk upright. They simply refused to listen to an artist during his or her performance, and fist fights were commonplace. I struggled manfully, but after nearly being brained by a large glass ashtray on the Wednesday night, I cut my act in half and shot off at the earliest possible chance.

On the Thursday night, the compère, a stiff arrogant type with illusions of grandiose importance, strutted into what passed for a dressing room and loftily explained that a open cast miner had asked him if I would mind if he did a song?

"He's asked before you know, silly chap, gets pissed, I'll tell him you won't allow it, hey?" I took my nose out of my whisky glass and said, "Let him sing by all means, in fact, mate, he can warble bleedin' Handel's Largo for all I care." The compère sniffed and stormed out. I was glad that I could put off going on that stage for an extra moment, and who knows, I thought, mayhap the miner will warm them up a bit for me. The compère asked for silence, didn't get it and a fat woman sat at a front stage table blew an oral fart at him. "Ladies and gentlemen, we have an audition tonight, a Welsh miner, who will sing for you. . . . Hush hush for Christ's sake," he snorted but to no avail. Idly I stood at the back of the auditorium and watched a tall, dark, sinewy man stride up to the leader of the awesome trio, and hand him a rolled up sheet of music. The man's face was pitted with black holes where the coal had struck him and his age was difficult to determine, for the ravages of toil had creased and etched his features into a mask. The audience took not a jot of notice, and carried on shouting and drinking and fumbling ladies on the knee. Eventually, the leader of the trio, who was the pianist, if you'll excuse the phrase, struck up the theme of the song which turned out to be a wonderful piece from *South Pacific* called *This Nearly Was Mine*.

In all the years I had been in show business, this voice was the first to grip my emotions. . . . I'd worked with artistes like Billy Eckstine and Matt Monro; Ronnie Hilton and Kenneth McKellar, but that miner's voice was a revelation. Deep and resonant, the liquid quality of it took you along on a harmonic tide of sweet melancholy. He was superb, and the noise subsided into an awed silence. When he'd concluded the song there was a stunned pause, then the whole room erupted into a great volume of approbation. Afterwards he came shyly into the dressing room and thanked me for letting him sing. I urged him to think seriously about a singing career: he didn't need tuition, his voice was a gift from the Muses. Just then his wife entered the room. She was a wiry, middle-aged woman, dark like her husband, but her eyes were narrow and suspicious, as was the tight line of her lips. "You should not be putting ideas into my man's head. . . . He's a miner and he has four childer. . . . Be off with you and stupid show business. . . ."

Throughout his wife's harangue, the dark man said not a word, he simply stood with his head bowed and his hands thrust into his pockets. In vain I pleaded with her to at least let me try to get a leading agent to hear him. Fiercely, she shook her head and her mouth assumed an even grimmer line. "No . . . he's a working man, not for the likes of him this stage thing. He'd only make a fool of himself." She gripped him by the lapel and her care-worn hands whitened. "Come home now." She almost hurled the words, and in her tone, I detected jealousy and trepidation about what might happen to her if he became successful as a singer. So often have I heard misguided ideas about show business: to some the world of entertainment is a weekly orgy. I've been in the game many years, and I've yet to see an orgy. Most performers are hard-working professionals who have a talent and a sense of morality far higher than the public they serve. Others look upon show business as a "get rich quick" job; it isn't. Stardom is gleaned through sheer toil and an ability to overcome bitter disappointments, and the rewards are few. This scarred miner had a talent that demanded to be heard, and yet I had to watch them both leave. That was the last I ever saw of him, and the last time I was ever to hear that wonderful rich voice of his. Years later, I was told that he had died in a pit accident.

There is a story that I enjoy relating. It occurred whilst I was appearing in Coventry at the New Theatre, for Newsome Productions. The bill for that particular week had the Shadows as top, a rising comedian, Ray Fell, and the usual chorus of dancers, singers and speciality acts. During the week's run, my car broke down and it had to be towed to a garage in Coventry, and as I had to return home on business one night, I caught the train to Manchester. The following day I set off back to Coventry only to find that a strike had halted the trains, and the only way I could get back in time for the show was to take a coach to the Midlands. I found myself sitting next to an elderly lady who appeared agitated, and when I asked her what the matter was, having lightheartedly assured her that I was not a potential rapist, she smiled nervously and asked would I mind changing seats with her husband who was seated opposite with a nun. Gallantly, I said of course not, the exchange was carried out and I found myself next to the old nun. Covertly I looked at my companion whose hands lay in her lap, hands that were like withered leaves in autumn. Her face had the hue of a sepia sky, and contentment rested twixt the creased texture of her skin. At Newcastle-under-Lyme, I bought her a cup of tea when the coach stopped, and after a hesitant start, we struck up a conversation. When I listened to the things that she had endured, my life as a comedian seemed futile and rather ridiculous. She had served her faith in the Far East and had been imprisoned by the Japanese; she had worked in India among the lost and the helpless; she had seen war in Africa and China. . . . Her life had been so full and passionate in its devotion, that I could do little else but gape and hang on to every word she uttered. She talked of Christmas Day in a mission, high in the hills of Assam, where the lepers sang carols; of the time she was held captive by rebels in Kurdistan and rescued hours before being shot. . . . The more she went on, the more my life became a vacuum. She interrupted my reverie: "Tell me, young man," she said softly, "what is your job?" What was my job? That was a laugh. "Er, I'm a comedian, ma'am," I replied. She nodded and asked me where I was appearing. I told her, the New Theatre. "Oh it's years since I went to see a show." She looked at me with twinkling eyes: "I don't suppose you could get me a ticket to see you?" Numbly I said yes, and that was that. Once back at the theatre I arranged a ticket for her, never for one moment expecting that she would turn up. The show that night went badly; there wasn't a big attendance and I "died" in my spot. Glumly, after the show, I sat drinking alone and feeling rather despondent, when the door opened after a short rap on the panel, and I rose to my feet in confusion as my old nun entered with a bright smile on her face. "Very good," she said. "Really enjoyed it." I muttered something about how much better it would have been if we'd had a decent audience, and rambled on until she put her hand up and stayed my diatribe. "Young man, God gave you a talent, and you made me laugh a lot . . . and by just that alone, you have justified your very existence." She embraced me with a warm smile and with that, she waved and left.

Her words made me feel that perhaps my life wasn't so empty after all; that by making people laugh for a moment in time, I had created something that would be lasting in future reflection.

I spent Christmas in pantomime at the Gaumont Cinema in Doncaster. It was my first panto, and I was in the good company of the Rockin' Berries and comic Mike Burton. We played a fortnight there, then went on to Hanley in the Midlands, where a flu epidemic had decimated the population, to such a degree I might add, that the deep freeze units in supermarkets were being used to store dead bodies. The pantomime ended its run in Gloucester and although the show hadn't broken records, it was one of the happiest seasons I've ever known, and it was my first taste of being "Top Of The Bill". I was now "resting" again, which is a theatrical jargon meaning out of work. I attempted to write again, this time a novel about the working men's clubs, but even as I penned my experiences, I had little faith in their being published. In my desk drawer I still kept all the rejection notices and they tended to moderate my ambitions to write. The manuscript was dropped hurriedly into a waste paper basket when, ashen faced, I rushed Meg into hospital when she complained of pains in her abdomen. Once again history repeated itself in the hospital ward as I paced up and down. It was a long drawn out delivery, but I was aroused from a vacant bed in a deserted ward by a radiant nurse, who, almost berserk with delight, informed me that I was the father of a bouncing baby boy, born at one o'clock in the morning on March 3rd 1967. I raced up the corridor skittling astonished staff aside, and stood with humility, watching my wife holding our baby son, whom we instantly christened Stuart Jason Dawson, a name we'd had for our first child who miscarried. What price the medical profession, I thought; the words came back: "You will never be a father" and here I was, the father of two!

We spent the summer of '67 once again in Blackpool, at the Central Pier. It was the strangest bill ever put together. Top of the bill was a huge American singer, Solomon King, who'd had a massive hit with a song called *She Wears My Ring*. He should have worn it through his nose for he turned out to be an incredible bore. On that amazing show was a street busker, one Don Partridge, who'd shot to fame with a song entitled *Rosie*. I didn't understand anything about him, nor the other comic on the bill, Ray Martine, whose humour was acid and vulgar. (We went on to become firm friends, however.) Then there was Joan Savage, a great wee pro, and a man with a dog that howled whenever he sang. His name was Jim Couton and I never saw him without his stage make-up on. Lastly, but not least was a Liverpool singer and comedian, Steve Montgomery, and his aim in life appeared to be to make love to every woman in sight. I myself have often veered to that idea, but with a face and body like mine, it has to be pure fantasy, I'm afraid.

Despite the almost lunatic bill, the show did well, much to everybody's surprise, and I came out of it unharmed in spite of vice squad policemen mingling with patrons on the pier in order to crack down on a suspected drug ring, operated, rumour had it, from within our show.

Solomon King was christened by the cast "The Alabama Elephant" and it had more than a ring of truth about it. Don Partridge sometimes didn't turn up for the show and on several occasions was seen with drum on back and mouth organ rack bobbing next to his throat, loping off on God knows what dastardly errand. Ray Martine minced about a lot and was sacked, but re-instated, and one of the dancers, a black haired lass with a perceptible glide in her eye found herself pregnant through the attentions of a fair-ground barker. There was, apparently, abandonment of all kinds, but I never saw as much as a buttock groped in that show. My dressing room wasn't a dressing room, it was a hole under the stairs and the space was to say the least confining, for instance, mice who crept in it had to stand on their back legs to shuffle through.

I played a curious role in that season; that of a sort of amateur para-medic. . . . It started when one of the dancers came to see me in my hole, and she said in her inimitable style, "Can you 'elp me? I ain't 'ad a period for two months, but I don't think I'm up the tub like." In a relaxed posture I drew out from her that no, she 'adn't 'ad it off and had no bleedin' intention of doin' like. From what small iota of knowledge I had of medicine, I suggested that perhaps she was a trifle anaemic and should therefore restore iron to her plasma by eating lightly fried liver. . . . This she did and lo! a day or two later she re-entered my hole in a delighted state to inform me that she'd commenced her menstrual cycle once more. . . . That did it, I became the saviour for all feminine ills: "thrush", "mammary secretion". . . . I began to see a future for myself as a back street abortionist should show business fail me.

But all in all, I enjoyed that remarkable season and as the chill of October drilled into our marrows on the sea-drenched pier, I felt a pang of sadness at the closing of the show. A small tale of how destiny can twist our lives: one night I came off stage, and I'd done so well, I was by now moved to second on the bill and was responsible for enticing customers in. As I mopped my forehead before crouching to gain entrance into my hole, Wally Stewart, the company manager, tugged my sleeve and said, "You had a visitor whilst you were on stage, Les." I lit a cigarette and made some comment about nobody being here now, and Wally said gently, "He had to go and find digs somewhere. . . . He'd had a rough time at a club and he'd been paid off. He didn't want you to see him the way he was . . . Les, it was Max Wall."

With a resigned smile, Wally went back to his office and I braved the buffeting wind and leaned on the rail at the pier end. Memories came flooding back. . . . The hopes that were dashed when Max disgraced himself in the public's eye; nights I had spent huddled on park benches; the smell of grease in café kitchens; the auditions and the failures. . . . Then Max had been a giant in the theatrical orbit, and I, so low. Years later, when the genius that was and still is Max Wall placed him back on top, no one was more pleased than I.

So many things were happening for me, that my home life was non-existent and Julie and Stuart were growing up without me being there to see them develop. When I did get home, Meg was fully in control and I felt that I wasn't needed, and, of course, in a sense that was correct; she had had to be a father as well, and although I realised it, the pain of seeing their closeness caused anger. Why, oh why, do we allow the shallow magnet of ambition to blind us to the true attraction of things that really matter? Those years can never be returned; it is the past. Newspapers found me good copy and I seemed to be in every daily in the realm, with photographs of my mournful countenance in morose profile in all popular tabloids. Jim Casey and I, along with Daphne Oxenford and Robert Dorning, Eli Woods and Colin Edwin did a radio series, and to this day Daphne and Colin and I are still at it, with . . . yes, Jim Casey.

I knew in my heart that I was pushing it and that burning the candle at both ends would eventually take its toll. I played every town in the country and drank a lot of 'em dry. . . . Something had to snap and it did, in Kidderminster during cabaret. I was nearing the end of my act and just about to sing *Bye Bye Blackbird* when the harsh lights began to spin and sweat poured down my face and body; I could feel the floor moving and my eyes no longer focused, then an ebony blanket fell on me. "Les," I heard a voice call out. It belonged to the agent who'd booked me for the venue, Billy Forrest, and he looked down at me in concern. I was in his house on the settee and I knew that I was fortunate to have been given a warning. But two days later, I was off again and the booze flowed and the midnight oil drained away into early dawns. . . . I'd wake up in unfamiliar places and see a stranger in the mirror, and oh, I swear by all that was holy, that this time. . . . But it would be years before common sense took charge.

IMAGES

The Queen drew closer to where Les Dawson stood and she would soon be introduced to the diminutive comedian. Her Majesty would see a crumpled man with hair in disarray and with a face that life had battered. . . . What she wouldn't see was the little man in the dole queue at Hammersmith with holes in his shoes. After he had drawn his pittance, the little man would walk back to his tiny room with a bag of chips for his evening meal and having consumed that, meet his only friend in a back street pub, where the little man would listen to his friend talk about his career in films. The friend would wax forth about his notices in a recent film with Dirk Bogarde, and the younger Dawson hung on every word. Later Dawson, the little man, would creep up the stairs of his digs because he owed a month's back rent, and the landlady wanted him out. He would then pull the one blanket around his shoulders and dream of an impossible future.

The following night, his friend didn't turn up and he never would again, because he had gassed himself to death in his own lonely flat. Dawson spent what money he had left on drink and he never felt the hands of the publican when he threw Dawson into the street for brawling. . . .

I think that moment was the lowest ebb in my life; lying supine in the wet gutter with a neon sign flickering above me . . . Lost and alone and seemingly without hope. I spent the rest of the night in a Salvation Army Hostel with other derelicts listening dully to the words of an earnest uniformed man . . . I was twenty-two years of age.

CURTAIN RISING

I took some time off to be with my family; instinctively I knew that my marriage was becoming unhappy with my continued absence; Meg was always the stronger partner and she had almost made a life for herself and Julie and Stuart, and I had changed, for the worse really: I was too ambitious for my own good. I fretted at the inactivity at home and longed for the travelling again. However, Meg and I had to bury our problems because my father was causing us both concern. Since we had left Keston Avenue, he had gone into a decline; the house wasn't being looked after, and what was even more hurtful, he wasn't looking after himself. In vain I pleaded with him to come and live with us, but no, on that subject he was firm to the point of stubbornness. He was a worry but the tempo of my career was increasing: Meg and I took the children to London where I taped a potential situation comedy called *State Of The Union* for the BBC. It was a good idea and with excellent people such as Patsy Rowlands and Michael Robbins in it, I thought it a foregone conclusion. . . . It wasn't. The national papers slated it and me, and as a result, producer Ronnie Taylor and director John Ammonds lost interest. It did me good in a strange way to realise that not everything I undertook was bound to be an unqualified success; mind you it hurt to read the reviews.

I took the family with me on the road to the north east again and we stayed with our friend, the Reverend Bill Hall. I didn't realise how tired I was becoming and Stuart was teething, so his cries at night robbed me of sleep. The outcome of this was, I suppose, inevitable: at the conclusion of the week's engagement, whilst driving home in the early hours of Sunday morning, I fell asleep at the wheel of my Vauxhall Cresta saloon and I crashed the vehicle at speed into a tree. The damage was horrendous: Meg's eyes were full of glass splinters and Julie had sustained heavy bruising. Passers-by helped us from the wreckage and the police took us to Leeds Infirmary where Meg's sight was mercifully saved.

Christmas loomed and Norman Murray was delighted that he had booked me at the Leeds Grand Theatre on the Batchelors' Christmas Show. The Batchelors were a top group of the day and their records were sold in millions. It ranks as one of the greatest seasons I've ever played, mainly because I was received very well by the audience who nightly packed the theatre to see a truly mammoth show. On that bill were people who are not merely friends but superlative artists: Arthur Worsley, in my view the funniest ventriloquist of all time, and Norman Collier, a clown in the great tradition of that most noble of callings. The show was a small hit, and what's more, it was to be a turning point in my career. . . . The magic propensities of our Unsworth bungalow had weaved another spell.

At risk of making too big an issue of the bungalow, it did seem as if a force for good was at work. Julie, who was then four years old, often used to stand in the hallway on her way to bed, and I would see her talking to a wall. One night I picked her up in my arms and I asked her why she chatted away to the wall. The hairs rose on my neck when she said scornfully, "Not talking to a wall, Daddy, I talk with the Grey Lady."

Years later I was to become interested in the para-normal, but at that period it put the willies up me to hear my first born speak of such things.

"Aren't you afraid of the Grey Lady?" I said inanely. Julie looked at me with eyes much older than a four-year-old's and whispered gently, as if talking to an idiot, "She's lovely, Daddy, and she has a bad foot, poor lady limps."

About this time, we had an extra three bedrooms put in the roof of the bungalow and my tiny son, aged two and a half, loftily informed me in between racing up and down in his cowboy suit, that "Somethink gus in me room at night, Dad, wid a poorly leg." By now I was searching for a squatter, but in a matter-of-fact fashion, Julie said, "It's only the Grey Lady dragging her foot." A few months later, Meg attended a wives' club meeting and the group was given a talk by a woman who claimed to possess psychic powers. She said to my wife, "You have a presence in your house, but do not be afraid, it is an element of Good. I get the impression that the spirit is lame." There you have it, and I rest my case.

I came off stage one night during the run at Leeds, and found a tall young man with a pint of beer in one hand and a cricket bat in the other, waiting outside my dressing room door. His name, he told me, was John Duncan, he was a producer for Yorkshire Television, and could he speak to me? He changed my life that night. The reason for the visit, he said, was to ask me if I'd care to do a "pilot" variety show for the company. We chatted and we drank and discovered that he had ideas very akin to mine. We had reached the stage of mulling over a title for the show, when a dancer, who throughout the season had played merry hell with my libido, popped her pretty head round the door and asked me to go to a party. I gave her a long smouldering look and answered in the affirmative; then I made some remark to the effect that the winsome lass would be mine that night. She grinned and said, "No chance, Dawson." She turned to John Duncan and carried on, "We don't take any notice of what Les says." After she'd left, Duncan looked at me and chortled, "That's it. . . . We'll call the show *Sez Les*." We did and that television show was to last eight marvellous years.

The run ended at Leeds and I had several cabaret engagements to fill and also a *Good Old Days* TV programme to do for the producer, Barney Colehan. In late March, just three weeks before I was scheduled to tape the pilot show for Yorkshire, I undertook a week's engagement at the Mersey Hotel, Manchester. One night, as was increasingly becoming my want, I stayed after hours for a drink and heard the sound of Glenn Miller-style music coming from upstairs in the hotel. On my inquiring about it, the landlord of the hotel invited me to go upstairs and see for myself. In a large room I saw sixteen musicians under the leadership of Syd Lawrence, whom I knew as a trumpet player with the Northern Dance Orchestra, playing the whole Glenn Miller range of music, and I knew there and then that I had to have them for the show. There was a selfish motive: I love the sound of a big band, and nobody featured them on a variety show on the air at the time, so we would have a "first". The same evening I telephoned John Duncan; the following night he came to hear them and he agreed with me: we had to have them as a base for the show. Syd and the boys were elated by the idea and the die was cast.

The orchestra were sat on two tiers against a glittering back-cloth, and over the announcement "Ladies and gentle-men. . . . Welcome to *Sez Les*", the band struck up and on came the Irving Davies dancers: beautiful girls and four superb male dancers, who performed routines that became the talk of the business. During the final part of the dance, I came on:

> "Good evening, ladies and gentlemen, this is another pilot show. . . . Frankly, I've done more pilots than the Battle of Britain, but who knows? perhaps tonight I'll finally get into the big money. Our big band sound is provided by Syd Lawrence and his boys. . . . Boys! They're so long in the tooth when they have a tooth filled their gums get metal fatigue. The band used to perform for the troops . . . at Bannockburn.
>
> Tonight we have a feast of entertainment for you. . . . Singers who sing, dancers who dance, and show girls who show us what it's all about."

The show went well, and I can never thank John Duncan enough for his faith in me. Today, John runs a book shop, but if I had my way, he'd be back in the studios. He had ideas and was never afraid to stand by them. The upshot of the pilot programme was that I was commissioned to tape six variety shows under the heading of *Sez Les*. From the moment they went out, they were a huge success, and I thank all the people who helped me so very much: writers David Nobbs and Barry Cryer; floor manager, now a producer, Don Clay-ton; back room boy Terry Hughes, and not forgetting the lads who moved the scenery and gave me all the help I asked for. The head of Yorkshire Television in those pioneering days was Donald Baverstock, who didn't really care for the

variety side of programming; in fact once, when I was offered
the sensational young Osmonds, he turned to me and said in
his thick Welsh accent, "What the bloody hell do you want
Negro blues singers for?" That was Don, and yet I liked him
and what's more, he listened to John Duncan.

After the success of the first six shows of *Sez Les*, another
series was mooted and agreed. By now I was becoming
well-known as a television celebrity and I tasted the wine of
all that: the autograph hunters and the gapes from people in
the streets as I walked past . . . it was heady stuff. In clubs,
I packed them in: from "Caesar's Palace" in Luton to the
Bailey circuit in the north, I could do no wrong. The ultimate
triumph came when I was booked to appear on the *Sunday
Night At The London Palladium* TV show: for all artistes the
supreme accolade at the time. I went giddy as I shared the
limelight with American singer Tony Bennett and drummer
Buddy Rich, and, compère once again, Dickie Henderson. I
was away from home and living a whirlwind existence. . . .
Night clubs in London welcomed me, as did the chic salons
of Mayfair. Women flattered me and my head was turning.
My writings were now being accepted by magazines: *Punch,
Woman's Own*. There were the parties and the hangovers; the
gambling and the guilt. . . .

The success of *Sez Les* led to an idea by Barry Cryer and Ray
Cameron called *Jokers Wild*. Six top comics telling jokes and
trying to outdo one another. . . . The show was a smash and
I became even more well known through that series. . . . It
seemed the world was my oyster, and I was now a regular
panellist on such game shows as *The Golden Shot* with Bob
Monkhouse, whom I'd worked with in summer season at
Scarborough; *Celebrity Squares* with Bob again; *The Generation
Game* with Bruce Forsyth. During the years 1967 to 1969, I
popped up on every major television programme doing guest
appearances apart from hosting *Sez Les* and *Jokers Wild*. All
this, coupled with appearing at every prominent night club
from Wales to Perthshire, helped to dispel any worries over
finance. . . . Money was no longer a burning issue with the
Dawsons, but despite the comfort of a reasonably padded
bank account, the harsher realities of life still kept up more
than a nodding acquaintance: Meg suffered another bad

miscarriage and I had to stem her torment by delivering the foetus myself because the doctor was late in arriving. The miscarriage didn't have the same emotional impact this time because we had two fine children and for that blessing, Meg and I were content. Our new found wealth enabled me to purchase a new car and to buy Meg a low mileage Triumph Stag sports car. . . . Meg had finally passed her driving test, how I'll never know; even today when she drives down a main road, the cat's eyes squint. . . . She doesn't have a radiator grill fitted on her cars, she uses a pedestrian strainer.

My father's health was visibly failing and he was causing me a lot of concern. Every time I went to visit him, I saw the signs of a man giving up the fight for life and pride. The house was becoming squalid and uncared for, and still he refused to come and live with me. Finally I managed to talk him into going for a medical check up and I drove him to Crumpsall Hospital in Manchester. Whilst he was being examined, I smoked heavily and paced the all too familiar hospital corridor. When he emerged his face was ashen, but when he saw me draw towards him, he forced a smile and tried to reassure me: "Not too good, son, I've got to take it easy for a bit, then I should be all back to normal." What I didn't know was after the medical examination, the doctor confronted my father with the chilling news that he had lung cancer.

This time Meg was adamant, I think she knew the truth before I did, and my father came to live with us.

More bad news followed. I was playing a week's engagement at "Caesar's Palace", Luton, when Meg rang to say her father had passed away after a long illness; I was full of grave forebodings.

A strike at the TV studios brought me a much needed rest from the work load and I scampered about our bungalow doing jobs that had piled up whilst I had been away. Frankly when it comes to "do-it-yourself" I'm about as much use as a one-legged man in an arse-kicking competition, but I sallied forth with hammer and screwdriver, putting shelves up that usually fell down and so on. My son Stuart and I decided to clean out a spare room one morning; well it wasn't a room in the proper sense of the word, it was more worthy of the title "cupboard". Little Stuart, resplendent in a Lone Ranger outfit, happily hurled himself into the task by tossing acquired garbage to the four winds. During one such impassioned fling, I noticed he held a large sheaf of foolscap in his hand, we wrestled good naturedly for it and when my offspring had finally become disenchanted with the clean up, I sat down and was agreeably surprised to find that I was reading my first effort at writing a novel, the one I thought I'd thrown away. As I perused the manuscript I decided there and then that I would have another go at it. Once I got reshaping and rewriting it, I was absorbed by the project. . . . Pictures came alive from the words and I spent every waking moment on it, with coffee and Scotch handy at my side. The bungalow spirit must have been beaming upon my efforts because three years later it was published by Sphere Books under the title *A Card For The Clubs*. Dawson was launched as an author, and I give thanks to my friend and mentor Eddie Lamb for having confidence in me. The book, a searing indictment of the conditions in working men's clubs, became a best seller and a novel that every performer who had endured those venues read avidly. From the grip of a small boy, a sheaf of damp, forgotten pages hoisted on to a new plateau a comedian who still remembered the words of an old teacher, addressing an ill-kempt urchin, "You have the talent to become a fine writer." I hope that one day I will be.

As March 1970 threw its last tantrum, my father was taken into Christie's Hospital, Manchester and I knew he would never leave that place. He was pitifully thin and slept most of the time. I would often sit by his bed and remember him as he was; a friendly man who, because of the war, had mislaid the role of a father in a boy's formative years. On April 10th 1970, as I sat by his hospital bed, Les Dawson senior fluttered his eyes once, called out my mother's name, and died. An overwhelming feeling of loneliness shrouded me as I realised that I had no immediate family left . . . and that all the fame in the world could never alter the decrees of Fate. In a strange way, I got to know my father better through death than I had ever done in life. I was back at his old council house, going through the awesome business of settling up a person's estate, when I came across a sealed letter, addressed to me. It had obviously been left in a position where it would have been impossible not to have noticed it. As I read that final chapter of his life, the man's enormous courage shone like a beacon from the print . . . and I wept like a child.

"Dear Son,

By the time you read this note I've left you, I will be gone and hopefully, reunited with your mother. I was told I hadn't much hope to recover, and frankly, I'd known that fact for some time. Please son, settle everything up for me, there is an insurance policy that should cover the cost of the funeral with a bit left over so buy the kiddies something nice.

I'm very proud of you, Les, and you have a fine wife in Meg, in so many ways she reminded me of your mother, and she was the best person in the world, and when she died, something in me died also. When I went away in the army, you were just a little thing, and can you imagine how I felt when I came home to find you standing by your mother? There you were, fourteen years old and growing up so fast. . . . I didn't know what to say to you, son.

I never had much money, but what I did have, was a wonderful wife and a son. Mother and I would have liked more children as you know, but when your brother Terry passed away, your mother couldn't have any more so that was that.

The rent has been paid to the end of the month and all other bills have been seen to. God bless you my son, I'll tell your mother how well you are doing, she would have loved to see you get on, she loved you so. . . . Be a man my son.

Dad"

It was dawn before I went home. My eyes were red, and my soul cried out for one last chance to tell him that I loved him, but there was just the echo of silence in that dead house. As per his wishes I had my father cremated, and I took the ashes and buried them in my mother's grave; he was only sixty-five years of age.

In 1970 I played Scarborough, yet again at the Floral Hall, with Kenneth McKellar and the young entertainer, Bobby Bennett. The business wasn't bad but I knew it could have been better and I began to wonder if I hadn't over-exposed myself on television. Within myself, I was unable to come to terms with so many things, I felt disgruntled, and as the ratings for *Sez Les* sank, so did my spirits. As if to compensate, the tempo of my private life increased: clubs, late night drinking, and I became obsessed with that most trite of dictums, 'Wine, Women and Song'. I no longer packed them in when I appeared at cabaret venues and bitterness in regard to show business and performers was my forte; I was envious of the success of other artistes who were seemingly in control of their futures. . . . Limbo period.

I had always undertaken charitable work, not to prove what a good chap I was, but the one code I have always tried to maintain is in the maxim, "Put back into life what you take out." I believe in that creed and so many rewards come from doing just that. It is indeed better to give than to receive, but now, I flatly refused to open garden fêtes and the like: why the hell should I? was my platform, who the bloody hell cared about me and so on . . . the wail of the idiot.

The last straw came with some particularly bad press for the fourth *Sez Les* series, and the show dropped out of the national ratings altogether. At the time, I was appearing at a club in Derby, where previously I had stormed them. This time however, the place was only half full and out came the bottle. At risk of making this meandering book a hymn to my wife, it was she, that much maligned lady, who took a hand in things and jerked me back to my sense.

She was sat knitting early one evening as I prepared for the drive to Derby. She was listening patiently to my stentorian discourse on the fickle public, agents, comics stealing my act, etc., etc., when the telephone rang. I picked up the receiver and a cultured female voice introduced itself as a certain Mrs somebody or other who worked at a home for mentally handicapped children and would I kindly go along on my way to Derby and open a new wing, please, it will only take a few minutes, Mr Dawson, it's in Buxton and I am led to

understand that is the route you take on your way to Derby
. . . I sneered over the receiver, "No I can't do it, I'm too
busy, sorry. . . ." Meg took the instrument from my grasp,
elbowed me out of the way and said, "Oh hello, no, my
husband is wrong, he can come along on Saturday afternoon
to open the wing for you. . . . Yes, well I do his engagements
for him and he is available to appear for you. . . . Thank
you." "What the hell did you say that for?" I asked angrily.
She gave me a look of withering scorn. "I'm disgusted at
your attitude, it's about time you pulled yourself together.
Don't blame a home for retarded children for the state you're
in." With that, she stalked off into the kitchen.

Saturday came and sullenly I drove off to Buxton. I arrived
there about ten minutes before I was due to open the new
wing, because in a fit of pique I had deliberately stopped off
for a few drinks at a moorland pub. As I drove up a winding
drive to a rather dilapidated Georgian house, every window
was jammed with children peering out. On the door step, a
tall grey-haired lady with anxious features gave me a smile
of agitated relief as I braked the car. "Oh, Mr Dawson," she
breathed in a cultured tone, "I thought you'd forgotten us."
I shrugged and mentally decided to get away as quickly as
possible. We entered the house and mounted a naked staircase
into a large high-ceilinged room where a tea urn stood on a
trestle table. A harassed-looking woman raced over to me
and haltingly asked if I'd like a cup of tea? I said yes and for
a few minutes we stood around making small talk until
suddenly a crowd of children, some in wheel chairs and others
with distinctive mongoloid features, were herded into the
room. The condition of some of the children was heart
rending; spastic limbs jerking; some crawling towards me
and others with open mouths and empty eyes. The lady who
had greeted me on the drive way glanced at me and said very
softly, "I don't think you realise what your coming here
today has done for these children, Mr Dawson. . . . You
know, they haven't got much of a chance in life." I nodded
dumbly and the last ounce of indifference flew from my soul;
I picked the kids up and I played with them and signed pieces
of paper for them, and before I realised it, I'd spent three
hours with those bright-eyed scraps of humanity who for
reasons known only to God himself had been the victims of

a genetic malfunction. I shook hands with my hostess, and she said with great sincerity, "You will never know what you've done today." I searched her face, lightly kissed her on the cheek and replied, "Madam, you'll never know what this visit has done for me." As I was about to drive away to continue the journey to Derby, a little girl came running to the car. She clambered up on to my knee when I opened the door. "I've got a present for you," she said solemnly, and she handed me a toffee that she had clutched in her grimy fingers. "I love you," she said and hugged me tightly. I stopped the car about a mile from the home; I dried my tears and all bitterness drained away. It had taken poor mentally ill children to put things in perspective.

My act that final night at Derby went superbly, and the main ingredient that created the success was that there was warmth back in me.

On the lighter side of charity, a vicar kept telephoning me to open a garden fête and to judge a children's fancy dress contest. As his vicarage was in Hull, and I lived in Bury, not unreasonably I tried to put the saintly man off, but no, he was quite adamant: "Please, Mr Dawson . . . I beseech you." Reluctantly I agreed to attend and off I drove across the lofty Pennines in a rain storm of quite incredible ferocity. With eyes aching and body stiff, I arrived at the vicarage and the rain still poured down. I got out of the car and as I was approaching the vicarage door, a small woman with a crepe hat marched towards me and said in ringing tones, "It never rained when Vera Lynn opened our fête." With that, she hit me on the shoulder with an umbrella. Inside the hallway the vicar, a tall gloomy man, bade me welcome and took me into a sort of vast conservatory where a throng of sodden people were steaming in groups. The kids were crying because their fancy dress clung to them now like paper mâché shreds. I was hoisted on to a makeshift podium and the vicar called for silence from the moist assembly. "Ladies and gentlemen, welcome to our fête, alas the weather has not been kind, but here is a gentleman who will lighten the day for us. I'd like to take this opportunity of thanking Les Dawson for coming today, I'm very grateful because I tried everybody else first." With that he handed me a whistling microphone and as I began to say a few words, a lean, hungry-looking female shouted in a booming voice, "Piss off." Needless to say, I was most gratified to escape from Hull.

My work improved and the next series of *Sez Les*, despite not having Syd Lawrence on the show, shot back into the ratings. Top stars like David Essex, Cleo Laine, Shirley Bassey, Olivia Newton John, Humphrey Lyttelton and many more became almost regulars on the programme.

As 1970 slid into '71, Meg broke the news that she was once more with child. Because of her history of miscarriages, she had to take to her bed more than she would have wished, but we didn't want to take any chances whatsoever. That winter, I was appearing in *Babes in the Wood* at the Grand Theatre in Leeds, and we were playing to tremendous business. It was a strong bill: Ronnie Hilton, Wyn Calvin, the Dallas Boys. It was a great season from a work point of view, as well as having a social scene enjoyed by all; many a publican may still muse about that halcyon winter when his profits soared to an all-time apex. . . . In the northern vernacular, "We supped Leeds dry." Occasionally also, I pass a gaunt, unprepossessing house in a Leeds suburb, and I recall parties that would make Lord Longford's dandruff bristle. . . . But enough of that. . . .

The pantomime completed its run in a blaze of triumph, and there was no time for a holiday. Instead it was back to work on a new *Sez Les* and the satisfaction of seeing my book *A Card For The Clubs* published. The night it was unleashed on the public, I spent a quiet evening looking through a heap of my rejection slips from virtually every publisher in the country, and I experienced a tremendous thrill in burning the whole damn lot . . . I'd done it! I had written a novel. The year sped by; Julie was going to school, Stuart was growing into a fine lad, Meg was contented, and I began to look round for a larger house. Like most people, I found income tax was a problem and I was advised to invest in property as a way of trying to salvage some of my earnings by obtaining a bigger mortgage. It puzzles me still that in this day and age, one has to get into debt to save money!

Meanwhile, I signed to appear for the summer season at the Queen's Theatre, Blackpool with Dora Bryan and Ronnie Hilton. It seemed Blackpool had been selected by the Fates to be a major part of my destiny. Success brings many things, but one aspect of it that saddened me was the "hate mail" that started trickling in: letters from anonymous morons, that at first upset me. After all, I reasoned, all I strived to do was entertain, so why did I inspire such vitriol?

I didn't mind in the least the shoal of eccentrics who wrote to me: the greatness of the British Isles lies in the fact that we are an eccentric race, and that is our secret weapon against the world, the weapon that always baffles the foe. For years, a man who informed me that he was in touch with Mars was a source of great interest to me, until he wrote saying that the Martians had taken over Bognor Regis and were going to turn it into a brothel. I haven't heard from him since and I just hope he's happy wherever they've put him. A clergyman from the Midlands with homosexual tendencies kept inviting me to go on a cycling holiday with him through the Dutch tulip fields, and a loony from Arbroath claimed, in a peculiar note to me, that he was the real Prince Philip.

When Julie's school holidays came round I moved the whole family with me for the summer in Blackpool, and Meg and I after a couple of weeks' safaris in St Anne's, a high class area six miles from Blackpool, decided that was where we would like to settle down.

In the period before I opened up at Blackpool, Meg and I had done the rounds of estate agents, and I must give them credit for imagination:

House 1, in Cheshire, was described as "Charming neo-Tudor dwelling with extensive countryside views".

That turned out to be a terraced slum overlooking a raddled field near a bacon warehouse.

House 2, near Southport, was described glowingly as, "Split level executive-style house, with sunken gardens".

The gardens were sunken all right, as was the house as well. A vast crack twixt bedrooms and living room made the place look as if it was leering at you, and the dampness was so bad, we would have had to have gutters on our pyjamas.

House 3, in the Lake District, was described thus: "Off the beaten track in charming woodland setting; slight renovation required".

That turned out to be a shack between two dead elms and in front of it was a pond of quite unique odours. When one threw a stone into its depths, the smell that emerged was positively mauve. The whole place was off the beaten track, that part was accurate, in fact the nearest town was Oslo. Meg and I had reached the stage of near hysteria by this time, and it appeared that we were never to be allowed to depart from Bury.

Meanwhile the summer season was going well and the business was good. So agitated was I over Meg expecting the baby at any time, that as soon as she felt a twinge of pain, I would rush her into hospital. It reached the point when doctors would remove me bodily as I babbled on. Finally she was admitted into Bury Hospital on the night of July 17th.

During Meg's confinement, I was like an overweight Dervish: the stage door telephone was out of bounds to the rest of the cast, and as soon as I came off stage, I would bound in a frenzy to the instrument and demand in a high nervous voice to know about the wife's condition: was there any sign of the baby? Was Meg in pain? . . . In short, I was a bloody pest and my highly strung attitude was driving the rest of the cast mad. Julie and Stuart were being looked after by Meg's mother at the flat we'd taken for the season, and she, poor woman, was nearly out of her mind with the antics of her son-in-law. On the night of the 20th, I had been wrenched off the telephone and hurled on to the stage for my sketch with Dora Bryan, when suddenly I felt a presence behind me. I turned and saw the spectre of Jimmy Tarbuck, bottle of champagne in his hand, standing with an enormous grin on his face: "You're a dad again, Dawson, phone the wife and I'll carry on for you," he chuckled. I darted off. "Mr Dawson, you have a fine healthy daughter, and Mrs Dawson is well," the female voice on the other end of the line informed me . . . I leant against the wall and frankly cried a little, mostly with relief and also for the gift of something so precious.

I drove away from Blackpool that night and made a beeline for the maternity hospital; nobody could have stopped me charging into the ward to gaze at the sight of my wife and daughter. Meg, I discovered, had not had an easy time with the delivery, and I decided there and then that she would not go through any more suffering. . . . She'd had enough. The staff at the hospital were marvellous and I can never thank those wonderful people at Bury enough for allowing me to stay overnight in an empty ward.

We called the baby Pamela Jayne, and her christening at Blackpool was a riot. Really, it was more like a show business regatta; all the pro's were in attendance and after forgetting the name of the church, we tried several, one a Mormon tabernacle, before we pulled up in convoy at the right church, only to find we'd lost the baby en route. I was about to get in touch with the FBI when the car carrying one of the harassed godparents finally braked to a halt. Needless to say, the drink flowed in cataracts that evening, and the last offspring of the Dawson loins was well and truly accepted into society.

Although the show at the Queen's Theatre heralded the arrival of Pamela Jayne, it was nearly the demise of her father. Two days before we christened Pamela, as the full company took the finale bow, scenery fell with a crash, knocked one of the artistes, Roger Mistin, unconscious and ripped the side of my eye in a deep gash. I was rushed to Victoria Hospital and thanks to a young nurse who acted promptly, no scar remains.

I'd like to go forward a few years for this story, which occurred when I was again appearing in Blackpool. The summer season at the ABC Theatre was drawing to an end, and the chilled winds from across the Irish Sea had started to thin out the holidaymakers on the beaches. Towards the close of the penultimate week there, the deputy mayor asked me to draw a lottery ticket at the Town Hall.

I must admit that I made my way to the ceremony a bit begrudgingly: after all I had performed many gala openings and garden fêtes in the name of charity and I thought I'd done my share, plus the fact that the ticket was to be drawn at mid-day, and I was still suffering from the effects of the night before's drinking bout.

The hangover was cured by a few more glasses of delight in the mayor's parlour prior to the ticket drawing drama, which was for the goodly sum of one thousand pounds. . . . Not bad.

With due pomp, portly Dawson, face aflush with spirits, drew from the drum a numbered piece of stiff material and

in his stentorian bellow announced to the local press representative and councillors the number of the lucky winner. The
name was checked and as the fortunate one lived close by, it
was thought that it might be a nice touch to have him or her
brought to the Town Hall immediately if possible for a
photograph with the deputy mayor and myself. As the taste
for acquiring more alcohol had increased, I readily agreed and
off went the mayoral car to bring the winner. . . .

The car pulled up outside a rather seedy address. The driver
knocked on the door: there was no answer. At that moment,
the window of the house next door opened and a woman
informed the driver that the occupant had just been taken to
the hospital a couple of hours before. The driver, sensing the
story wasn't at an end, drove to the hospital.

He was stunned to find that the winner of the thousand
pound lottery had been rushed into care after taking an
overdose. . . . The ticket owner had less than two pounds in
his bank account, and despair had driven him to find a way
out of his predicament by taking his own life.

He'd recovered enough to be told that he was a richer man
by a thousand pounds and today he has a thriving business,
apparently. . . . I like to think that a higher authority guided
my hand in that drum of tickets, who knows?

There is always a feeling of melancholy when a show ends
its run and the summer season when Pamela was born was
no different. Performers come together at the commencement
and by the close of it, they've become like a family and it's a
wrench to say goodbye. It had been hard work because not
only did I perform six nights a week, on the Sundays I hosted
a television programme called *International Cabaret* which
was shot at the Talk Of The Town in London. In many ways
it was an odd ball show: mostly European artistes took part
in it and the language barrier was a problem. The producer's
drinking habits didn't help matters . . . he wasn't a man, he
was a perambulating distillery. . . . It was a relief when that
show finished, the smell of alcohol hung about the room at
the Talk like a dandy's after shave.

Because of the patter I used in which the wife's mother was
mentioned, I suddenly became the country's leading Male

Chauvinist Pig. Sinister ladies would creep up to me, jab me with quivering digits and say the most awful things about my parentage, or lack of it. One rather odd lunatic in a flowered beret threatened to have me castrated if I didn't stem the scathing flow directed at the wife's mother. . . . In fact, Meg's mother enjoyed it! She was a celebrity in her own right, and wore the sort of injured expression probably used by Joan of Arc. The letters from outraged females poured in by the bushel – and why? All I ever said were things like:

"The wife's mother has things that many men desire . . . muscles and a duelling scar."

"She's so fat, she doesn't have elastic in her knickers . . . it's Swish Rail."

"For Christmas I bought her a fireside chair . . . unfortunately it fused."

"Women are like elephants, nice to look at, but who wants to own one?"

"I said to the wife once, would you like coq au vin? She said I prefer it in bed."

"The wife said what's Rachel Welch got that I haven't got? I said nothing . . . it's just fresher."

Hmm. . . . They have a point. So it was with trepidation that I launched a new character on the *Sez Les* series – Cosmo Smallpiece, who, complete with thick glasses and a frantic sex drive, went into a frenzy at anything that remotely suggested sex. I made one rule with Cosmo, however: no matter how he leered, he never actually touched a member of the opposite sex. Cosmo stormed the nation, the men loved him as the secret character they all possessed, and to my astonishment the women liked him. . . . Once again the fair sex had me baffled. As an instance of this, one night my agent Norman Murray and I were in the Savoy Hotel for dinner. Prior to the cabaret coming on, a tall, beautifully groomed lady drifted languidly towards our table dragging a mink coat behind her. She paused, waved her cigarette lighter at me and said in a well modulated tone, "Ah, it is you, you odd little man, I have something to say to you." This is it, I thought, I'm going to be ripped asunder in no mean fashion.

Other diners were glancing covertly as I stood and bowed slightly, and waited for the onslaught. She coolly appraised me and snapped her fingers at a peppery sort of "Hooray Henry" at her rear. He handed her a pair of bifocals, the sort I used for Cosmo, and she put them on and clenched her fist in the phallic symbol and went: "Knickers Knackers Knockers" which was Cosmo's war cry. The dining salon burst into laughter and I slumped back in my seat stunned. Over a cocktail I asked her why she liked the character of Cosmo Smallpiece; after all, I reasoned, the man was a sexual deviant. She smiled and replied, "Of course he is, Dawson, but he is at least honest. A woman would know exactly how she stood."

Let's make one thing clear. I adore the ladies and whoever christened them the weaker sex must have been an insane recluse. . . . One afternoon in one of my few excursions home, I idly noticed two men approach the bungalow opposite in a stealthy manner. I didn't think much about it until, a few moments later, I saw a figure inside the bungalow flit by the window. I knew the occupants were out and I grew uneasy. Just then I saw the lady whose bungalow it was walking down the road and fumbling in her handbag for her key. I went out and asked her had she any workmen in? She looked puzzled and shook her head. I escorted her to the front door and saw, with an increased tempo of the heart, that the door had been forced open. With faltering bravado, I tiptoed into the hall in time to see a large man run into a bedroom. Without thinking I chased after him and struck him on the temple. He lunged at me and we grappled in silence with only fear as the referee. My neighbour screamed as the burglar and I fought with fist and foot and head. Luckily he suddenly surrendered as I twisted his arm up his back. He indicated that his accomplice was hiding in a clothes closet; the accomplice at that point opened the door and made as if to go for me. Thank God that despite the many years of abuse that my body has undergone, the reflexes were in fine fettle. I jammed the door on his hand with my foot and the tableau took on an element of farce. It seemed an eon before the police arrived; my neighbour was ashen and trembling, and I remember thinking to myself that she, poor soul, would never recover from the drama. To my astonishment, a newspaper reporter materialised on the scene and asked my neighbour if she would have a photograph taken with me. I jumped up to protest that in her condition it would be out of the question. . . . But I don't know women, do I? Within five minutes she had fixed her hair and make-up, changed into a floral garment, and sat in almost rehearsed pose. I spent the night in bed with a blinding headache and nerves twanging like a hillbilly's banjo.

One of the country's greatest theatres is without a doubt the Alexandra in Birmingham, and when Norman telephoned me to say that I was booked to appear there for the winter's pantomime, I was elated. The impresario and chairman of the theatre was Derek Salburg, whose father, Leon, had run the theatre for years and was a legend. Derek, when I met him at our preliminary meeting in Blackpool, did not impress me one iota: a small agitated man with worry lining every crease in his face, he depressed me. The pantomime was to be *Robinson Crusoe*, with yours truly top of the bill as Billy Crusoe, a new pop group called the New World who had a monster hit in the music charts, and that marvellous Dame, Jack Tripp. Derek threw out every idea I had for comic business and I felt like stowing away on a freighter, only there aren't many in Birmingham.

The show opened to rave reviews and the business was tremendous, but every time I mentioned this fact to Derek, and frankly we didn't get on, he would merely shake his head, and mutter, "Could be better. . . . Could be better." It was getting me down and when a member of the New World poured a bucket of cold water over a traffic warden and we made the headlines with it, I began to think of digging a tunnel to get out of it all. One night Jack Tripp said, "Take no notice of Derek, if you say one thing, he'll say something opposite." Derek always called into our dressing rooms to say hello before a performance, so one first house, I waited for his knock, and when it came, I put my head in my hands and slumped on to the table. He came in, saw me and almost yelled, "What's the matter . . . are you ill?" I wearily shook my head: "No Derek, it's nothing like that . . . I just feel that I've let you down by not drawing the audiences in . . . I'm sorry about the rotten business," I moaned. He stared at me open-mouthed. "Rotten? It's the best business we've done in years, thanks to you, Les," he said. I wagged my finger at him and laughed. "Got you, you old bugger," I shouted. He glared at me and then roared with laughter; from that moment on, we became firm friends and I hope we still are. Derek Salburg was of the old school and a gentleman in every sense of the word. Despite some sad personal problems, his regard for people was unmatched. The one thing he had had to live with was the memory of his father, and everywhere the ghost of Leon Salburg threw a shadow. There were brass plaques in abundance: "Leon's Bar", "Leon's Room". The man had never been allowed to rest and the work that Derek had done was often forgotten. The theatre is the poorer for the retirement of men like Derek and my affection is as strong as ever.

I was tired and I hadn't seen much of the family. When I did return home for the odd weekend, Meg seemed to be unenthusiastic about my presence, and the kids were furtive too. Several times when I answered the telephone the line went dead. I began to suspect that Meg was having an affair. By the middle of January, the cast of the pantomime were acting strangely, and I became almost paranoid. Then one night whilst on the phone to Meg I heard our door bell ring, Meg went off the line to answer it and my son, Stuart, picked up the receiver and squealed about a man who had been to the house asking about my army career, amongst other things. When Meg came back on the phone, I questioned her about the "man" and she said oh, he was from the gas about a fault on the stove and he thought he'd been in the forces with me. That night I slouched off to a night club firmly convinced that my marriage was on the way out. . . . Who could blame her? Away for weeks on end; no angel myself, drinking too much. . . .

I'd made one record, a song called *Send Her Roses* for Chapter One Records, run by Les Reed. It hadn't done well really, but a song plugger by name Tommy Sanderson had asked me to tape another song in London. I'd put him off time and time again, but finally, I agreed to take the night train to

London on the Saturday after the show and tape the song on the Sunday. This meant of course that I couldn't go home for the weekend and when I telephoned Meg to tell her this fact, she sounded relieved. . . . So I was right, there was somebody else. I was virtually carried on to the train that bitter evening by Mike Bullock, the manager of the Alexandra Theatre, and I sat the whole journey through the chill of the night, morose and ill-shaven. Tommy Sanderson and his wife were at the station to meet me, and away we drove to their modest home in Hampton. On Sunday we entered a sound studio and I sang to a backing track. My voice was awful, tired and hoarse, and on top of everything else, my agent phoned to say that I was due to go to Thames Television to do a small walk-on piece with Hughie Green. I couldn't believe it. . . . I shouted down the line that it was bloody impossible, but Tommy said he'd run me to Teddington in time for the show. Over and over again, I did the song and it got worse. Eventually I threw the head set down and cried that enough was enough. In silence we drove to Thames TV and all I wanted to do was drink. Royston Mayoh, an old friend now a senior producer there, walked over and shook my hand warmly and away we went, as I thought to the bar, but no. Royston marched me to a dressing room where bottles of Scotch were standing in welcome upon a table. I was furious. I demanded to know why we couldn't go and see the many friends I had in the bar? Sorry, Les, Royston apologised, but there was an executive party being held there. He left with an excuse and I was alone with my thoughts. . . . A broken marriage, a career that seemingly was in decline, what the hell was happening? Suddenly, as is the way of television, all became a hustle. . . . Make up, fuss, lights, I'm tired, sod all this. The whisky in my gut is sour and rank. . . . Introduction from Hughie Green, in a daze I walk on to the stage area; small talk, a few laughs but a nervously eager audience. . . . What the hell is going on? Frank Carson, the Irish comedian, comes on with a parcel. . . . What's he saying? Have I brought a present for Hughie's birthday? I feel numb and I am sarcastic in my rejoinder. Hughie makes some remark about me opening his present from Frank. I rip open the parcel, inside is a red book and I see the title, "This Is Your Life". I roar with glee, of course that explains everything! They've caught

Hughie Green. I hand Green the partly revealed book and I wink at the audience; they roar back when I say to Hughie, "You'll love this, mate." "Take the rest of the paper off, Les," he says firmly. Hey? what the hell . . . I do so and there beneath the title I read dizzily "Les Dawson". At that moment Eamonn Andrews pats me on the back and booms, "Les Dawson, singer, comedian and pianist . . . This Is Your Life."

The studio erupts and I cling to Andrews for support as the whole place swims out of focus. . . . There is no way I can carry on. I'm pale and trembling and I have to be led away, and the bar is opened especially for me as I try to recover my composure.

I kept wondering who the hell would come on. . . . Would they have traced the negress who I lived with on the Left Bank? What about that French Canadian cutie in Soho? I rummaged through my memory banks; too many corners, dark ingles of indiscretion. . . . Surely they wouldn't have found the German stripper who I'd promised to take to England just before my marriage? Who would be aware of the vagrant and drunk, the pot washer and boxer? I worried needlessly.

First to join me with Eamonn was Meg, who, true to her lights, burst into tears and held me close. No wonder the telephone had clicked off at home when I answered it, the research department for *This Is Your Life* had been in close contact with Meg all the last few weeks. I confess to being emotional as the likes of Hughie Green, Dickie Henderson, Dora Bryan, Norman Collier came on. . . . Then old friends like Betty Lawrence who had fed me when I was down and out; dear Ken Cowx; my old Hoover boss, George Walker, and finally, the entire Syd Lawrence orchestra. . . . It was a night I will never forget, and when my two eldest children Julie and Stuart rushed breathlessly into my arms, the floodgates opened.

When I hear people say that a lot of celebrities know they are due to appear on *This Is Your Life* I would dearly love them to see the video of mine: my face is drawn and pale, and I assure you, it's not an experience I would want to repeat. But it was well put together and apart from one moment in the programme when Eamonn Andrews asked me about playing the piano in the Parisian brothel, there was nothing to cause dismay. Meg still tells our friends that she was frightened by the state of me when the show started, and that she would never enter into such a subterfuge again. Still, the evening of the programme did have its benefits: Meg and I made love in our London hotel in the manner of a teenage honeymoon. . . .

FIRST ACT

Change was in the air at Yorkshire Television. The company no longer had a pioneer feel about it, Donald Bavistock had gone and then John Duncan, the man who had made it all come true for me with *Sez Les*, decided to leave with Donald Bavistock as well. It was a wrench. John had been a good friend and I saw that things would be different from now on. Paul Fox, a veritable dynamo of a man, took over Yorkshire TV and the company became part of Trident Television. The company was growing into maturity, and it had to, of course . . . but the old days had been fun. Now, the unions had a large say in things and no longer could one man move an object if he didn't belong to the right union – it was a trifle wearisome. I introduced two new characters about the same time that John Cleese came into the show; the characters, based on typical Lancashire women, were called Cissie and Ada, and the man who has now spent many years with me, playing Cissie against my Ada, was Roy Barraclough, a fine sensitive actor. We hit a rapport straight away. "Cissie and Ada" have now become a cult, but even in those far off years, we knew they were destined to be a hit.

As '73 cruised along, the press had another field day with *Sez Les* and looking back, they were right. I'd been a long time with Yorkshire and I was taking them for granted, as they were taking me for granted. The wind of change was in the air in more ways than one and I knew that soon Yorkshire TV and I would be parting company, although I had just signed another two year deal with them. In '73 I took the family off to Madeira for a much needed vacation, and to give myself a period in which to think about the future. When I returned home, Norman rang me to say would I do a charity

show? I was rather preoccupied at the time and, only half
listening to him, I agreed. . . . The charity show was the
Royal Command Performance. Long after Norman had rung
off, I stood stock still with the receiver in my hand. . . . Me
on a Royal Command Performance. . . . An overweight,
baggy little man who used to be shouted off stages and
abused had been chosen to appear on the most prestigious
variety show in the whole world. . . . Me. The Les Dawson
who had once served Shirley Bassey with spaghetti in an
Italian restaurant; the Les Dawson who had washed taxi cabs
to earn a few bob; the same little man who had shivered on
the Embankment, now to appear before his monarch. . . .

I alighted from the taxi outside the stage door of the London
Palladium and a surge of autograph hunters surrounded me.
My feet were not actually touching the ground as I scribbled
away merrily. I came down to earth when one enormous
lady thrust herself forward and yelled in an unmistakable
Lancashire accent, "My 'oover's never been bloody right
since you serviced it, you little sod." But I did detect a note
of pride in her voice. Was there ever such a day? Old George,
the famous stage door keeper, handed me a key and in his
vibrant Cockney tones, wished me "Ole the luck in the
world, Les." I shared a dressing room with Cliff Richard and
Ronnie Corbett, and a heap of telegrams awaited me from
friends and pro's alike. The magnitude of the evening's cast
overwhelmed me: Cliff Richard, Dick Emery, Rudolf Nureyev, Peters and Lee, the hit recording duo, Francis Van
Dyke, Philippe Genty and Company from France, the Second
Generation dancers. . . . I felt dwarfed by the glittering caval-
cade . . . all those and Duke Ellington as well.

That day crawled along. I fluffed my rehearsal because of
nerves and I turned to the bottle for a little sustaining
courage. . . . Ronnie Corbett said that he felt quite at ease,
then promptly put my dress shirt on and vanished under its
folds. . . . No, nerves are part of that wonderful theatrical
event, it wouldn't be the same without them. As the time
approached, the tannoy spluttered into life and we were
treated to a running commentary regarding Her Majesty's
journey to the theatre. The knots inside my gut tightened

unbearably. The very air was electric and damp with energised perspiration; last minute mutterings to oneself; singers clearing tense throats; musicians in the pit blowing down cold tubes; sidelong smiles to one another as the disembodied voice tells us that the Queen has entered the theatre, is shaking hands with Bernard Delfont. . . . Now the first lady of the land is settling herself in the Royal Box; the national anthem strikes the proud chord. . . . A moment's silence as the last cough ceases then the most magic of all theatrical phrases: "Overture and Beginners please." It's on.

Artiste after artiste went up to the side of the stage like gladiators for the arena. I paced the floor of the dressing room, vainly trying to remember my lines. . . . I heard the laughter that Ronnie Corbett received and my heart sank; how could I, a red nosed club and pub comic ever hope to entertain the Queen? Had I bitten off more than I could chew? On and on. . . . Oh Christ the waiting. . . .

Little Corbett comes into the dressing room, leaving solid applause behind him. The strain has gone now from him and he gives me a grimace of pity. I can't smile back, my lips are dry and my heart is pounding like a sledge hammer . . . Rudolf Nureyev is on stage, and the roar from the audience is a respectful tribute to his talent. . . . Wait a minute, Nureyev on? You fool, Dawson, you're next on, get up and into the wings for your cue . . . I watch him dancing with such animal grace that he must indeed be a God. I glance at the Royal Box: Her Majesty and Prince Philip watch attentively . . . I can't go on, I cannot even hope to follow this. Madness all of it; out of my depth. . . . Meg is out there, my Meg, what will happen if I forget one line? Millions will see my downfall on their screens. . . . Sorry, Mother, sorry, Dad, I'm going to fail you. . . . I gape as the great dancer takes call after call from a wildly delighted audience. He stands erect and proud as he accepts the ovations. . . . I'm on.

That walk to the centre microphone is the longest I have ever taken. For me there is no announcement, no play on music, nothing but a silence that is as profound as an absolute zero. The Queen is looking at her programme: she doesn't know who I am. The audience is hushed and am I imagining it? Are they puzzled? I begin my act.

> "In 1645, Prince Rupert's mercenaries smashed Cromwell's left flank at Naseby, and in 1871, the Franco-Prussian War took a serious turn at the siege of Rouen, and in 1952 from the Kyles of Bute came the first report of an outbreak of sporran rash . . . (A few titters) None of this has anything at all to do with the act tonight, but it just shows how your mind wanders when you're worried."

There is a split second of silence and then roars of laughter. I take a sly look at the Royal Box and see the Queen and Prince Philip laugh hugely. The tension evaporates, I carry on with more confidence in my delivery:

> "Forgive me if I appear nervous, there's so many stars on this show, I'm the only one I've never heard of. The last time I appeared at the London Palladium, it was the same year that the Queen got married. I can remember turning to the producer and saying I hope she'll be very happy with Prince Albert.
>
> When I arrived at the theatre tonight, Mr Bernard Delfont himself, personally . . . ignored me. I was so flabbergasted, I damn near dropped my begging bowl.
>
> The wife's mother is outside in the car, I would have brought her in but I've lost the keys to the boot. To add to my trough of woe, she came to live with us three months ago. As soon as I heard the knock on the door I knew it was her because the mice were throwing themselves on the traps. . . ."

I finished my act to a thunderous reception: it had been my night, I could do no wrong, and at the cessation of my performance, Her Majesty and Prince Philip applauded me soundly. But the look on my little Meg's face was the one that really gave me the greatest thrill. All we had endured had been for this single evening. I searched my wife's features as she sat there with a vast beam of a smile; my lady in the front row of the London Palladium. As I came off stage, Billy

18. With two dear friends, Hattie Jacques and Eric Sykes

19. The diminutive Dawson with writers Galton and Simpson – a superb
example of a ham sandwich

20.   I used to box like Cooper. Not Henry, Gladys!

21.   A scene from YTV's *Dawson Cinema*. The longest custard pie fight
sequence since my honeymoon night

22. The pagan Dawson with Buddhist statue in Hong Kong, 1976. Everyone whispered in the temple – I couldn't tell talk from mutter

23. The celebrated Ada Sidebottom, the thinking man's sex symbol

24.   Filming *The Dawson Watch*, BBC-1

25.   With Shirley Bassey on her show. Note the near panic in her eyes. My singing voice filled the studio – the audience left to make room for it

26. Our home in Lytham St Anne's – detached property surrounded by mortgages

27. The Dawson family. My son Stuart Jason, daughters Julie Helen and Pamela Jayne with their mum, Meg. The fat fellow in the middle pays the bills

28.   My biggest creation ever, the Roly Polys. They were built when meat
was cheap

29. His Royal Highness ignoring my plea for adoption

30. Roger Moore, Twiggy and lil' ole me with Prince Charles. He still wouldn't call me cousin. Note Dame Anna Neagle watching in case I fell over

31. Prince Michael of Kent with the princess meeting the new King Rat who at the time was still sober

32. A face with all the charm of an ill-used sock

Marsh, one of London's leading theatrical agents, embraced me warmly and whispered, "Great, Les, you've never worked better."

Back in the dressing room, all my fellow performers gathered round and with enormous sincerity congratulated me. I sat down, wondering when my pulses would stop racing. . . . Before me the wilderness years went by as if in a film sequence. . . . That time when I escaped from a club through a toilet window to avoid a drunken audience ready to beat me up for an alleged insult. . . . The times I slept in the car to avoid paying for digs. . . . The times I was "paid off" by beer-reeking concert secretaries. . . . Going without meals to buy a pair of decent shoes, and now, this moment.

It was finale time and in order of appearance, the artistes took their final curtain. It's a time that most pro's hate: it's known as the "Who's Best". As I hove into the lights the applause grew in intensity and I could have basked in the sound of it for the rest of eternity.

Now had come the moment to line up and be introduced to Her Royal Majesty. I thought she'd never get to me but suddenly she was there, and I took her proffered hand and bowed. She wore a radiant smile and her eyes, such beautiful eyes, were awash with warmth as she said quietly, "Thank you very much, you were most entertaining." I couldn't help my next remark: "Thank you, ma'am, I was very nervous, I hope it didn't show too much?" She looked at me and went on, "It didn't show at all, and really you have no need to be nervous, it was very good." Those words filled my every fibre. What nobody ever knew, was that before the show had commenced, I'd had a small posy of flowers delivered and placed discreetly on a chair at the back of the stalls; on the card was a message that went: "Hope you enjoy the show, Mum and Dad. Love, Les." The fact that they were not here to share my joy marred the happiness I was experiencing, but in my heart of hearts, I knew that somewhere they would be nodding with satisfaction.

At the party afterwards, Meg met me at the entrance and we threw ourselves into each other's arms. We both cried a little and laughed a lot. My agent Norman was wreathed in a cloud of grins, as was his close secretary Anne Chudleigh, who in the not too distant future would be a partner with

Norman, and I would boast having two agents for the price of one. I have had wonderful meetings with Royalty since then, but never will an occasion arise, I fear, to match the elation of that night, one to remember for ever.

It was back to the grindstone once again and I had to face a daunting task: doing my own show on German Television, speaking in German and appearing before a German audience; it had never been done before and I now know why. It started with a meeting in London with the head of a TV company in Berlin called SFB. The head of the station, one Herr Leibshitz, or something like that, proposed that I get some sketches together, ones which he'd already been shown I might add, and the whole show would be an hour's segment within another show, called *The Paul Kunz Show*. Kunz was a band leader who played the Glenn Miller style. The arrangements were hammered out and this was it:

Because my knowledge of German was skimpy, an actor called George Sewell, who'd made his name in the serial *Special Branch*, would come along to act in the sketches. George spoke fluent German and obviously would be invaluable as an interpreter and tutor for me, the added bonus being that George was and still is a marvellous actor. Also on our show would be Kenny Ball and his Jazzmen . . . old drinking buddies of mine, so things would certainly be lively in old Berlin. But firstly, Norman, myself and my *Sez Les* producer Bill Hitchcock, a great friend and help to me, flew out to Berlin to settle things regarding props, music, etc.

As we circled over Tempelhof Airport, the aerial view of West Berlin depressed me. If ever there was a city that epitomised the brutality and ignorance of man, it is Berlin with that dreadful wall snaking through it. I have known and loved many European cities: Brussels, Rome, Paris and even Vienna, despite the stench of the so-called "Blue Danube", have entranced me. I have been fortunate enough to amble through the narrow streets of Amsterdam in the dying embers of autumn; to have strolled through the Prado in Madrid's summer heat and to have sat for hours toying with thick black coffee in Istanbul. . . . But of Berlin, I remember only the hostile checkpoints and the wreaths clinging to the gaunt wall, garlands hung in memory of those who have died in seeking freedom. It was in this mood that I entered the functional building that housed SFB Television.

The following saga of that visit is the one that had convulsed Michael Parkinson when I did his chat show. It was funny then in hindsight, but at the time it was a pointer to the German mentality. Bill Hitchcock, Norman Murray and I sat at a long, plain and – dare I say it? – functional table. We were flanked by thin-lipped, blue-eyed executives and large ladies with braided hair and scrubbed faces. The minutes ticked away as we sat in silence waiting for the arrival of Herr Leibshitz. When the door was flung open the entire group hurled themselves to their feet and I fully expected a snatch of the *Horst Wessel*.

In halting German I bade Herr Leibshitz good afternoon, and he in halting English said, "Herr Dawson, please, you tell mine interpreter vot sketches you haf got for us, yes?" I nodded, half hoping a bottle of Schnapps would materialise but it didn't. Round the table marched a formidable figure of a woman. Tall, blonde, heavily built in a leather frock, with a pair of arms reminiscent of gammon steaks, she sat next to me with notebook and functional pen at the ready. I cleared my throat, trying to ignore the grins from Bill and Norman opposite me. "Well, the first sketch concerns a small car in between two larger cars." I broke off as the massive blonde told the rest of the table the idea in German. I went on: "The driver of the small car wants to get out but the space is too small for the driver to negotiate properly, so I stand there guiding the driver of the small car out." I stopped as Gretel jabbered away to the stony-faced group. When she'd finished the German translation, I coughed and continued: "Back-wards and forwards I make the small car go in an effort to get it out; finally when I do, the driver thanks me and I get in the front large car and also drive away."

My Gretel glared at me. "Herr Dawson, if you owned the first car, why didn't you just drive away in the first place? Then you would not have had to go to so much trouble getting the middle car out." I didn't know what the hell to say, I simply managed a weak smile and muttered, "Er, well that's the joke you see." She sniffed and rattled away in German to the others. They in turn gazed at me as if I'd just given birth to a reindeer and said not a word. Gretel spoke:

"Vot else you have, Herr Dawson?" Bill was nearly under the table and Norman's eyes were moist.

"Well, let me see. . . . There is a man sweeping the street." Gretel stopped me with a hand like a dinner gong, and repeated what I'd said in German. She then poked me with her pen. "Continue, please," she cooed. "The man sweeps the street one way." Gretel interrupted my flow and interpreted my deathless prose and I caught two words that sounded as if humour was still alive in the Reich. . . . The words were "Ein Farht". Alas, it didn't mean a good old fashioned anal trump, it meant, "One Way". Rather tense by now I went on: "The man then sweeps the street the other way, and when the dirt is in a heap, he lifts up the pavement and sweeps the dirt under it." Mein Gretel looked at me with a mixture of pity and Teutonic triumph and trumpeted, "No good, Herr Dawson, in Germany the pavements don't lift up."

That night in the Berlin Hilton I got pissed. I was all for getting out of the contract, after that afternoon's fiasco in particular, but no, I was told, the die was well and truly cast, and in late November in freezing conditions we arrived back in Berlin to do the show. The snow lay thick on the ground and the city was more miserable than ever; blackened buildings against the blinding white and a cutting wind that slivered the skin. Kenny Ball and his lads got me through the week with booze and I thank the Lord for allowing them to be with me. We taped the show on the Friday, having pre-recorded a lot of material during the week, so at least that took a load off my back.

Before a programme in this country, we use a comedian to "warm up" the audience – I used to do the same thing years ago for the Harry Worth series. . . . Here in bonnie Berlin, the man they used must have spent years as a cheer leader for the Gestapo; he bullied the audience into a frightened submission as they entered the studio, and they sat in their hard seats, cowed and meek. Two well-known German actors had been included in the cast, and I started off the show with one of them, a great brute of a chap with a face like a raped ox. The idea was that we would speak in German as we welcomed each other to the show, then some remark would spark off a free for all with custard pies. Unfortunately, after the first few were thrown, the German got carried away and started the Third World War. . . . He pelted me with an avalanche of quivering edible matter and followed that attack with a punch. Half blinded with custard, I crawled towards him and pulled him to the floor. All this of course was unrehearsed, and as he fell I bludgeoned him with the biggest pie I could find and then drove a swift fist into his rotund midriff. He gasped and tried to gouge out my right eye, but was thwarted by my knee on his testicles. The audience was in an uproar; they, poor souls, thought it was part of the act; little did they know it was a fight to a flour and water death. Eventually, Paul Kunz strolled on and somehow put an end to the brawl; Kenny Ball staggered on in a cloud of alcohol and wailed into a jazz number whilst I and the German actor went off to get changed and even as we went off stage the crackpot tried to trip me up.

During the show I found the key to German humour; when in doubt, blow as many raspberries as you can. It worked: the audience were in hysterics. After the programme Kenny Ball and I and George Sewell and Bill got the entire German technical staff absolutely pissed to oblivion. . . . But I have never been asked back.

On the plane back home, I reflected that the seventies had certainly started with a bang for me. . . . Two successive years in pantomime at the Grand Theatre, Leeds: *Babes In The Wood* and the following year, *Goody Two Shoes*. Then *This Is Your Life* and of course the Royal Variety Performance and my debut at the Alexandra Theatre, Birmingham, not to mention the fact of appearing with a homicidal maniac in merry old Berlin. . . . Yes, son, it had been quite a start.

I arrived back home just in time to pick the wife up and return to London for the annual Water Rats' Ball, held at the Grosvenor House, Park Lane. The Grand Order of Water Rats is a society of show business people dedicated to 'philanthropy, conviviality and good fellowship'. It has a fine record of fund raising and charitable work, and is truly a brotherhood in that all its members work for the common good. It is said that to be elected to the position of King Rat is the greatest compliment any man associated with the entertainment industry can receive.

I wasn't a member of that most noble of orders then, and Meg and I had been invited by Terry Cantor, who alas is no longer with us. She and I sat open mouthed on the top table with famous people such as Stanley Baker, Tony Curtis, Roger Moore, Henry Cooper, Vera Lynn, Prince Philip . . . and the ultimate thrill when my name was mentioned, the applause from all the guests. . . . The Rats are a fine brotherhood, and although I didn't know it then, I was being earmarked as a potential member. After the ball, Meg and I lay in the luxury of the hotel apartment, and we both remembered that dreadful cold water flat we once used to shiver in, with a drunken landlady and her coloured lover as neighbours, three flights up a ramshackle tenement. . . . I do realise that I have a tendency to dwell on the days gone by, but it does keep one's feet firmly on the ground.

SECOND ACT

1974 was supposed to be my penultimate year with Yorkshire
Television. They had offered me a year's contract with an
option for one more. I discussed it with Norman and Anne,
my agents, and we felt that now was the time for change. We
had one year left of the existing contract and we decided to
get away from the *Sez Les* style show and branch out . . .
and we did just that. Firstly Roy Barraclough and I did a
situation comedy programme called *Holiday With Strings*, a
spoof package tour with a cheap aeroplane service. The cast
that was assembled was a formidable one: Mollie Sugden,
Patricia Hayes, Frank Thornton and several well known
supporting actors. Even today, that show is still being
screened, especially on transatlantic flights; it was a fun programme and fun to do.

Holiday With Strings was just a one-off show, which was
the biggest mistake I ever made. . . . I should have followed
it up with at least a series of six. Written by Ray Galton and
Alan Simpson, *Holiday With Strings* would have become a
landmark in television. I think that the one thing that has kept
me active in the television medium, is that I have never been
afraid to try other ideas, no matter how much they may be
the wrong ones. . . . For one's own sake, it is important that
change be the most important factor in a career. One of my
favourite one-offs was directed by Ronnie Baxter and called
Dawson's Electric Cinema. It was an hour of unashamed nostalgia, in which I played various members of my family who
ran a veritable flea-pit of a picture house. I played my father
and my son Stuart played me as a young lad. The press hated
it and the public didn't actually fall over either, but it's a thing
I'm glad to have done, and the silent screen custard pie
throwing routine is in the cinema archives now and is shown

to students. The film was bled with sepia to age it, and I defy anybody to tell the difference between it and say a fifty-year-old film.

The next project was an unusual one: Alan Plater, the writer, had an idea which we titled *The Loner*. In this I played a man coming from nowhere, going nowhere, and it was about what happens to him in transit. There was a trilogy of them, and like most things I'd done, frankly, it was ahead of its time. It was performed without an audience present and the whole thing was shot as a black comedy. Again, I incurred the wrath of the press, they simply could not see the situation, and Yorkshire dropped the idea of doing any more.

As spring paved the way for summer, Galton and Simpson, who saw me as a successor to Tony Hancock, wrote a six part series called *Dawson's Weekly*. Again Roy Barraclough joined me in what I consider one of the funniest situation comedy shows ever created. They were finished by early August but were not screened until 1975 because of internal problems, and then when they were shown it was in the summer at seven o'clock in the evening, and naturally, the ratings were poor. Once more into the breach came the press and they hammered it as a series, but in the view of ordinary television watchers, it was a success. I began to wonder what the hell you had to do to glean a newspaper credit. Looking back on those wonderful years spent with Yorkshire Television, it's the work load that satisfies me the most.

Meg was becoming increasingly important to me on charity appearances, although I strongly suspect that meeting her favourite stars had a lot to do with it. On one night alone at the Leeds convention for Stars For Spastics Organisation, she met and had her photograph taken with Cary Grant, David Niven and Douglas Fairbanks Junior. I must admit, though, that I still get a thrill from meeting names from the theatre and public life in general. Douglas Bader made a big impression on me with his resolute courage, as did Orson Welles. At the National Theatre, during a charity show called *Night Of A Thousand Stars*, Sir John Gielgud actually spoke to me! Sir John Mills was most pleasant and I found Donald Sinden a pure delight. It was a nice time in my life and I revelled in it. Every London nightspot welcomed me and dawn was a constant companion.

I don't think my wife will object if I recount a week in my life that was out of time in a sense. . . . I flew down to South Wales to play a cabaret date in a small ivy-encrusted club that had once been a fine house. It was in the Usk Valley, surely one of the loveliest places on earth. Towering hills with mantles of greenery flowing down to heaving meadows and beckoning woods, escorted by a meandering river and darting minnows. . . . It captivated me, and one night I met a girl whose beauty took my breath away. We would roam the hills, with her quoting poetry, her wild eyes glowing and her hair flung behind her with the wind going through the tresses; we sat in darkling corners of inns which smelt of age and stood alone with the scented air of the Brecons filling our lungs. . . . It was a week that was worthy of a Victorian novelist; there was no sexual desire in our companionship, nor would I have wanted it . . . my feelings for her were the passions of the soul only. She took me to her secret valley where time hung in a misty melancholy, and I wanted to stay in that place forever. . . . Finally it was time to go home. She stood barefoot on the sweeping grass, held out her arms to me as I made to clamber into the car and whispered, "Good-bye, my boy . . . forever."

I don't know why I mentioned that story, but in this day and age of lust and depravity which hides under the name of progress and unisex, I think it stands out as a tribute to the real depth of understanding between men and women. Years later, I might add, I returned to Usk, but I never saw her again nor was I able to find her secret valley. It was after living through that enchanted week, that I understood James Hilton's *Lost Horizon*. It was odd really, but I felt spiritually cleansed by the encounter.

You'll have noticed that I do tend to meander instead of keeping some sort of chronological order, and for this I make no apology. In writing about one's own life, it is the memory of people who touched it that gives the autobiography the stimulus of interest. . . . Just now I recalled an incident which gave me the greatest joy of all. . . . Years ago as a Hoover sales representative, I was called out on Christmas Eve to an ill-painted terraced house in a rough area of Manchester called

Greenheys. As I have said before, I was used to slums, but when I saw this street, I automatically gripped the small hammer that I kept in my overcoat pocket in case I was attacked, such was the feel of the place. Twice before, I had been leapt upon by thugs in back streets and the hammer was a comfort.

It was snowing and the pallid light from the rusty lamps created wavering shadows as I approached the house. I knocked for some time, received no answer and was about to walk away when the scarred door opened. A woman stood there, her eyes reddened by grief, and she still had a handkerchief gripped in her care worn hands. I mumbled something about coming at a bad time, and that I could call again. . . . She shook her head and haltingly said that her washing machine had broken down and she needed it for the children's clothing. . . . She let me into a barely furnished room which smelt of dampness and body sweat. Four small children, two boys and two girls, were sitting with thumbs in their mouths on naked floorboards, and they too looked as if the tears had only just subsided. With his head in his hands, seated by a tiny fire, I saw the husband. His shoulders were trembling with emotion and it was obvious he was sobbing silently. Never had I seen such a scene of despair, and my first thought was to get away from it as quickly as possible. Christmas Eve and no tree here; no gifts on display and no decorations. . . .

"Excuse me," I said. "It's obvious that I've come at a bad time. . . . Let me return some other time." The woman shook her head yet again as tears sprang to her eyes and she said, "No, you are here now. . . I'm sorry about this, my husband has lost his wages and his bonus for Christmas was in it as well. . . ." I walked into the cramped, dirty kitchen where filthy rags were piled up in a heap on the floor. The washing machine was a very old rusted one and I smelt burning rubber from the back of it. It wasn't a big job to fix it, and I decided not to charge them . . . it would be my Christmas gift to them.

When I told her that there would be no charge for the repair, the woman thanked me and her husband, his face lined with sorrow, nodded gratefully and also thanked me. I couldn't very well bid them a merry Christmas, so I simply walked to the door. On the way out, I saw a battered Hoover vacuum cleaner that had seen better days. The woman saw me look at it and she said with a sigh that the cleaner had stopped working that very night. Well, I was here, so what the hell. . . . I tipped the machine up on its side and as I took the bottom off it I saw a brown packet lodged between the brushes and the casing. I hooked it out . . . it was the missing wage packet. It had apparently fallen off the table and got caught in the mechanism. I sensed that I was about to make one family the happiest in the realm. "Well I'll be off now, oh by the way, may I wish you all a very merry Christmas," I boomed, and as I did I threw the wage packet to the husband. He stared at it, then at me and he was off his chair in a trice. He hugged me in a bearlike grip and the wife kissed me and the kids flung themselves around my legs . . . and oh yes, I was crying as well. Before I could stop her, the wife rushed out with some of the money out of the packet, and she returned with a couple of bottles from the nearby public house, and we stood in that most impoverished of dwellings and drank as the kids sang a Christmas carol. Outside as I commenced to trudge through the snow, I turned once and saw through the lighted window, a family radiant with happiness, and I was glad that I had been Santa Claus that night.

Meanwhile back we are in 1974 and I taped another *Sez Les* series. My producer Bill Hitchcock was worrying me. I knew that Bill was an alcoholic but he'd always contrived to hide it, even from me. . . . But now, the drink was showing up the ravages of excess on his face. I myself was quite exhausted and urgently needed a holiday. When the last episode was in the can, we held a party and Bill threw his arms around me, saying, "It's been great working together, Les, I've enjoyed every minute of it." I smiled back and replied, "There'll be others, Bill." He stared at me for a long period. "Will there?" he said.

Two days later Meg and the kids and I flew off to Cyprus. We hadn't been in the hotel more than a couple of hours and I woke from a nap to find Meg holding my hand. "There was a phone call from John; I took it, whilst you were asleep, love," she said quietly. I blinked. John Foster, one of my friends . . . what had he phoned for? I was soon to know as

Meg whispered, "It's Bill, Les, he's dead." My Bill, dead? The drink had claimed him with a cardiac arrest. Meg knew I had to be by myself and I spent the night alone and remembering. . . .

Bill's death marred the happiness of that holiday in Cyprus and on top of that Turkey was making threats to the Cypriot government; in fact as my family flew out from Nicosia, the Turks had commenced hostilities. My heart was saddened by the rape of that most beautiful of islands. We came home to the news that our bungalow had been sold; this created a mild panic, because although Meg and I had decided on living in St Anne's, we hadn't as yet found the home we wanted. Time and time again I travelled to St Anne's looking at everything that estate agents had on their books, but to no avail. Then, while I was having a drink with a musician friend of mine in Blackpool, he casually mentioned that he'd heard there was a place for sale in Islay Road, which lay between Lytham and St Anne's, but it was not yet announced to the public. He said he thought the house was called "Garth". I had nothing to lose and I was being pressed to leave our bungalow as soon as possible, so I took a chance and went to see the premises. I drove down Islay Road and fell under the spell of that unmade track that wound round some extremely handsome properties. Then I saw "Garth". It was the sort of house I'd always wanted, a large, white, Georgian style house with simple yet impressive lines. It straddled a massive stretch of lawn with mature trees sheltering the perimeter. I rang the bell and a courtly man opened the thick, studded oak door, I apologised for calling without an appointment, but he brushed that aside and bade me enter. As soon as I saw the kitchen, I knew that Meg would want this house: it was the sort of kitchen you hold a polo match in, still leaving room for the odd rugby scrum. There and then, I did the deal without even telephoning Meg about the decision. I arrived home in Bury, picked up Pamela who wasn't yet at school, scolded Meg into action and away we went back to see the house, with myself hoping against hope that she liked it.

All the way across, she grumbled, "It'll be like all the others, people don't leave nice houses . . . never do . . . I'm fed up and I object to being dragged over here." On and on she went as all women do. As we turned into Islay Road, she seemed impressed and I deliberately slowed down as we passed majestic "Garth". She prodded me: "That's the sort of house I'd like, but you never see them for sale," she groaned.

When I drove the car into the drive leading to the front door of "Garth" she looked at me open-mouthed and could no more than croak the question: was this it? I nodded with a wide grin. As I had thought, she went berserk when she saw the vast kitchen and I had before me a very happy lady.

The next three weeks were hectic; apart from getting all our furniture ready for removal, I was trying to finish my second novel, *The Spy Who Came* and get it off to a most impatient publisher. Finally as the day dawned for us to vacate our small bungalow, Meg and I grew sad at the thought of leaving the place which had given us both so much to look forward to, and I swear to this day that the bungalow seemed sad as well. The *TV Times* were there to photograph our departure, as well as the local vicar and a knot of neighbours. The furniture was stowed into the furniture van and off it lumbered. Meg and I stood looking at the empty abode and my wife cried openly, then turned her head away and got into the car. I don't know why I did it, but I re-entered the bungalow and talked to the element that had been a part of our lives there. . . . "Wish Meg and me luck, whoever you are," I whispered self-consciously as I looked at the naked rooms. Just before I closed the front door forever, I shouted into the interior, "Why don't you come with us?" Did I imagine a chuckle from the living room?

Whilst Meg enjoyed spending money on our new home I was kept busy with club dates and some TV work, plus agreeing to put in a summer season at Southport, which hadn't had one since the old Garrick Theatre closed fifteen years previously. Frankly it was a gamble; a new theatre in a resort that was nowadays simply a day tripper's outing. The town was not the town I remembered: the magnificent Lord Street with its elegant shops and Victorian arcades. Still it was a challenge and the deal was finalised. The bill was to be: top of the bill, Les Dawson, with the Irish singing star, Dana, Bobby Bennett the young comedian-impressionist, and a speciality act from Australia, Jumping Jack, who did the funniest things I've ever seen on a trampoline. We had six pretty dancers and we started rehearsals in June.

Opening night, apart from a few incidents such as a drunken orchestra and a dancer who fell down a hole, went well enough and the advance bookings seemed quite favourable. Afterwards came the opening night party, which caused me to totter out into the night air and straight into the arms of a policeman; luckily I wasn't driving that evening, so nothing was said when I threw up on his trousers. I soon sobered up when I got home. Meg was looking very worried, and she ushered me upstairs to Julie's bedroom. "What on earth's the matter?" I demanded. Meg picked Julie up and I saw that her eyes were swollen and closed. "She was playing with Stuart, and from what I can make out, the pages of a book went across her eyes," Meg said. I examined Julie as best I could, and I became concerned myself, it looked painful and sore. The following day I telephoned a leading eye specialist in Preston, and he promised to see Julie at home that afternoon.

I had to leave to get to the theatre for the first house but Meg promised to telephone me after the specialist had been. From the outset the show that evening went splendidly: Bobby Bennett was in fine form; Dana had them shouting for more and Jumping Jack murdered them. I was stood in the wings fiddling with my bow tie, ready to go on when the stage door keeper came over to tell me that Meg was on the phone. I had a couple of minutes spare so I took the call, and when I did, my world stopped. The specialist had taken one look at Julie's eyes, and immediately had her rushed to Preston Infirmary. . . . The pages of the book had split the cornea of one eye and severely damaged the other one. There was every possibility that she would be blind.

From the auditorium came the sound of laughter as I slumped against the telephone stand. . . . My little girl; no no no no. . . . A hand jerking me. . . . What's that? I'm on? On where? I can't go on stage and make them laugh; my daughter might never see again. . . . In the name of Christ what do they want? Somehow I did my act and the audience screamed, but at the finish, did they perhaps wonder why I walked off the stage in tears?

I got through the second house with the help of two bottles

of whisky and as soon as the curtain fell I was driven away
to Preston, where Meg was already at Julie's bedside.

She lay there, my daughter, with her head enclosed in a
wooden frame and her face was white and drawn. To my
bombardment of questions Meg answered: yes, they'd
operated, not they didn't know the result yet and she burst
into tears. That night I walked into a church; I was alone and
I knelt and begged for my little girl's sight.

It was two weeks before we heard the verdict: her sight
had been saved. Though her left eye was as good as new, her
right eye would always be blurred slightly, but praise be. . . .
One night as I was coming out of the theatre, a loud-mouthed
woman, from Liverpool by her accent, turned to her blowsy
friend and screeched, "That's Les Dawson getting into that
bleedin' Jag. . . . All right for 'im, he's got it bleedin' made."

Bobby Bennett stopped me from going over to her. . . .
Got it made, hey?

With Julie's eyesight saved, I threw myself into a frenetic
workload of club and cabaret dates after the summer show
ended its run at the Floral Hall, Southport. . . . It had been
a minor triumph; the show had put the resort back on the
entertainment map, and the way was paved for other impresarios to stage productions there. Also I had found time to
finish off *The Spy Who Came* and that was due for publication
in the following year. Norman Murray had talks with Yorkshire Television, and we decided to stay on with the company
until 1977 at least. Frankly I was glad; having thought that
1975 was to be the end of our association, I had been troubled
at the thought of going elsewhere: all my friends were at
Yorkshire Television, and despite the changes that were
taking place, my innate need for people who understood my
changeable nature gave me a feeling of warmth and security.

Looking back, I enjoyed the seventies, although on the
broader issues of the time, black clouds were looming both
for the orbit of entertainment and the world in general.
Because of the somewhat odd gambling laws, venues which
supported cabaret by the casino now had to have more than
one entrance to them. . . . I never fully understood the machi-
nations of all that; if a person wanted to gamble his money

away, he would. The fact of premises having to have another door that didn't indicate gambling seemed to me to be bloody ridiculous. The upshot was, of course, that many of the big clubs on the circuit had to close their doors and the outlets for new talent were diminished. Although I had played some absolutely dreadful places in my grope to success, at least I had been able to learn my trade; now there was only a void for new performers.

A very wise sage once said, "There is no such thing as progress, only a state of change." Newspapers then carried the same headlines that depress the commuter today: the pound was in trouble, little wars kept boiling up. . . . There was drought and hunger, inflation and notable key figures having it away with broad bottomed ladies. In the Good Old US of A, President Nixon was proving so bent, even his underpants were cross threaded. What did trouble me was the barely perceptible crawl towards uniformity: cars began to look the same; boys and girls looked alike and the age of the Town Planner was at hand.

Suddenly, great chunks of familiar city centres became temporary deserts as busy little men fussed over the rise of frowning concrete cliffs that would house insurance companies and high-rise office towers; the planners forgot people and the cities emptied of life.

For anybody built like myself, life became almost intolerable. Thin was Beautiful. No longer did clothing emporiums possess suits for the fuller figured male, one had to be positively emaciated to get fitted, and on the social front Mods and Rockers knocked seven bells out of each other at Margate. . . . Meanwhile, I kept the breweries happy wherever I appeared.

Thus the seventies laid out the blue print for the 1980s . . . but much more was to happen, much more. My wife's mother, who had been ill for some time, came to live with us at "Garth". Sadly, not for long, she died in 1975. Our relationship had always been a mixed one, although strangely enough, of all the family, I think I probably understood her the best. She had ruled her brood according to her lights and her son and daughters were a credit to her vigilance. Despite the fact that I used her unmercifully as a basis for my act, and despite the fact that she often used to shake her fist under my nose, as I've mentioned before, she rather enjoyed the notoriety she gleaned from being my butt. Not wishing to upset Meg's family I had privately decided to drop mother-in-law jokes from my act when it became increasingly obvious that her health was failing. One night just before she left Meg and me to live with one of the other members of the family, I sat with her in the bedroom, and as is so often the case, the past predominated the conversation. We talked about my mother and my father and my father-in-law, all sadly missing from our lives. Suddenly she smiled at me, grabbed my arm and said, "Don't ever forget me when you do your 'turn'." I never have. Women like Ada Plant are few in number today, and if by keeping her name alive I help to forge a monument to such of her ilk, then I will continue to do so.

Thanks to various organs of propaganda, the so-called "class" struggle creates a lot of bitterness today: trade unions accusing management and vice versa; platoons of ardent pacifists and "do gooders" who undermine discipline . . . the list is dreary. All I know is that a good family background and a strong hand might well have changed the course of many a wayward soul; the so-called super powers may well snarl at each other, but the knowledge of each other's strength has staunched the flow of blood that seemed to occur every twenty-five years or so. . . . The power of the atom is with us; we cannot lock its awesome power away in our subconscious, surely we must learn to adapt to its presence now.

It may appear odd for a red-nosed variety comic to wax forth in this solemn manner, but do remember, a comedian has to be a bit of a philosopher, otherwise they'd take him away drooling in an unlettered van. All that is clear to me, having seen both ends of the social spectrum, can be encompassed in the wisest phrase I have ever heard. In years long gone, I was playing a South Wales mining social club. Hard people in even harder surroundings; slag heaps against the slate grey skies and the stark outline of the pit's wheel as a backcloth. It was not an easy week, there had been a bad accident at the coal face the day I arrived and a young miner had been badly injured. "There will be no show at this club tonight," a dark, gnarled man told me and so that evening I wandered around the grim village, with silent staring women with heavy shawls around their shoulders, standing by the open doors of the houses that led to the pit-head. In one small inn, a knot of miners were singing a hymn with only a mouth organ as accompaniment. I had but one drink and went back to my digs, run by a stout cheery lady, whose husband was blind. I sat with him and we drank dark beer by the struggling flames of the fire which threw grotesque shadows upon the whitewashed walls. His wife, in her merry fashion, told us that the young miner would recover and that lifted out spirits. On we talked and talked about every subject under the sun and finally, I asked my blind host, "What in your opinion can be done to improve the lot of humanity?" He smiled, and held out his great horny hand that had seen so much toil, patted my hand and in his soft burr, simply said, "Be kind." That was all.

Not so long ago, at a big charity luncheon, with expensive cigar smoke wreathed above sleek heads, I overheard a heavily jowled man with a large brandy in his well manicured hand, say, "Damned strikers, ought to shoot a few of the buggers, hey?" His companion, of the same ilk, snorted, "Too many bloody foreigners as well." I turned and repeated those words from the echo of time: "Be kind." One glared at me and muttered something about "bloody show business people". But isn't that the key? Be kind.

LAST ACT ON BEFORE THE INTERVAL

At Christmas 1975, instead of doing pantomime, I embarked on a series of one hour programmes for Yorkshire TV. The Christmas show wasn't exactly acclaimed by the general press and the viewing figures sank lower than a crippled diving bell. My second novel didn't blow the literary world and it looked as if I was about to enter the doldrums again. In the early part of the year, I hosted a television show from Caesar's Palace, Luton. Prince Philip was the royal guest and from the outset the show seemed to be heading for disaster. . . . There was too much interference and panic; technicians running about like headless roosters, and flushed producers altering the running order of the show every five minutes or so. It wasn't a bad bill, really: myself as host, Charlie Smithers, a fine Cockney comedian, Peters and Lee, still top of the music charts and the dancer Peter Gordeno and his girls. . . .

The club was packed to the rafters and I had had far too much to drink. Prince Philip arrived and seemed in good spirits. He was flanked by Bill Cotton Junior and several nose-in-the-air equerries. Amid the nervous tension, after a dance routine, I went on:

> "Good evening, as you all know we have a very impor-
> tant person with us tonight. . . . It gives me great
> pleasure to introduce, Bill Cotton . . . he's over there sat
> with a sailor.

> We have a great show for you tonight, with marvellous
> artistes. . . . From Leeds, the Jenny Lind of Yorkshire,
> Gladys Boothroyd, who sings *Nearer My God To Thee*
> and does a striptease in a bucket of ferrets. . . . Hard-
> bitten woman but very nice. . . . She has a damn good

sense of humour, at rehearsal she lost one of her ferrets but she had a hell of a smile on her face.

Sad to say we are short of an act, we should have had an Irish memory man on the bill, but he forgot to turn up. Make way now for my old friend Charlie Smithers, they say laugh and grow fat . . . his biggest fan is Twiggy."

The show went like a rocket; what should have been a disaster was a triumph and Prince Philip roared with laughter. After the show, George Savva, the club manager, had arranged a room in which the prince could relax, but he refused and said he wanted to meet the performers. I was found in my usual juxtaposition to the bar, oblivious of the approach of the prince. Suddenly he was there at my side. "Hello, Dawson," he said. "Damn good show, enjoyed it." I stiffened and replied, "Thank you, sir, hope I didn't offend in any way?" He shook his head and went on, "Are you still living in the north?" "Of course, sir, is there anywhere else to live?" He merely smiled and we had a drink as he informed me that he had accompanied Her Majesty to Rochdale to open a shopping precinct, and that someone had presented her with a parcel of black puddings. . . . "Delicious things, Dawson," he said. "We had them fried for breakfast." It must have been the drink that made me feckless as I remarked, "Sorry, sir, traditionally, a black pudding should be boiled." He cocked his head at me and retorted, "Don't talk such rot, Dawson, you fry the blessed things." From that moment on, I confess I forgot I was talking to a prince of the realm, I argued and to his amusement, got hot under the collar about the flaming black puddings. Ashen-faced officials listened to the harangue in horror and the press were kept back as we went at it. The realisation dawned on me that if this went on I would probably be transported to the Tower, and the argument fizzled out as my bravado evaporated. Prince Philip was vastly amused by it all, though, and I cannot pay him a high enough compliment in his attitude to this perspiring little idiot who stood under his chin.

A few weeks later I attended a charity drive at the Grosvenor House in London with Donald Sinden and the chief speaker was Prince Philip. At the end of his speech, he concluded by saying, "So don't forget, send any monies you can for this

very worthwhile cause, and failing that . . . black puddings."
There was a short, stunned silence and the prince turned to
me and said, "That didn't go very well, Dawson." I stood
up and said, "You should have boiled 'em, sir." We both
roared and the audience were to be forever mystified by the
duologue.

Many times I was to blunder in the presence of royalty. . . .
I still must be the only comedian to take his trousers off in
front of the Queen. . . .

It happened at a big charity affair attended by the Queen
and Prince Philip in a circus tent in Windsor Great Park. . . .
It was an incredible event with famous circus performers,
including the Flying Terrels who performed a fantastic aerial
feat, the triple somersault on the high wire. Every name in
show business seemed to be there that night: Telly Savalas,
of *Kojak* fame . . . Elton John and Mike Yarwood . . . Ronnie
Barker and David Frost; there was no end to the parade of
stars. Eric Sykes, my old friend, and I shared a caravan and
throughout the day, ensured that the distillers' profits rose.
It was good to embrace Olivia Newton John once more, and
it was nice to chat to Leo Sayer and Bruce Forsyth. . . . Fine.
Only one problem, I hadn't a clue what to do as an act, I'd
forgotten to work one out. The huge tent was overflowing
with public, dignitaries and talent; if I blew this I'd be back
working welfare clubs; and the worse aspect of all, Meg and
the kids were due in.

I strode up and down the perimeter of the Big Top, getting
in the way of circus workers banging in pegs and wrestling
with guy ropes, and not a germ of an idea flowered. It was
the sight of my wife drifting into view that finally galvanised
me into mental action: I recalled a sketch that I'd done on *Sez
Les* five years previous. Frankly, it hadn't been one of the
best things I'd ever done but it was the best I could come up
with. . . .

It consisted of me dressing in a pair of knickers, a pair of
trousers that didn't match the jacket, and a shirt that was
obviously too small. I shudder even now typing the format
out. . . . Bruce Forsyth introduced me as "Signor Macaroni,
the great Italian tenor". In trepidation I walked into the centre
of the mighty ring that was bathed by dazzling lights and I
sang *Some Enchanted Evening* from the musical *South Pacific*.

After three bars of music, Bruce came on behind me and demanded his jacket back, saying how dare I pinch it from the caravan. Protesting at the interruption, I shrugged the jacket off and handed it to him. Once more I launched myself into the song. Again, after a few bars, one of the boy dancers, a very slim lad, trotted towards me and in a shrill voice asked me for the shirt on my back. As I unbuttoned the garment, abusing the dancer all the time, another dancer came on asking for the trousers. . . . At that point I got the first laugh. Alone now with just the pair of frilly knickers in front of my monarch, who seemed a trifle stunned by this time, I resumed the song, and after what seemed a long period, a girl draped in just a towel sauntered on, stood next to me and simply glared at the knickers. . . . That was enough, thank God, the place fell about, as I made a rude gesture and chased the girl off.

I must state, that after that little lot I received a few curious glances from the other performers, and indeed on the finale walk down, Her Majesty gazed at me keenly.

After I had appeared at the National Theatre in the previously mentioned *Night Of A Thousand Stars*, Her Royal Highness, the Princess Alexandra, came backstage to meet the stars. She entered the room only to find Dawson and the actor Patrick Cargill on hands and knees, worse for drink, dishevelled and playing marbles with olives. That was the first time I ever heard a royal sniff.

It was a year of working hard and playing hard, and it was taking its toll of my health; late nights and too much drink had raddled my figure into a shapeless abomination and I could get winded just by playing Cluedo. There were the parties and the so-called jet set that only suffered you because you were a name, and matters came to a head after a hard and long night with Billy Connolly. We finished up at about nine in the morning at a record company's party. We'd been at it for over twenty-four hours and if I had breathed on anyone they would have been arrested. I staggered into the bright light of day with eyes full of grit and a mouth coated like a chicken run. Where I roamed in search of a cab, I know not, but I found myself in a back street where some derelicts were sprawled on a heap of rubble. One of the human flotsam teetered towards me, ill kempt in a torn raincoat, begrimed face unshaven. He stared at me, and I sobered up in an instant. . . . I knew that face, it belonged to a comedian who at one time had been a bill topper in variety. . . . He paled at the sight of me, began to scrabble back to his lost companions, and I heard these words torn from his very soul: "God, why am I not dead?" I still enjoy a drink but after that incident, it never ever got the better of me again, nor will it.

Summer that year was spent in Scarborough, at the Floral Hall yet again. The business suffered at first because the weather that year was the hottest for almost a decade: day after day the sun blistered down in shimmering waves and the glare from the sea tormented the eyes. There was no escape from the heat and finally people started coming into the theatre to get cool, and the business improved. Meg and the children had gone home after only a fortnight's stay in the resort, and in the past, I would have been delighted to be free to kick over the traces. . . . Now, I missed them. I was finally growing up.

The summer season ground to a halt and although it had been a most pleasurable run, I was eagerly looking forward to my next engagement at the Mandarin Hotel, Hong Kong. . . . Hong Kong, the very name inspired me; the mystery of the East. . . . Thanks to show business, I'd seen a lot of the world, but the Far East . . . that was a new world to conquer.

I took the family, of course, and as usual we dragged along everything but the kitchen sink. The customs had a field day with excess baggage fees and quips. The flight out to Hong Kong was a slow one; almost twenty-four hours across Europe, the Middle East and the long descent over the Ganges, with the Himalayas yawning in the distance. Finally, the "jumbo" shuddered to a halt on the runway at New Delhi airport; the heat was appalling and one elderly chap passed out. For some reason or another there seemed to be a flap on at the air terminus and enormous, fierce men in military dress herded we passengers into a customs shed. All the baggage was hurled off the plane, and in the sweltering cavern of the customs shed, the contents were minutely scrutinised. It had to happen, did it not? My son had secreted his toy machine gun in one of our myriad of suitcases, and when a hefty Indian official opened the lid of the suitcase, Stuart's toy gun started rat-tat-tatting. At least two men dived for cover and rifles wavered in every direction. Calm was eventually restored after a rather indignant Dawson senior was allowed to demonstrate that the gun really was a toy, but I still got the distinct impression that half the Punjab cavalry was at hand to cut me down.

We were shepherded back on to the aircraft. I was as usual trailing behind the other passengers and as I heaved a sweating foot on to the first rung of the steel stairway that would take me back inside the jumbo, a tall, bearded, swarthy Indian official grabbed my arm and pulled me off the rung. "Please, you come with me . . . now." Did I resist? Did I hell as like; off I trotted at his side, with the faces of the passengers pressed in alarm at the portholes. I glimpsed my wife's face creased with worry as the lithe gentleman hauled me away. . . . I could see the headlines in the press: "Les Dawson held in India. British Consul to see comedian in his cell." My imagination ran riot, as I was flanked by six soldiers with cocked rifles who then proceeded to march me at a spanking pace into a large room with a whirring fan blowing moist, tepid air in every direction. Sat a table was a man who looked as if he'd sprung from the pages of Kipling's Frontier Yarns; broad in the shoulder with a hawk-like nose jutting in the manner of a peninsula, from a face that had a scar running from his eyebrow to his ear. He wore quite the biggest turban I've ever seen and I began to tremble as he wagged a brown finger the size of an average sausage in my bloodless countenance. I searched my mind in an effort to think what I had done wrong. . . . Passport was in order, was it not? Had they found a quantity of heroin in a pair of my underpants? Was I thought to be a spy for a rival curry republic? My kids would all be mature adults when I got out of this mess: the wife would probably remarry and if I ever did get paroled, the government would probably disown me and I'd finish up a beachcomber in the Isle of Man.

The seated official held out his hand, I shook it and suddenly he grinned: "Welcome to India, Mr Dawson, I saw you in pantomime in Birmingham and it was very good you know. . . . My brother and his family took me, you might know them, they live in Nuneaton." With that he broke off his conversation and offered me a large gin and tonic. The passengers will, I feel sure, never forget the sight of a small, slightly intoxicated comedian being escorted back to the aircraft, which was by now over an hour late in taking off. To my kids I was a hero; to the passengers, a pain in the arse; to my wife – well her remark sums the whole peculiar situation up: "He'd find a bloody drink in the Sahara desert," she said not too unkindly.

Slowly the giant aeroplane commenced its descent to our final destination: Hong Kong . . . what a view! Ribbons of garish illumination threading from the island across to glittering Kowloon and brooding China. The humidity threw a blanket of damp heat in our faces as the family and I trooped off the jumbo into the airport lounge, only to be met with hordes of Chinese porters and spectators, all pulling their faces like my character, Cosmo. I couldn't believe it. "Oh God, not here as well," sighed the wife as the Yellow Peril surrounded us making disgusting sounds with pouted lips. A car was waiting to transport us to the Mandarin Hotel, and the driver bobbed and tittered as he drove along under the tunnel to the hotel. The Mandarin was breathtaking to look at, ranking as it does so high in the world of innkeeping.

The accommodation for our stay in Hong Kong was the last word in sheer luxury; we had a suite that was so large it prompted my son to remark, "I wish I'd brought my library cards." Leaving them to the gruesome task of unpacking, I went to investigate the cabaret room which was situated on the twenty-fifth floor. I was taking over from that great American comedian, Morry Amsterdam, who turned out to be a most genuine person. The room wasn't full for his last night's stint, the response to his act was not exactly tumultuous, and I felt the stirrings of unease at the thought of my debut. . . . I need not have harboured such misgivings.

I opened on the Friday night and the room was crammed with British army and naval personnel. . . . The act went well:

"Good evening, what a thrill to be in Hong Kong, which is a sort of Isle of Man with rice.

Amazing place this, four million Chinese and I still can't find a decent laundry.

We flew over here with British Airways, I said to the stewardess, do these planes crash often? She said only once.

Great plane . . . it was an early jet, a bag of charcoal and an oven.

Over India, the pilot did a loop the loop, he said how was that for skill? Half the people on the ground thought we were going to have an accident . . . I said half the people up here have just had one."

I was going great. I'd forgotten just one thing . . . jet lag. Suddenly I found I was repeating myself over and over again, but the audience was obviously used to this phenomenon, and as I groped along they roared encouragement. I finished up in the early hours toasting Britain, the Forces and Anglo-Chinese relations and finally I was carried back to my quarters. One thing that never failed to stun me was the sight on television of my *Sez Les* series dubbed in Chinese. . . . The dialogue sounded like bubbles in a bath. Meg and I were invited everywhere, and my excuse for drinking was my horror of dehydration, due to the humidity: Meg never seemed to be sympathetic regarding this matter, but that's women for you. . . .

Meg and the kids had to return home in order to pack the children off to school, and I was left to my own devices. . . . I watched their flight soar away from Hong Kong, and I trotted off to Kowloon to sample the delights of oriental night life. Which I did, often. After the show I was oft to be discovered in the Ginza or the Bottoms Up Club in a state of high disorder, usually with a retinue of grinning Chinese behind me all pulling faces, à la Cosmo. Then I began to get worried. I'd had no word from Meg that they had arrived home safely, and when I read a news bulletin that a plane had crashed in India, I panicked. For three days I tried telephoning my home number, my agent, and finally the British Consul in Bombay, all to no avail. Finally, one night I phoned home and to my relief, a sleepy Meg answered the call. I'd forgotten that in Britain the time was 3.30 a.m. but the wife forcibly reminded me of the fact, then calmly told me to "hang on" whilst she went for a pee. . . . So good was the line from the hotel to my home, I could hear the loo flush, and mentally I totted up the cost of that bladder evacuation. As it turned out, she'd been adrift in Bombay after missing the 'plane and they'd had a rough passage.

It was a wonderful season and the business was the best they had enjoyed since Dave Allen had appeared there. One night it came home to me just how powerful the television media really was. I trotted on stage only to find that the entire audience was Japanese. The English-speaking cabaret manager was at hand, and I stammered out to him that it was pointless me even attempting to go on: as I have been known to have trouble being understood in Tamworth, there was no way that I could see how the Sons of Nippon would grasp my humour. "Meester Dowsan," the manager said politely, "they book room to see you." I tried. Oh I tried. . . . For ten minutes, nothing. They peered at me like a colony of chimps and the silence was so intense I could hear them hiss. I shrugged, and put the Cosmo bifocals on, made a rude international gesture with my clenched fist and outstretched arm, pulled my lips together in a leering fashion and the whole room exploded. Thick glasses made an appearance; the Jap tourists stood up and copied my gestures and facial expressions, and the night was saved.

The eastern way of life fascinated me. I haunted the Buddhist temples, and found myself drawn to that religion. For a long time, I had been interested in many spiritual philosophies, but in Buddhism, I found I could relate my beliefs better than in the more militant western dogmas. It was there in Hong Kong that the germ of a book was born, although it would be a long time before I actually brought it to fruition.

I was sad at leaving Hong Kong. I had made many friends there; the RAF had flown me in helicopters all over the island and Macao. . . . The navy had sailed me into the South China Sea, nearly getting us arrested by a Red Chinese naval gunboat in the process. . . . The army had taken me into the New Territories, and due to a friendship with a high ranking Red China embassy official, I had been granted a visa to visit Canton in Red China proper.

I flew out one hot night and a small knot of friends waved little Dawson off into the wide blue yonder, but being Dawson of course the flight had a touch of the grotesque about it. I was sat on the aircraft next to a huge, rough-looking man who turned out to be a mining engineer. He was Australian, and he was frightened of nothing . . . except flying. He was drinking at the airport and he was still at it when I sat down alongside him. I tried to ignore him crying quietly to himself, but as the mighty VC10 engines shrieked into life, he grabbed me around the neck and started to screw my neck out of its torso socket. None of the other passengers seemed to notice the commotion, and I was alone, grappling with a powerful, fear-crazed animal. Somehow I managed to get breath back in my aching lungs and I had to punch him, to little effect I might add, on his head. He started blubbering again, so I shoved his bottle of vodka down his throat and he sucked at it like a new born calf. That was the pattern of the journey to Calcutta: I'd ram the vodka down him until he passed out into troubled stupor, then when he jerked back to consciousness again, I would summons the stewardess for another supply and repeat the dosage. He had to be carried off the plane when we landed; I assisted his bulk down the gangway, and the stewardess glared at me and snarled, "That wasn't a nice thing to do, getting that poor man drunk, you ought to be ashamed of yourself." The bruises on my battered larynx took a week to clear up.

Back home, I taped a Christmas Special for Yorkshire Television, but I wasn't happy about it. . . . I felt stale and I was glad when Norman informed me that Yorkshire were not taking up the option on my contract. There was just one more series of four one-hour specials to be completed and that would sever my long ties with Yorkshire. The Christmas Special, as I feared, received bad press, and frankly I deserved it; I needed to get away from the studios and start to reappraise my career. In 1977, the last show for Yorkshire was "put in the can". As the last sketch, a "Hunchback Of Notre Dame" send-up, ended, all the crew, producers and men I'd worked with for all those years, gathered on the set in front of the studio audience, and they sang a parody of the Gilbert O'Sullivan song hit *Claire*. The sincerity of the lads brought me to the brink of tears as the emotion in the studio ran high: so many years . . . some good, some, well, you can't win them all. After a party with the company heads, I stood outside the familiar buildings and took one long last look. . . . What the future held, I knew not, but I had the confidence and experience behind me to tackle anything that came along. I felt that at last, the little man had found himself.

I started on another book, *The Cosmo Guide To Male Liberation,* which was not destined to set the literary world aflame; the book in itself wasn't bad, but the publisher was indifferent to suggestions that I should go forth and promote it in bookshops, and it died a natural death. I spent the summer of that year in Blackpool again, this time at the ABC Theatre, where it had all begun for me, and the season got off to a good start, despite the opposition from my friend, Danny La Rue, who was at the Opera House, and Little and Large, who were starring at the North Pier. Once again I had a stalwart cast with me: Ken McKellar, Bobby Bennett and Jumping Jack, and it was a pleasant season. I took up golf, and I have never improved my game a jot since. In fact I have spent so much time in bunkers, I suffer from sandfly fever, but at least it's a nice stroll when I do play.

It was during this period that the BBC approached me to join them. Frankly, I wasn't too sure, I still smarted from the *State Of The Union* debacle I had gone through, and after the warmth of Yorkshire Television, the BBC seemed a trifle austere. At any rate, I signed with the Corporation to tape six shows to be called *The Les Dawson Show* – with the bubbling young singer, Lulu. When the summer season ended, I immediately went back to London to start work on the series. It took some getting used to, working for the BBC again, but this time I was known, and I was treated with courtesy and friendliness. Lulu and I hit it off straight away and I enjoyed working with her. . . . John Ammonds produced the series and I thought it would be liked by the general public. During '77, I taped the first Des O'Connor chat show, a second Mike Parkinson chattie, and a *Summer Time Special* at Yarmouth for the BBC . . . and still had to find time to appear with Nanette Newman on her show. . . . I was in danger of over exposure. I was on the box more than the test card, and the national press were quick to point this out. When the first show with Lulu and me went out on Saturdays at the peak period, they panned it, and the public switched off en masse. The series was a flop.

Obviously I was depressed. It seemed that everything I tried to do was courted by disaster. My wife told me in no uncertain terms what she thought: (1) Nobody understood what I was trying to do. (2) I should have stayed with Yorkshire TV. (3) Give television a rest. The way things were going, it looked as if I might be in for an enforced absence.

Our show alternated every other Saturday with Mike Yarwood's show . . . his ratings were very high in the charts, mine, non existent.

I still don't know why *The Les Dawson Show* went so badly; it was funny and different in many ways to other things I'd done, but it simply did not jell, and as pantomime crept into view, this time at Bradford Alhambra, I had to take serious stock indeed.

Once more, I found myself looking at a career that had seen more ups and downs than a section of the Alps. . . . Had the friendly ghost from Unsworth decided that enough was enough? Only time would tell.

INTERVAL

I never imagined what a chore it can be writing about one's own life. There are so many things and events that become clouded by the passage of time. What may seem mundane to me, may be of immeasurable interest to others, and vice versa. The one thing that did come home to me, was how much the fabric of relationships with other people shapes your thoughts. Trivial matters that possibly forge your future actions and mayhap mould your character. As I have written previously, courage, either moral or physical, has never been my strong suit, but did a small isolated incident in Germany help to inject a change in my genetic coding? It is during my Army service, we are out in the wilderness firing live ammunition. Twenty pounder shells from our tanks roaring miles towards invisible targets. . . . It is summer and the heat shimmers and we boil in our tank suits. I place a shell in the breech of the gun; I fire the mechanism, nothing happens, but the firing pin has struck the shell. The officer in my Centurion goes white, and he dives off the tank and leaves me alone with the driver. The whole area clears as the huge metal monsters veer away from potential disaster. . . . I cannot take the risk of clearing the shell from the breech. . . . I am alone. I recall being unable to think clearly at the time, then suddenly a calmness settles my nerves. I tell the driver to get out and I drive the tank back to the camp with every fibre, every sinew taut . . . but I do it.

During a particular depression in my career, a man sent me a painting in oils that he had done of me from a photograph in a magazine. It was good, and why I'll never know, instead of writing to thank him for it, I went to his home, a grey council house on a sprawling estate outside Manchester. His wife beamed when she saw me and ushered me inside. When I saw her husband, the man who'd painted my image, I couldn't utter a word. . . . He was completely paralysed; he'd painted me by holding the brush in the only part of his body where he had movement: his right foot. Was it he who gave me the will to fight on?

I knew that I learned compassion for others from a man who was blind from birth who nightly scoured derelict areas of Manchester with food for the homeless and the forgotten. Once when I was with him, a ragged, thin alcoholic stumbled out of the shadows, and fell at his feet when the blind man gave him some food from his holdall. As the tramp wolfed the food down like a wild creature, the blind man said to me, "It's a terrible thing, son, when a man loses all dignity." He held on to my arm as I guided him away from the mess of rubble. "Life is a wonderful thing, providing you share it with others," he said softly as he tapped his way home.

So much is talked about show business as a futile, immoral and egotistical experience, that performers are looked upon as latter day gypsies and thieves . . . indeed, we pay more for car insurance and accommodation quite often because we are considered "shiftless". Yet a performer can create more happiness than any well meaning social platitude. . . . There is one story about the world of entertainment that I hold sacred; it is true.

Enzio Pinsa was a great operatic tenor. He was eulogised on both sides of the Atlantic, and the fame had made him feel he was almost a God. Nobody was allowed near the great man, and his retinue had to be servile in his presence. One night after his triumph debut at the Metropolitan Opera House in New York, a trim, well dressed man asked at the stage door if it was possible to speak to Pinsa, who refused point blank. Every night henceforward the quiet man waited in the hope of an audience with the supreme tenor, until one evening, the manager of the Opera House begged Pinsa just to meet the man. Grudgingly, Pinsa agreed to see him and get rid of him. The man thanked Pinsa for the interview, which purported to engage the tenor to appear at a concert in South America at a vast fee and with free air transport for the whole orchestra. Intrigued by the money involved, plus the man's obvious wealth, Pinsa agreed to do the concert. The whole cast was flown down but because of bad weather conditions, they arrived just in time to get on stage, which was set in the open air with bright lights around the perimeter. Irritated and tired, Pinsa sang for over an hour, and did not once receive any applause. Pinsa stumbled off the stage, his ego in ruins and he said to the man who was standing in the shadows, "Sir, you have humbled me, I have failed you and as a penance I will waive the fee." The man stepped from the shadows and his face was wet with tears. "Failed?" he said in a trembling voice. "You have brought a touch of God here tonight, Señor Pinsa." With that the whole arena was lit up, and the audience was seen sitting there . . . all of them lepers.

CURTAIN UP . . . NEXT ACT.

The 1977–1978 pantomime at Bradford Alhambra Theatre. The subject? Babes in the Wood. The cast as follows: myself as "Nurse Ada", Roy Barraclough as the "Bad Robber", Tammy Jones as Robin Hood and from the television series *The Avengers* Patrick Newell, as the Sheriff of Nottingham. Also we have Peter Goodwright, playing my son, and a young girl from St Anne's playing Maid Marion. Add if you will the name of my old friend, Eli Woods, and you have the ingredients for a wonderful show. . . . Wrong.

Firstly, after only two nights, Patrick Newell, the sheriff, decides he's not fit enough and vanishes, so I have to take a man out of the "merry men" to be the sheriff. Secondly, the weather is bloody awful, it's so cold, brass monkeys are effeminate, and three of my merry men go down with flu! On the opening night, Tammy prances on stage and slips on her arse and Roy Barraclough is alarmed to find that he has a gastric ulcer. The snow is so deep, nothing can move and one night we have to put the audience up in a sauna bath. After three weeks, I'm down to one merry man and Roy has to go for treatment. My Maid Marion isn't too happy, so she leaves the show as well. One memorable evening, in the scene where they are about to hang Robin Hood, I haven't anyone to do it, so she has to put the noose around her own neck, as I shout from the wings, "Hang him."

By now, I am fairly close to a nervous breakdown, as my cast is whittled down one by one. . . . The merry man has to rush off stage and rush back on again as the sheriff's man, and he is knackered. On top of all this the fairy accuses my freshly recruited sheriff of "flashing" his privates at her. In one heartwarming scene, a stage hand who is clearly pissed drops in the wrong scenery and we find ourselves in a woodland glade where it should have been the interior of a humble cottage. Afterwards as I drink to forget in my dressing room, the fairy enters complete with wand, and informs me that the sheriff has been "showing it again". I call the sheriff in and the tableau is a comic gem . . . I'm sat in a wig, pink knickers and bra, Fairy is in a sticky-out gossamer gown with wand at the ready, and the sheriff is dressed in doublet and hose and plumed hat. I ask Fairy to repeat the accusation, and she does so with an air of disdain. The sheriff, quivering in his patched hose, denies the charge and says it is all a mis-understanding. . . . At the time Fairy was passing his dress-ing room door, the towel around his middle dropped off revealing his masculinity. At that moment of high drama, a lame cleaning lady hobbles into my dressing room and asks, "What's up, Les? Has he been showing his cock again?"

The weather never improved and the business drained away to a trickle. Meanwhile Eli was off ill and now my strolling band of players was so depleted, we could have staged the damn panto in a phone box with room for the orchestra. I only managed to get home a few times as the road conditions were frightful. On one occasion when I did contrive to get over the Pennines, I couldn't get back, I was stuck atop the hills in a blinding snow storm. The police made everybody turn around and go back to Lancashire. I implored one befrosted constable, who was sinking rapidly into a mountain of snow, to let me through as I had a pantomime to put on. . . . His answer opened my vocabulary up to a whole new range of curses, and I slid back to Lancashire.

With so few artistes left, the nightly finale became an exercise in pure farce: the merry man took his call, went off, put a different hat on and came on for another call. The king stepped forward, took his bow, sprinted off and returned as a jester. How the hell we got through it, I'll never know, but finally the thing ground to an end and I clambered out of Bradford, numbed. Arrow Books commissioned me to write a book of anecdotes and so I had the proud sum of four literary pieces on the book shelves. There was one disturbing feature about this period: Meg wasn't in the best of health. She was tired all the time and began to complain of a lump in her breast. She saw our local doctor, but he brushed her fears away; it was nothing to worry about, he said, it was merely mastitis of the mammary.

The Les Dawson Show ended its run on television, and nobody noticed its demise. But I knew it had harmed my career, for when I played cabaret dates, the halls had vacant tables, history was repeating its charms. The BBC came up with an idea for a series during the summer run at the Spa Theatre, Bridlington in 1978. It was a spin off from an American show hosted by that sardonic comedian Alan King. The idea was a sort of comic "watchdog" programme. I saw a video of it and the theme was to take on all the situations that beset people, like the law or medicine and put humour into stock procedures such as house conveyancing or the National Health. The programme appealed to me, and we arranged to start taping the series in late September. . . . Meanwhile, I had to face Bridlington for ten weeks, a daunting project. In essence, Bridlington is quite a pleasant resort; nice harbour full of character, the people the salt of the earth and the theatre was a gem; trouble with the place was it was mainly a day tripper's paradise, and at night it had little to offer. The main diet was fish and chips or, for the very adventurous, crab salads. It was a good bill: myself, Tammy Jones, Stu Francis and a dog act called the Wedgwoods. Meg and the kids took one hard look at Bridlington and went home after a fortnight, as did Stu's wife, Wendy. . . . So Stu and I moved into my large flat and shared expenses. His companionship saved my sanity, and we managed to manufacture our own fun.

The ten weeks passed, and the show had done very good business indeed, so I felt mollified even to the point of becoming an addict of crab salads. Back in London, the new series went into rehearsals. It was called *The Dawson Watch* and it was produced by Peter Whitmore, a very able man who steered the show along nicely. The set was in the shape of a giant computer with two or three lovely long-legged girls walking about with note books and pencils to give it an air of efficiency. *The Dawson Watch,* although not perfect, did much to wipe out the memory of the previous series and to my astonishment, it appealed to a higher intellectual bracket. Ratings were always around the nine million mark, and to my intense satisfaction, it raised fury with people involved in the subject we touched on. Solicitors howled for my blood; so did estate agents and in one case, the Bank of England. That suited me, for I never have courted popularity, being different has always been my forte, and I had got through to people with this type of show. After the first series had completed its run, I was optimistic, especially when I saw the advance bookings for the 1978–79 pantomime at the Birmingham Hippodrome: £250,000 in the kitty before we even opened. I was getting back on top again.

The Birmingham pantomime was a very successful one, and with a cast that included Julie Rogers, Roger DeCourcey, Eli Woods and dear old Danny O'Dea, it was also a happy one. Meg and the kids came down on New Year's Eve to a party that I had arranged and we caroused into the early morning.

After the panto season, I wrote a few magazine articles and made a start on a new novel, tentatively entitled *Hitler Was My Mother-in-Law*. Also I did a commercial for, of all things, "Glow Worm" boilers. I was to be dressed up as a glow worm, which turned out to mean I wore a pink padded one-piece suit with a bulb on the arse end which lit up. It took a full day at Shepperton Studios to get the thing right, which wasn't easy, because the crew on the project – lighting, cameras, the whole shoot – couldn't stop falling about when my arse illuminated. Still, the money was a Godsend, HM Inspector of Taxes was still delving into my linen for every groat he could steal.

A new *Dawson Watch* series was being planned, and indeed the crew and I filmed in the Wye Valley for five weeks, so I was away from home yet again. Once the actual outside shots were in the can, all that was left to do were the studio rehearsals in London. I arrived back home tired and worried about Meg, especially when I saw her. She was listless and almost indifferent to everything around her, which was never like my Meg. Despite the assurances of our local doctor that the lump on her breast was nothing to worry about, she was far from satisfied. We made arrangements to get her to a specialist. . . . With what we had undergone before in medical matters, I was suspicious of the average GP.

Before I could contact a specialist, Meg went for a cervical cancer test: just routine. She mentioned the lump in her breast.

The doctor, a woman, examined it. She made an indentation with her finger; the breast dimpled. . . . Meg, my Meg. . . . The doctor had an anxious look on her face, Meg told me later with a wry expression. Events moved too swiftly for me to grasp. . . . Two days later my wife's illness was diagnosed: breast cancer. Our world collapsed at the utterance of those most dreadful words. . . . Meg was taken quickly into hospital for tests. . . . I roamed the house, frantic and sick. . . . Where are the jokes and smart remarks now, Dawson? My children got me through the next day and as night fell, I drove to the hospital, unshaven and frightened. Meg was sitting up in the austere hospital room; she smiled. How can she smile? It was she who had the strength that night, not I. . . . Who's this coming in? Oh yes, of course, the specialist who's treating my wife, the man who's done the tests. . . . He's efficient and firm as he tells me that Meg will have to have her breast off. . . . What the hell. . . . Inside my gut is churning and I want to run away and take Meg with me. . . . No, no . . . this sort of thing happens in films. Oh you can weep at the sadness on celluloid, but it's merely make believe, it doesn't happen in real life. . . . No, no, God, you took our babies away from us; you can't have my Meg.

Where was all the ambition now? A thousand laughs I had given . . . couldn't someone somewhere give me one?

Eldest girl Julie did the housework and the cooking, and the other two, Stuart and Pamela, well . . . diamonds the pair of them; once again demonstrating an inner strength that I did not possess. The operation was over, the breast removed, and before I entered the spartan room, the specialist drew me into a corner of the sickly lit corridor: "The operation has been a complete success, there are no signs of malignancy left. . . . She'll need you more than ever now, you must realise it's a very traumatic experience for a woman to go through." He shook my hand in what seemed a sympathetic manner. I tiptoed into the room just as Meg was coming round from the anaesthesia, and I gripped her hand as she regained consciousness. Her dear sweet face, so pale. . . . Remember all the wisecracks, Dawson? The ones directed at her in all those sleazy dumps. . . .

"Take my wife . . . please."

I'm not saying she's ugly, but when she went to see a horror film the audience thought she was making a personal appearance. . . ."

Funny. There she is now, Les, alone in that bed, and she's looking at you with love beyond any other. Meg's family creep into the room and so do my three children. The relatives mean well but their tears don't hold a promise of hope. . . . It was at this moment that I said something which many will condemn me for, but I knew my wife and what she thought of her relationship with me after so many years. . . . It was when Meg whispered to me the words that ripped through my heart: "Hello, love. Tell me the truth, have they taken it off?" I knew that her main worry had been that if they hadn't removed it, it might indicate that it was inoperable, as had happened to a friend of hers.

I kissed her lightly on the forehead. "They've taken it away, love, and it was all right, a success . . . you're going to be fine," I chortled brightly. She smiled and replied, "So it's all over." What made me say it I don't know . . . I leant over her, shook my head in mock solemnity and intoned, "No, love, you still have one more operation to go." The circle of relatives stood in shock at my pronouncement, only my kids had a rough idea what I was trying to do. Meg stared at me: "What do you mean, another operation? I thought you said. . . ." I didn't let her finish. "Just one more operation. They're going to take the other one off and put it in the middle." She opened her mouth and laughed. "Now I know it's going to be all right," she said firmly and held me close. I left the room saying that I wanted to talk to the specialist. . . . Outside in the corridor, alone and trembling, I broke down and sobbed with the grief of the tormented echoed down the ages.

Obviously I had cancelled a lot of engagements but the television series had to go on and I didn't want to be away from Meg for the whole week of rehearsal for show one. On this matter the BBC, and Peter Whitmore in particular, were kindness itself: the whole crew moved to Lytham and we rehearsed in the Clifton Arms. This meant that I only had to go to London on the day to tape the show.

Meg improved, but the operation left a mental scar. One night I had to take her to the bathroom, as she was still weak. The way she kept looking at me as I helped her along the landing made me realise how self-conscious she was about the missing breast and the subsequent stitches down her left side. In the bathroom, I took her dressing gown off in preparation for getting her eased into the bath; the scar was livid and jagged, and as she saw me look at it, she trembled and whispered, "Not very pretty is it?" I did not reply. I kissed the scar, helped her into the bath water, and as I went to leave, I merely remarked, "The one you've still got is nicer than most. . . . Just means I'll have to love you that bit more now."

The second *Dawson Watch* went better than the first series had done, and the public took to it. Norman and Anne, my agents, rang me up in late August to say that I would be headlining *Babes In The Wood* for the pantomime season of 1980–81 at the Liverpool Empire with Julie Rogers, Don McLean, Eli Woods and the Rocking Berries. Whilst he was on the telephone, Norman casually mentioned that I had been chosen for another Royal Variety Performance in November. . . . Naturally I was overwhelmed by my inclusion. Meg got stronger and with the bond of love that our family had, she lost her reluctance to mingle with people; there had been a time after the operation when, not unnaturally, she had felt less than a woman and had tended to withdraw into herself. . . . However, the kids and I flatly refused to allow her to become paranoid, and once again the power of humour worked.

It was a busy time, and a happy one, with Meg on the mend, a successful panto season ahead, good television reaction, and another Royal Variety Show. This year, Her Majesty would watch the marathon music hall from the Theatre Royal, Drury Lane, because at the London Palladium, the traditional home of the Royal Variety Show, *The King And I* was still pulling the customers in, and the sets couldn't be taken out. . . . So, Drury Lane.

There is a legend that the ghost of an actor roams the Theatre Royal, and the spirit hates any form of stage work that is not that of the immortal Bard. I scoffed at such a thing. . . . Wrong.

From the morning we taut performers wandered through the busy streets towards the old theatre, spectral energy was at work. Firstly, for no apparent reason, the lighting failed after being checked repeatedly. Tempers flared over the most trivial matters and several musicians turned up pissed.

Yul Brynner, who is the King of Siam in his view, blocked my passage as I was en route to the bar and thundered, "I am Yul Brynner. . . . Who are you?" I smirked and the American comedian Red Buttons turned away with shoulders shaking as I said to the gnome-like Mr Brynner, "I saw you in that great film *The Magnificent Five*." He peered at me as if I'd slid off a specimen jar. "No, no," he said vigorously. "It was *The Magnificent Seven*." I smiled and cracked, "No, I went to see it early." He snorted, turned and said something that sounded naughty in Russian to a languid ballet dancer with a box office crotch, then stormed off. Carol Channing, the American star who's played *Hello Dolly* on Broadway since Tiberius had a teething rash, pranced about with her garish make-up on all day like something out of a coven, and Elaine Stritch, another Broadway veteran with a viper's tongue, looked through us all until she fell down the stage stairs. Rehearsals were bloody awful, nobody was given time to finish their prospective acts; the sound went peculiar and worried technicians were running about like raped pullets. I shared a dressing room with Red Buttons and dear lamented Reg Bosanquet, whom I had a lot of time for: he was simply a nice man. As a bonus, our little dressing room would be graced on the night by James Mason, whose sole task would be to introduce the two Russian ballet stars, one of them, the chap with the box office balls.

Her Majesty arrived, and the formalities over, the show went on with a whimper. The ghost cackled as dancers staggered and nearly fell, as Carol Channing's voice went during her number, and then the sprite must have really enjoyed himself when the Yul Brynner bit with Virginia McKenna turned into a near shambles with a sound defect. Reg and I busied ourselves with strong spirits . . . if disaster was inevitable, why not meet it with a tum full of the blender's art? It was my turn for the ghost to have a go at – and he did, mightily.

I walked on to the stage, shot a quick glance at Her Majesty – she wore a radiant smile – and I went into my act. No, that's not quite correct. I didn't go into anything because the microphone didn't work, did it? Helplessly, as I shouted inane remarks over the dead mike, I shot darting glances into the wings for the sight of a sound engineer . . . nothing. Finally, with the audience as dead as mutton, I walked off stage to find someone to get the sound back. As I walked off on the prompt side of the stage, two men strolled on from the other side, carrying not one but two microphones. Hastily, I discarded the one I'd taken off and returned beaming to the centre of the stage, only to find that the two freshly acquired mikes were also quite dead. Panic, dear reader, took over, and a film of sweat began to slither down my face. Whilst I was busy barking into the useless appliances to the descant of sniggers from the audience, a small man on his knees started to crawl across the stage behind me. I perceived that he too was laden with a microphone and lead which he essayed to place on top of the piano. "I don't do a double act," I yelled in a strangled cry, and just at that moment, there was an almighty rumble from the sound system which resembled the wrath of God himself. Flinging my arms wide and beyond caring anymore, I shouted: "Don't blame me, Lord, I'm new at this!"

The rest of what was left of my act went by in a dream . . . I was shattered and I saw my career floating before me like a dead ox down the Irrawaddy. Poor James Mason, the only member of our dressing room coterie who refused a drink and went on totally sober, couldn't pronounce the names of the Russian ballet dancers and wandered off the stage in an advanced stratum of confusion. Mercifully the show ended and I awaited the arrival of security men in vans to take me into custody. We were arranged in something like an orderly crocodile to meet Her Majesty, and when she entered the foyer, her eyes were sparkling. Eventually she got to me, and to my surprise, she grinned widely and said, "Oh I did enjoy it all. . . . Tell me, all the things that went wrong, was it planned that way or did they really happen? I should jolly well keep the mistakes in." I stood open-mouthed as she went by.

Between the Royal Variety Show and the commencement of the pantomime season in Liverpool, I trotted around the sceptred isle doing cabaret dates plus a nightmare TV for Esther Rantzen. . . . I say nightmare because her show, now as it was then the popular *That's Life,* was in full swing and she persuaded me to take part in one of her most idiotic ideas: to judge the worst laugh from a contingent of macabre contestants who brayed in the studio like well groped hyenas. Dressed as a sort of "specialist", I sat opposite these howling morons and attempted to choose the most inane cackle. The climax to this sort of entrance exam for Bedlam, was the advent of . . . wait for it! A laughing horse. Yes. I sat there in a small room at Lime Grove, still reeling from the human cacophony, when quite without warning, a large dray horse of enormous proportions had its head thrust through an open window. The expression on its face suggested the strain of an awkward bowel movement. Suddenly a man's face appeared by the side of the animal, and he said cheerfully, "Are you ready?" Numbly I nodded and the horse glared at me, bared its teeth and whinnied. I discovered later that the cheerful man had achieved the "horse laugh" by kicking the quadruped up its exposed arse.

Liverpool opened her heart to our pantomime and we had a marvellous time in a city that I have a great affection for. The town planners may have savagely hacked the soul of Liverpool to shreds, but the people are magnificent. Despite the sound problems in the cavernous Empire Theatre, which were severe, the audiences gave us total support and I for one was sorry when the run ended. I took Meg and the kids on a cruise to the West Indies, and apart from a riot in St Lucia, two cracked ribs in Barbados, and giving a taxi driver in Puerto Rico a hundred pound tip . . . I came back home rested and ready for the next challenge on TV, a pilot show with a gang of kids who called themselves Kids International. There is an old saw in our business which says simply, "Never work with dogs or kids." How true.

   Ernie Maxim, a veteran BBC producer with a good track record, became a firm friend as the planning for the show went ahead with what we hoped would be original innovations, and in this particular assumption, in one respect I struck pure gold. Buried deep in the catacombs of the BBC Television Centre, I chanced upon a wild-haired genius who was to make most of my future variety shows with the corporation a major talking point. . . . He was a wizard at electronics and he gave me the idea for a piano that could do anything – and it did.

Apart from Roy Barraclough and myself, plus the odd guest spot, the rest of the show was, as the name implied, Kids International. We had black kids, yellow kids, big kids, little kids . . . the studio began to look like an orphanage. Yet despite the assembly, when it came to talent, only two of the youngsters had any true gift: a young coloured lad who danced like a budding Fred Astaire, and another tot who played the piano in the style of Oscar Peterson.

The show went on before a studio audience on a Friday night and from the moment I introduced the trick piano, which, on the first occasion, grew in size as I leant on it, then collapsed as I played it, the show was an uproar. When the programme went out on the air, the nation took it to their hearts: the viewing figures were enormous, but even more significant, the appreciation figure which is gleaned by researchers calling on householders up and down the country was the biggest in the corporation's history. So it was decreed that we should do a series featuring the children. The pace of life was hotting up and several of my friends began to express concern as to the state of my health. Late night revels, and a sheer inability to say a firm "no" to offers of work did nothing to create confidence in my fitness; baggy-eyed and overweight, snatching sleep on motorway journeys in a mist of alcohol, Les Dawson was looking enough like the Missing Link to give Darwin eternal satisfaction. Little did I know then that one day in the not too distant future, I would be battling for my very life.

We taped six Kids International shows and they all became big hits with the viewing public. The things that my backroom boy did with our piano were the main triumph. One week he made the instrument rear up on its back legs and box; another week it walked away from me and I shot it; on one programme it did a striptease. . . . Whatever I asked my little boffin to do with the piano, he did it.

Everybody was enthusiastic about my involvement with Kids International and many high ranking BBC bosses reckoned that the series could become an annual thing . . .

I totally disagreed. When I mentioned earlier about never working with kids or dogs, I didn't mean it in the accepted show business sense, that children usually steal the limelight from established performers: I saw it differently. There is one thing that people often forget when they see a child perform: children grow up, and that is exactly what had happened with Kids International. When we did the pilot show some of the youngsters had been appealing, but by the time we did the actual series, they looked like urban terrorists. Many of them were taller than me and frankly impudent and bold; gone forever the waif-like innocence.

1981 was a busy year yet again. I flew to Vienna and Madeira for conference work; cabaret work was dwindling rapidly and it looked as if the golden years of the night club circuits were finally at an end, so those conferences were a Godsend.

1981 was also yet another year of personal tragedy. In November, as usual, Meg and I attended the Annual Water Rats' Ball at the Grosvenor House Hotel on Park Lane. It is always a marvellous occasion and my pride in being a Water Rat is self-evident. The ball is a riotous affair: the wine flows, as does the comradeship between the professional artistes, and it is a night to remember. During the cabaret, Meg seemed troubled with her back and she had turned pale. Normally we stayed in the Great Room until the wee small hours, but on this night Meg asked me to take her upstairs because she felt "under the weather". After she had fallen asleep, I returned to my table of guests as she had requested I do, and frankly I didn't think there was much to worry about.

When Meg and I returned home, she seemed a trifle better and the doctor called and eased my concern by saying she'd got a little sciatica problem. Julie was at home at the time, awaiting admittance to nursing training, so at least I could carry on working away as the breadwinner. I had to be in London for a photography session for a saucy calendar in which Cosmo leered at lovely undressed girls – and that was a labour of love, I can tell you.

I had signed to do pantomime at the beautiful Richmond Theatre in Richmond, Surrey with a star-studded cast: Bernard Bresslaw, Christopher Timothy, Rula Lenska and dear

old Arthur Askey, who at the time was not in the best of
health himself. I was staying with a friend of mine in his flat
in Twickenham for the winter and all seemed set for another
good season. The weather was cold and we had daily snow
flurries, but the box office was always busy, which augured
well. Arthur Askey, however, was a different kettle of fish.
The old boy was in pain and I had to make a decision, to
write him out of the main plot and leave him to make one
appearance to do his act. I knew in my heart of hearts that
dear Arthur would never complete the pantomime run and
he agreed with my decision to free him from making more
appearances on stage. Towards the end of the rehearsals, I
returned to the flat with my friend John Foster: the idea was
a brief shower and into the West End for yet another tussle
with Bacchus. I had a moment to spare so I rang home to see
if my brood were managing without the master. . . . Julie
answered my call. . . . What? Mum not well? Meg crying
into the line sobbing with fear. . . . In God's name, what
now? Cancer in her back? Not sciatica. . . . Xray results taken
show that she has the disease in her back? My world exploded
into a mist of pain and anger. Hadn't she gone through
enough? John took the phone from my lifeless fingers and
told Meg we were coming home straight away. I rang Norman and Anne and told them I would have to skip the
remainder of the rehearsals and also would not work on
Christmas Eve . . . I had to be with my wife, nothing else
mattered.

    We drove north in silence, my mind a vortex of troubled
images. . . . How could I go on without her? Although I'd
often put my career before the home never once had I ceased
to love that little lady who shared so much pain with me. . . .
How could there be a God? Silently I raged at the unfairness
of life: just as we seemed to be established, again Fate stepped
in to destroy our happiness. In my mind I saw the young
couple with no money, staring into shop windows and dreaming about better times; such wonderful days, when dreams
were all we had apart from rude animal health.

    Meg and I clung together and we cried and our marvellous
children rallied around us; through our tears, as a family we
vowed we would fight this terrible new foe between us. Meg
had treatment at Christie's Hospital in Manchester, the one

in which my father had spent his last days, and so upon returning there, more poignant memories returned. Word about Meg's illness leaked out and the press had to be kept at bay, otherwise they would have created a circus out of it. The treatment was successful in the sense that for a time it contained the cancer in the bone, and the specialist advised me to carry on as if everything was fine. After talking it over with the family, I did just that. I returned to the pantomime leaving Meg in the hands of the three greatest kids in the world.

I went home every weekend despite the appalling weather and Meg recovered enough to bring the children down to Richmond to join me at New Year. For a time the clouds of sadness lifted. Every day was now a bonus; the future meant nothing to me, I didn't even want to contemplate it.

Three weeks later Arthur Askey had to leave the pantomime; both his legs were amputated, and a short time later the Great Old Man of Variety died. It seemed strange to pass his dressing room, empty now, not hearing that well known cry which he always gave me: "Hello, Playmate."

The pantomime ended a very successful run and, with relief, I returned home to be with my family.

PENULTIMATE ACT

Having cancelled a lot of engagements because of my wife's latest health setback, I had time in mid-1982 to enjoy family life and to see the children mature into their teens. I was also able to catch up with my writing once more. Although I knew now that I would never be a millionaire from writing my style of novel, nevertheless I enjoyed it, and what was also very satisfying was that I had by now achieved a reputation among publishers for creating books that sold reasonably well: *A Card For The Clubs, The Spy Who Came, The Cosmo Smallpiece Guide To Male Liberation, The Dawson Joke Book*, and the book of puns to end all puns, and my greatest disaster, *The Malady Lingers On* (ouch). Once again I battled with my golf game which had made me the laughing stock of most courses including my own club, Fairhaven, where I held an annual Golf Classic in conjunction with my friend Richard Gill, of the Dalmeny Hotel, St Anne's. The tournament had been running for four years and was popular with footballers, snooker players and theatricals. As then, the Classic is basically a fun match, which always leaves me with a damn good excuse for making a bugger of my game. To give you some idea how bad I am, in one pro-celebrity game sponsored by my old friend Gordon Banks, the ex England goalkeeper, I didn't only lose seven golf balls, I lost a five iron as well. My caddie, a most amiable man, finally snapped on the ninth hole and stormed off back to the clubhouse leaving me alone in a ditch.

On another dreadful day in which I had hit a pheasant up the anus and nearly decapitated "Hurricane Higgins", I finally had my moment of pure bliss: with a video camera whirling away merrily, I sank a forty foot putt on the ninth green, and tears sprang to the eyes as cheers and applause greeted my

triumph. Just at the time my arms were stretched out to my
public, the video cameraman informed me that he hadn't
captured my magnificent putt, because he'd run out of
film. . . . He was so sorry and could I do it again? It took the
combined weight of four competitors to stop me bending my
putter around the fool's neck.

During one recent golf classic, I found myself in the last
bunker trying to get the ball from under a mound of sand
that resembled the Chilterns. At that desperate moment
in time, a squat lady dragging a mucus-smeared child poked
me with her not inconsiderable digit, and said in a booming baritone, "Give 'er your autograph." With that pronouncement, she handed me a matchbox cover and a pen-
cil. "What is the little girl's name, madam?" She blew a
wreath of Woodbine smoke in my right eye and replied
proudly, "Samantha Rebecca Louise". All that on a matchbox
cover.
   It is always nice to be asked for one's autograph, but so
often I wish the person who requests it would have something
decent to write on. Over the years I have scrawled on Kleenex
Tissues, cigarette packets, toilet paper, plaster cast knees,
bandages and once on a pair of outsize knickers.
   My name has been emblazoned on shoulders, armpits,
tennis balls, train tickets and on a doctor's prescription. In
the service of dispensing autographs, I have been bitten by a
corgi, infected with chicken pox and a sinister flu virus. I
have had a small boy hit me in the groin with a rocket gun
once: his family laughed merrily as I writhed on the ground
in acute testicular agony, with the father of the brat saying to
an interested audience, "'E's a funny little bleeder, isn't 'e?"
   My clothes sport cigarette burns, toffee smears, lipstick
stains, beer stains, face powder residues and mascara. . . . I
have been pillaged, punctured and pricked with umbrella
ferrules, hat pins, tie pins and knitting needles. On one
occasion, however, after a stout matron had pulled me into
her bosom which resulted in facial lacerations from her bra
strap, I retaliated by twanging her garters with gusto. A rather
nice lady once asked me to autograph her inner thigh. . . .
Naturally I readily agreed. She placed her leg over my
shoulder and pulled her skirt up to reveal a very pleasing

length of flesh pelmeted at the top by a pair of skimpy drawers. I was sorely tempted to write "Engelbert Humperdinck" along it, but after all one is a gentleman so I compromised my rising lust at the thought of the shadowed delight above, and I signed the thigh . . . Leeeeeees Daaaaaaaw-sssooooon.

But keep asking, dear public, the day you don't means that I have reached the sunset of my career and all that remains is to write my autobiography. . . . Wait a minute. . . .

Meg's health seemed to improve with every passing day, but although my worry over her condition eased, I decided not to be away from home for a lengthy period. I signed to appear in pantomime at the Davenport Theatre, Stockport for the 1982–83 season: Stockport is only an hour's journey away from St Anne's, so my burden was considerably lessened. In October I taped the radio series *Listen to Les* for Jim Casey, then flew down to London for a television script. We had decided to use the trick piano again as the main comedy prop, and I had two new characters that I wanted to introduce. One was called "Zebidiah Twine", a sort of failed variety act who was a drunk . . . some of my contemporaries suggested that the character was an extension of myself. Twine would wear a faded frock coat and his nose would be a bright red and most of his teeth would be blacked out as well. The other character was one that I had been toying with for a while: a northern mill owner called Arkwright, who merely stood stock still and talked into the camera about his rise to prosperity and his wife and children, who had ginger hair and freckles, then Arkwright would introduce his best friend who, yes you've guessed, had ginger hair and freckles. The idea was that week by week the family grew into dozens of kids, some coloured but all with ginger hair and freckles. I wanted the new series to have a talking point; something that would have the public's interest, because frankly, a lot of television was so moribund that nobody remarked on what they'd seen, and I have always believed that the medium of TV succeeds only by the public exchanging likes or dislikes about what they've viewed. . . . But I couldn't think of a damn gimmick, until I did a variety show in Brighton and the show opened with the usual bunch of half starved dancers gyrating to a rock tempo: that's it, I thought . . . why not break all the rules and have fat dancers on stage?

I put the idea to the producer and the BBC. They looked at me as if I'd gone bananas, and I nearly gave up the idea, but something stiffened my resolve, and finally, with muttered threats like "Be it on your own head", we auditioned over seven hundred vast, blubbery ladies with thighs and buttocks usually only evinced on buffalo herds in Dakota. Finally we chose seven substantial females who could all tap dance; six were chosen because they were fat enough to be obvious, but not to be in any way grotesque. The only exception was a performer who had appeared for years on the northern club circuit with her husband in an act called "The Mighty Atom and Roy". She, known to us all as Mo, was short and huge but incredibly light on her feet, and she was a natural comic. We went into rehearsals and the studio crew gaped when they saw the vista of so much flesh, and my boss and friend Jim Moir went about with darkling expressions of grave foreboding. The night came to tape the first show, and at the dress run Jim turned to me and said, "Well at least you'll get some laughs from them in your patter." I shook my head. "No, Jim," I said. "If I do that it will be a burlesque. No, I'm just going to accept them for what they are." Jim strode away, muttering. At my insistence, we had a curtain draped across the shooting area of the studio so that the audience would not be able to see the fatties line up. . . . Then I suddenly remembered I hadn't got a name for my big girls. . . . At that moment was born the name that would soon have half the country talking about them. . . . "The Roly Polys".

Make up over, warm up man on set. . . . A few flutters in the Dawson tum . . . usual before a show of course, but a slight concern. . . . Would my creation of the Roly Polys go well with the studio audience? On you go, Dawson . . . to the audience, few gags and a chat with the people, put 'em at ease. . . . Floor manager's signal: start the recording. Titles on: *The Les Dawson Show*. . . . Music and intro to me. . . .

"Good evening, ladies and gentlemen, and welcome to the show. . . . A show, what is a show? A show is lights." (At the flick of my finger a weak forty watt bulb lit up.) "A show, my friends, is music." (At a signal, a float was pushed on and sitting on the float which was designed as a sort of "Palm Court" set, three very old ladies, two playing violins and one murdering the cello, hove into view and the song they were playing was *Run Rabbit Run*.) "But above all, ladies and gentlemen . . . a show means girls, and we have 'em. . . . Let's hear it for . . . La Femme."

The curtains rose and I held my breath as the first Roly Poly tap-danced on. . . . There was a silence from the audience that seemed to last for an eternity. . . . On came the others. . . .

Even before Mighty Mo came on the laughter rose into absolute hysterics as the floor shook with my Amazons, and when the incredible hulk of Mo appeared, the whole studio was convulsed and I knew I had a winner. As they danced and sang, applause for their ability took over from the laughter and they finished their six minute routine to a great ovation.

The following week I hired a penguin from a zoo, and all it did was waddle on to the stage and stand next to me. . . . I ignored it completely and the audience fell about. That became the pattern for the next six shows: The Roly Polys and a variety of animals. . . . One week I hired a camel that spat at me, then calmly evacuated all over the floor and two members of the audience had to be carried out in near hysteria. We had a kangaroo that kicked the hell out of me, then leapt off to God knows where. When the series was shown on the network, the public loved it – and the Roly Polys. I like to think that I was responsible for giving overweight ladies renewed pride when they saw their fellow womankind dancing with such vigour; at least for once I had no letters from any of those dreadful "Women's Lib" groups.

A few days off then on to Stockport for the pantomime, which ran for ten weeks and did nice business. Meg wasn't walking too well now and reluctantly, she had to use sticks in order to get about. My heart was full for the brave woman in my life; it seemed so unfair that at the age of forty-two, she should be thus crippled.

I found that I was a prey to every virus that lurked in the shadows that winter, my resistance to infection was nil and my drinking increased to combat the fatigue that was my constant companion. Norman insisted that I get myself and the family away for a holiday, and we sailed to the Greek Islands and the Middle East on the liner *Canberra* which had done such sterling work in the nasty little Falklands war.

On returning home, I taped a mammoth TV spectacular at the Coliseum Theatre which was a tribute to the lads who had fought in the Falklands. . . . The pubs were open all day near the theatre and I helped the Armed Forces and fellow artistes to drain the cellars. Roger Moore and I stood swaying together after the show as we lined up to meet Prince Charles. Frankly I was loaded and twice I was scolded for giggling by Dame Anna Neagle. Charles stood before me as I grinned inanely at him. He smiled as he shook my hand and said in his well known clipped accent, "Marvellous show, Mr Dawson, enjoyed it. Nice tribute for a job well done." Owlishly I wagged a finger at him and slurred, "Not over yet, sir . . . Argentina will seek revenge, mark my words." He looked at me horrified and replied, "Do you think there will be a war of attrition? I swayed and burped and answered, "Oh no, sir, they'll take all the keys off their tins of corn beef." The Prince threw his head back and roared, thank the Lord, and Tarbuck collapsed in a fit.

Yet again in 1983 I found myself taking part in a Royal Variety Show, again at Drury Lane. This time however the ghost only struck me. I had been working on a new television series and it wasn't going well. I had a new producer who had no sense of humour, in fact he had to make an appointment to see a joke, and it was getting me down, and in the condition I was in, my voice went on the very night of the show. Somehow I croaked my way through it, and afterwards Her Majesty was most sympathetic, but I felt that I had failed miserably.

Dear Meg was urging me to slow down but something inside of me wouldn't let me stop the relentless workload, and I took ill several times during the Stockport pantomime run, although I never missed a performance. The television series that I had been troubled with didn't do as well as the others; something was missing and I knew deep inside of me that I wasn't working as well as I should have been. The winter of 1983–84 was spent in pantomime at Wolverhampton with the Roly Polys and Michael Barrymore, a rising young comic, and we did the best business the theatre had ever known, and yet despite that, the theatre somehow lost money, which I found most odd.

After the dramas I had undergone with the last television variety series I wanted to get off the "box" for a time and concentrate on perhaps more stage work and writing. My latest book, *Les Dawson's Lancashire*, was out in hardback and doing much better on the market than my previous hardback offering, *The Amy Pluckett Letters* which I had written for Robson Books. I still think the title I gave the novel in the beginning was a better choice: *Hitler Was My Mother-in-Law*. But no, someone at the Robson publishing house wanted a more erudite title and a flop was spawned. Later on, the paper-back version of *Amy Pluckett* came out as *Hitler was My Mother-in-Law* and did much better.

Meg could only get around now with great difficulty. Walking was a problem even with her sticks, and she had to spend more time in bed, so there was no question of me working on shows in London for any length of time. . . . Doing another variety series for the BBC which would entail weeks away from home was out of the question. My elder daughter Julie was away in Nottingham training to be a nurse, and I had to be on hand to look after my son and younger daughter whilst their mother was so ill. It looked as if I would have to semi-retire. Meg had to be taken to Manchester for regular treatment and although my son aged seventeen was more than capable of looking after things, I didn't think it fair to heap such responsibility on his young shoulders, so I informed the BBC that the way things were, I would have to bow out. Obviously I was bitterly disappointed at the way my career had ground to a halt, but that was that.

Suddenly, towards the end of the pantomime run at Wolver-hampton, Norman and Anne, agents and friends for years, approached me with an idea that the BBC had mooted; simply that they, the BBC, wanted me to take over from Terry Wogan on the show he had made his very own: *Blankety Blank*. As every reader knows, Terry Wogan is a legend in broadcasting, and I don't think there has been a more popular figure in this country for years. He possesses everything I haven't got: good looks and charm. How could I, a dumpy, craggy-faced comic, hope to take over from such a man? It was also a dangerous thing to do, taking over from an established host of a popular show; years before a good coloured comedian called Charlie Williams, had taken over a programme called *The Golden Shot* from Bob Monkhouse, and it had virtually killed off Charlie's career. The BBC took me to the annual festival in the Swiss resort of Montreux, and between drinking bouts, expressed confidence that I could do *Blankety Blank* well. A press conference was held and I could see by the expressions on the faces of the journalists, that not many of them thought I could do it. Later that night, as I stood alone with a glass of wine and watched the moon dapple the surface of Lake Geneva, I knew that I had to take up the challenge . . . I had no choice. I still had a contract to fulfil with the BBC and I would only be away from home one day a week if I took *Blankety Blank*. It would be punishing but possible: a car would pick me up at home early Saturday morning, take me to London where I would tape two pro-grammes, then the car would bring me home on the same night, albeit the early hours of Sunday morning. That way, I could look after the children and my wife. There was another reason for having to take the quiz host job: money. The income tax had yet again denuded me of the filthy, and I have never been much of a saver.

My friends howled that I was out of my mind; my wife shook her head in disbelief and my confidence began to dissolve. It was decided that I would do a pilot run of the show to see what I was like on it. . . . I was awful. I couldn't remember the rules, and I floundered but one thing did emerge: it was funny. So, in early 1984, I hosted twelve *Blankety Blanks* and my fears were shortlived: the viewing figures went from five million to ten million; after a hesitant start, the show came naturally to me and the public obviously liked it. The first person to congratulate me on the success was Terry Wogan himself. But the weekly journey was tiring and my body was sending out warnings to ease up. Meg was a constant worry to me, she was in pain all the time, but her fortitude gave me the will to carry on. Summer came along and I was booked to appear in Blackpool for the summer season. . . . This was a Godsend, of course, and I was proud to be able to tell the world that I had broken all existing box office records at the Grand Theatre since its conception ninety years before.

My Roly Polys were a huge success in the summer show, as was my old friend and partner, Roy Barraclough. Our sketch of "Cissie and Ada" was now a classic and the holiday-makers loved it. After a short break, I taped another twelve *Blankety Blanks* in the autumn, but the fatigue was becoming apparent in my work, and I refused to do a pantomime season; it was obvious even to me that I had to rest up. Meg was only able to get about with great difficulty and it broke my heart to see the pain in her eyes. Frequently now, I found myself sliding into fits of depression and a feeling of "What the hell is life all about" soured my outlook.

After taping a show, instead of driving back home soon after the programme, I would get the driver to take me into the West End to the clubs, and there in those dimly lit places I would drink to excess. . . . I was at a very low ebb.

TOP OF THE BILL

In the mood I was in, I didn't feel like attending the Water Rats' Ball at Grosvenor House and Meg wasn't bothered too much about the function either. However, we had promised Stuart and Pamela that we would go, so I decided to pull myself together and off we went. Our custom is to make a weekend of the affair. Saturday with about fourteen friends we eat and drink and dance in an Italian restaurant owned by good friends of mine, and then Sunday evening, the Great Ball. Not only is it a wonderful night of merriment, it is also the time when the new officers of the Water Rats' Order are announced: the greatest accolade a performer can reach is to be nominated by his peers for the office of King Rat, and I always eagerly look forward to seeing who will be elected to that most distinguished of positions. Prince Michael of Kent and his lovely wife were the guests of honour, and it was a delight to see the stars in my Pamela's young eyes when she met the famous people who called to our table.

It was time for the announcement of the stars who had been chosen for office, and the vast room fell silent as Davy Kaye, the King Rat, stood up to intone the list. After each name, cheers rang out and I must say, I felt a slight twinge that I had never been considered for any post within the Order, but alas the way things had gone the last three years or so, I had never been able to attend a Lodge meeting nor do the Order much good in the way of promoting charity. For some time I had been the president of a mentally handicapped centre as well as a special school, and that was about all I could manage. However, the highspot, the announcement of the new officers approached. . . . Davy, to a drum roll, read out the name of the new Prince Rat and I leapt to my feet and applauded warmly at the name: "Prince Rat for 1985 is . . . Jimmy Tarbuck." The whole room rocked with applause. I sat down and drank deeply as Davy went on to introduce the new King Rat.

"Ladies and Gentlemen. . . . The new King Rat for 1985 is . . . LES DAWSON." I sat back stunned as to a man my fellow artistes stood to their feet and cheered and cheered. I saw genuine love on their faces; Meg was crying with joy and my son and daughter were slapping me on the back and beaming with pride. In a dream I rose to my feet, bowed to the assembly and made my bewildered way to the top table to say a few words of acknowledgement. Princess Michael went rather coy when I broke all tradition and kissed her firmly . . . much to the amusement of the prince.

The vast throng were still standing and applauding as I shook Davy Kaye's hand, but I wasn't in that room. I was that lonely kid again in a torn cardigan; I was the homeless twenty-odd-year-old . . . the fat comic "dying" in a sleazy club. . . . Scenes from the past were vividly real and all the heartache remembered so well. Here I was, top of the tree and the emotion of it all tore at my throat.

Did I really once sleep on a park bench? Had I lived through such pain and sadness? Little Dawson . . . King Rat.

At home over Christmas, I found myself looking at mementoes of the past: the Variety Club Awards, newspaper awards, faded photographs of a cocky young comedian starting out, unaware of the harsh future; the setbacks, the disappointments, the ups and downs of life, bitter sweet recollections now softened with the passing of time. Had it all been worth it?

On the way out of my study to join the family celebrating in the lounge, I glanced into the hall mirror. I saw a fat, creased, lived-in face, a face that Fate had knocked about a bit, and suddenly I laughed . . . I rubbed my chin and said out loud, "You did it, Dawson, God only knows how, but you made it. . . . Top of the tree, kid."

POSTSCRIPT

Most people ask themselves when they muse over their life: "Was it all worth the effort?" I was soon to find out.

Early 1985 saw me working on another batch of *Blankety Blanks* which I was not destined to complete. In March, I went with friends to the golf club to finalise the arrangements for my Golf Classic. It was an amiable lunchtime meeting in which several pints of lager were dispatched down the Dawson gullet. Excusing myself I went to the toilet for the human function of emptying the bladder, a normal, every day necessity . . . I found I couldn't pass water. I thought little of it until I arrived back home and the need became pressing, but again it was impossible to urinate, and by now pain was springing up in my stomach and kidneys. Julie was home from nursing, and at her insistence, I went to see my local doctor and asked him for something to help me. I explained airily that I had probably contracted a chill. In response, he ordered me on to his examination couch and he probed my prostate gland. His face was quite serious when he'd conducted his examination, and he told me that the gland was infected and swollen and that I would require surgery. This came as a blow to my masculine pride – I had never been in hospital, indeed, I had a morbid fear of such places. My doctor made an appointment for me to see a specialist on the Monday morning, which I said I couldn't fit in because I wanted very badly to get to London to attend the funeral of one of my old show business friends: singer Matt Monro, whose death had shaken me up very much.

I never got to Matt's funeral, nor was I able to do the last editions of *Blankety Blank*. Over the weekend the pain increased to a screaming pitch and I knew I couldn't take any more of it. They took me into Preston Royal Hospital. The operation was successful and joy of joys! with the instrument drawn through my penis into the bladder, I was able to expel water . . . I felt good. Arrangements were made for me to leave the hospital the following day. As I bade goodbye to Meg and the kids who had been to visit me, I wandered into the day room to watch anything on the television in order to pass the time along, and I began to shake violently and arched my back in pain.

Somehow I got myself back into bed and the shaking intensified. A worried nurse took my temperature and within seconds, there was a hive of activity in my room. . . . Ten minutes later I was in the intensive care ward, my kidneys had ceased to function, my blood pressure was almost nil and I was fighting for my life.

For three long days and nights, those wonderful surgeons fought to save me. Meg had been told that I had a fifty-fifty chance of pulling through. One specialist told her bluntly that my resistance was so low, I could not combat any infection.

Little did I know that the radio and the television were daily reporting my progress, little did I know that the national press had to be kept forcibly out of the hospital. . . . I knew none of this until the morning I opened my eyes, grinned at a pretty nurse and asked her for a date. . . . Thanks to God I had come through it all.

The answer to the question "Have all the things I've done been worth the effort?" came in the shape of sacks and sacks of mail from the public. Good will cards, get well cards, fruit, flowers filled the hospital to overflowing. There was a letter from an old age pensioner begging me to get well soon, and in the letter she'd pinned a pound note saying "Get yourself a tonic with this money." Thousands of children wrote to me expressing their concern and love. . . . Yes, love there was in that sick room and the letters bore mute testimony to that fact. Show business opened its heart and the affection brought tears to my eyes. A young nurse came into my room and helped me to read through the heaps of mail. At one point she looked up and said in a trembling voice, "It must be wonderful to know that so many people love you."

Yes, everything I had done had been worth it. I never knew how many lives had touched mine throughout the years.

When I came out of hospital with stern warnings to take it easy for a long time, the wife and I were lying in bed, she poor lass drowsy with pain killers, and I exhausted. We looked at each other, two souls who had been so close for twenty-five years. . . . Meg turned to me: "Look at us," she said with a wan smile. "A pair of crocks." I kissed her, held her close and said, "Sweetheart, we'll beat 'em yet." And do you know something? We will.